James Bowron

James Bowron

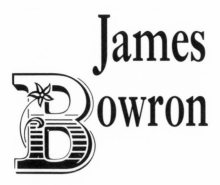

The Autobiography

of a New South

Industrialist

Robert J. Norrell

The University of

North Carolina Press

Chapel Hill and London

The paper in this book meets the guidelines for
permanence and durability of the Committee on
Production Guidelines for Book Longevity of the
Council on Library Resources.

95 94 93 92 91   5 4 3 2 1

Library of Congress Cataloging-in-Publication Data

Norrell, Robert J. (Robert Jefferson)
    James Bowron : the autobiography of a new
South industrialist / Robert J. Norrell.
        p.   cm.
    Includes bibliographical references and index.
ISBN 0-8078-1987-5 (alk. paper)
    1. Bowron, James.   2. Industrialists—United
States—History.   3. Iron industry and trade—
United States—History.   4. Steel industry and
trade—United States—History.   5. Tennessee—
Industries—History.   6. Alabama—Industries—
History.   I. Title.
HD9520.B69N67   1991
338.7′6691′092—dc20
[B]   91-9847
                                              CIP

For Paul Gaston

Contents

Illustrations

Acknowledgments

I owe one very large debt in the preparation of this manuscript to Betty M. Wedgeworth, who copied thousands of pages at the Xerox machine, typed a large portion of those pages onto the computer, and then tolerated months of my deletions and rearrangements. She did all this in good humor and with an abiding enthusiasm for the personality and character of James Bowron.

Others helped in important ways. George W. Prewett found numerous obscure reference works and did a helpful index to the original Bowron autobiography. Joyce Lamont of the Amelia Gayle Gorgas Library at the University of Alabama provided the original encouragement to do this project, and her associates Gunetta Rich and Clark Center helped me with the use of the Bowron manuscript material. Marvin Whiting, Don Veasey, and Jim Murray at the Birmingham Public Library Archives gave assistance in locating photographs. Whitney DeBardeleben made available the image of his remarkable great-great-grandfather.

James Bowron's descendants assisted the effort without knowing what it would yield. Richard Bowron encouraged this project from the beginning; his enthusiasm for it nurtured my own. Paul Bowron provided many helpful insights about his father in a long interview. James French lent me several good family photographs.

Lewis Bateman at the University of North Carolina Press is a strong, supportive, and honest editor with whom it has been a pleasure to work. He has become a valued friend. Mary Reid and Ron Maner at the Press made many suggestions for improving the manuscript.

It is a pleasure to dedicate this book to my mentor, Paul Gaston. Readers who know Professor Gaston and then get acquainted with James Bowron will find some irony in the dedication, for surely the two men would have shared few views on politics, religion, or race. But they have in common an idealistic impulse, a belief that the world—and the South, in particular—can be made a better place. Such idealism is hard to find in the late twentieth century, but I am sustained by the rare examples that do occur.

Introduction

James Bowron managed iron and steel operations in Tennessee and Alabama for the half-century after Reconstruction, the era of the New South. He had migrated to the United States in 1877 as the representative of rich, sophisticated fellow English Quakers who were developing a coal and iron company in Tennessee. He came intending to serve as assistant to his father, the general manager of the new concern, only to inherit the whole responsibility when the senior Bowron suddenly died. He was stranded, a young man with a young family in a foreign country—indeed, in what seemed to the mid-Victorian Englishman a wilderness. And yet he would make his way in the South and in fact would gain wealth and status there. Bowron credited Divine Providence for his rise. His autobiography suggests that his own character and determination also had much to do with his success.

The autobiography illuminates many areas, most particularly the history of southern industrialization. Bowron lends a rare perspective. Only a small portion of the wealthiest American capitalists were inclined to write their autobiographies, and no other southern businessman left a comparable work. Written first by journalists like Henry Grady and Richard Edmonds, the economic history of the South tended to emphasize the achievements of post–Civil War southern industry and to downplay the evidence of failure. The academic literature that followed has been more critical, though the early works were hardly free of boosterism. Bowron's account is more personal and in some ways more accessible than those of the economists and historians who have written on the subject, and he provides a far more sophisticated critique of the New South economy than most journalists attempted.[1]

In Tennessee Bowron encountered a racially divided, economically devastated region, yet one desperately hoping to overcome its preoccupation with agriculture. The New South welcomed all foreigners—northerners as well as Englishmen—who brought capital to build industries. Bowron moved quickly into the upper reaches of the southern iron industry, where he found a chaotic, often amoral, usually disorganized practice of business. But it was an environment tailor-made to his talents. Bowron had learned the practices of modern business through firsthand participation in his father's many enterprises in England. Early in his life he mastered the intricacies of credit, which prior to the development of modern national banking was often fraught with mystery. At an early age he became expert at delaying payment of debts, forestalling bankruptcy, and operating business with little capital. His mastery of finance would set him apart especially in the underdeveloped South. He stood out as one man who could raise money for undercapitalized corporations when most others did not know how to begin. He was honest when some fellow industrialists broke the law regularly. He ordered his affairs meticulously when too few understood or cared about proper accounting. He mastered the technology of the iron and steel industry when many southern entrepreneurs slighted it for land and stock speculation. Indeed, Bowron brought to the South many talents in short supply.

He worked in an emerging industry plagued with overproduction and overbuilding of iron-making capacity. He witnessed the sudden appearance of "boom" iron towns in the southern Appalachian hills in the 1880s and 1890s and was instrumental in the building of South Pittsburgh, Tennessee, one such town that enjoyed some success. Later, in Birmingham, Bowron became one of the South's most respected industrial boosters, not because he could match Henry Grady's superficial eloquence but because he commanded wide respect for his realistic view of southern economic potential. He led in the development of the Tennessee Coal and Iron Company (TCI), one of the South's most important industrial corporations and in time the dominant iron and steel producer in the South. At TCI he constantly wrestled with the problems of outside control. He resented how TCI's Wall Street directors selfishly manipulated the company's stock, exploited its credit needs, and failed to support steel production in Birmingham. Time and again Bowron indicted the colonial nature of the southern economy, though he conceded its apparent inevitability in the face of the South's capital shortage.

He often found himself a party to business practices of questionable wisdom and sometimes outright dishonesty. The worst abuses were "insider trading"; secret and profligate issuance of stock bonuses; stock "watering" (creation of stock that represented little or no real wealth); payoffs to politicians for special favors; falsification of company reports to stockholders; and a general inability to practice honest cost accounting. Bowron condemned the irresponsible practices of his TCI colleagues, and ultimately he left the company because of the board's insistence on paying stock dividends with borrowed money.

Bowron provides an internal view of the TCI management's attitude toward labor. Like most southern industrialists in the coal and iron trade, he viewed black labor as a great natural resource—just as the mineral deposits in the Appalachian hills were a unique southern advantage. He explained how TCI and other industrial corporations constantly worked to maintain dominance over their workers. The use of convict labor, almost all of it black, served as a hedge against unionization, but it also constantly vexed the industrialists. The convict-lease system was often expensive and usually the source of political bribery and social condemnation.

Bowron's career as an industrialist expanded and changed over the years. He helped to build the South's iron pipe industry and saw pipe become a major "finished" industrial product of the region. He invested in other, less successful enterprises linked to iron, particularly a stove works, and experienced the many difficulties associated with developing new industries. He helped to direct a major coal and land company in Birmingham and saw firsthand the close connections between town building, land speculation, and industrialization. Later in his career he took over a failed steel company and returned it to profitability in the 1910s. He would manage it until the day he died.

Bowron witnessed the emerging conflict between corporations and government in the early twentieth century, and he objected strongly to what he often saw as needless and unwarranted government interference. A staunch Republican and avowed protectionist, he thought that the Democratic agitations to lower tariffs and inflate the currency in the 1890s were foolhardy and destructive. In the twentieth century he became increasingly hostile to the national government. Regulations on trusts and railroad rates, in his view, damaged the prospects of southern industries. World War I, which brought federal controls that encouraged unionization, turned Bowron toward an even more hard-bitten antigovernment posture. He became shrill in his opposition to regulatory agencies and the unions. After the war he was strongly committed to the "open shop" movement that successfully undermined new unionism in the 1920s. Bowron's response perhaps typified the thinking of American businessmen after the war experience.

A highly disciplined, wholly systematic person, Bowron kept a diary for more than fifty years, making an entry every day of his life—except the last one—from the age of thirty-three. The Quaker background helped to create

such an avid diarist. From the time of the Reformation, English Quakers
had been taught the virtue of keeping records of personal habits and behav-
ior as a means of developing one's moral rectitude. Bowron's determination
to develop his diaries into an autobiography also owed something to the
tradition among radical Protestants of autobiography as an exercise in spiri-
tual self-examination. It was a means to evaluate the condition of one's soul.

The autobiography also represented the final gift of a loving and generous
father to a family he adored and guided with a firm hand for his entire adult
life. His children, not his small fortune, were Bowron's greatest legacy. The
father of fourteen, ten of whom survived to adulthood, he wanted to show
them by the story of his life what he had done right and wrong and to reveal
the processes of self-examination which would lead to a righteous life.
Throughout a demanding business career, he attended faithfully to each one
of his large brood, rearing children for fifty years. He was alternately tender
and tough, in the evening a chum at the billiard table, in the morning the
tyrant of the breakfast table. "When Dad was acting as parent," his youngest
child, Paul, said many years later, "you had better listen and do exactly what
he told you." Bowron maintained a private relationship with each child; he
gave each one tough, critical, but confidential counsel on important matters
far into adulthood. He kept a thoroughly Christian home, complete with his
own Bible reading each evening after dinner, but Paul Bowron insisted that
his father was not overbearing in his religiosity. To be sure, few if any chal-
lenges ever emerged. Like the children, both of Bowron's wives accepted his
authority in the home. The second Mrs. Bowron clearly shared his religious
fundamentalism and reformist impulse.[2]

Bowron was hardly shy about his own abilities. He explains that he was a
good student, that he had a marvelous memory, that he had a facility for
languages and arithmetic. He knew that he had a broad fund of general
knowledge, and he delighted in sharing it. He was aware of his strong voice,
his fine elocution, and his natural facility for expression. He relished making
speeches and took pride in his ability always to deliver them extemporaneously. He believed he knew more about the iron business than any other
man in the South. On the other hand, he was usually honest about his fail-
ings. He owned up to his poor handwriting. He dealt at some length on the
mistakes of his business decisions, and he pointed out the times he repeated
mistakes.

He never admitted, however, to a rather strong strain of self-righteous-
ness. Bowron came from a pious family, and as a young man he formed close
friendships with like-minded fellows in the Young Men's Christian Associ-

ation. He exerted a "muscular Christianity" that embraced Biblical fundamentalism and social reform at the same time. He took his strong spirituality
with him to America, where it was applied in various concerns—the YMCA,
the antimodernist reaction among Protestants of the early twentieth century,
and the Prohibition movement. He became more and more outspoken in his
fundamentalism in the later years of his life, at times sounding like the
narrow-minded "Booboisie" that Henry L. Mencken condemned in the
1920s. Bowron's views are important, however, for the clarity with which
they represent common, everyday sentiments among many Americans of the
late nineteenth and early twentieth centuries.

Bowron's views on southern industrialization are pertinent to several significant interpretations of the subject. Perhaps the first work they bring to mind
is Ethel Armes's 1910 book, *The Story of Coal and Iron in Alabama*. A broadly
researched and richly detailed account of the origins and early development
of Alabama's iron industry, Armes's work covers much of Bowron's territory.
It gives an expansive history of virtually every coal and iron enterprise in
Alabama from the state's white settlement to 1910. But it was written for the
Birmingham Chamber of Commerce and has a decidedly boosteristic tone.
Despite the fact that Armes had access to Bowron's diaries, her work offers
little of the direct criticism about business decisions that characterizes Bowron's reflections. As a result, her profiles of important men like the TCI
executives Henry DeBardeleben and Nathaniel Baxter are at best benign
and colorful and in some respects are inaccurate about their abilities as
industrial entrepreneurs. She rarely focused on the mismanagement resulting from outside control. She neglected the long struggle within TCI to
begin steel production and offers a misleading—but often-cited—explanation for why steel making happened when it did. Bowron thought Armes
had slighted his accomplishments, despite extensive assistance given her,
because he failed to contribute enough money toward her book's publication. "I suppose if I had been in a position to have made her a present of
$100 or $200," he wrote in the autobiography, "I would have had at least
one page devoted to my accomplishments and services in keeping the Tennessee Company through three financial panics and for [twenty] years out of
the hands of a receiver."[3]

  C. Vann Woodward's *Origins of the New South, 1877–1913*, though forty
years old, still commands the largest authority over the subject of southern

industrialization. Woodward emphasized the colonial nature of the South's post-Reconstruction economy and argued that outside control allowed only a slow and incomplete industrial evolution, rather than a dynamic, far-reaching economic revolution. According to Woodward, monopolistic capitalists like J. Pierpont Morgan gained control of the southern industrial economy and used resources exclusively for the sake of northern profits. Low-value-added manufacturing and extractive industries characterized the South's economic development in the late nineteenth and early twentieth centuries. In the steel industry, the South suffered from U.S. Steel's discriminating "Pittsburgh Plus" pricing; Birmingham steel was sold in the South for the set Pittsburgh price *plus* a phantom shipping cost from the Pennsylvania city. Woodward argued that the artificially high prices of steel had inhibited the development of more sophisticated manufacturing in the South. The resulting slow growth and low wages did little to overcome the poverty of the region's people, despite the claims of prosperity that New South promoters like Henry Grady had announced.[4]

Bowron's view upholds the Woodward interpretation on important points. From his perspective, outside control of TCI led to many decisions that handicapped industrial development in Alabama and Tennessee. New York directors never provided adequate capital for building and equipping modern plants. They sacrificed technological improvements for unprofitable expansion of pig iron production and for land speculation. Their first concern always was the price of the stock, whether they happened to be "bulling" or "bearing" it at the time. Bowron believed that the dominant stockholders usually seemed indifferent to the best advice of the southern managers, like himself, who wanted to improve output and produce more finished goods, in particular steel. TCI's John Inman epitomized the rapacious Wall Street director, and Bowron's insider view of him and others confirms in damning detail what Woodward outlined. Bowron's characterization of some boosters also mirrors the very negative assessment that Woodward gave of the New South publicists. Many of these men cared nothing for industrial production and genuine economic growth, Bowron believed, and everything for land speculation and the quick buck.

But Bowron takes a far more benevolent view than Woodward of the role of railroads, especially the Louisville and Nashville. In opposition to Woodward's emphasis on the railroads' exploitative tendencies, Bowron leaves the strong impression that Milton H. Smith, the L&N executive in the South, provided crucial financial support for iron and steel development when TCI's major stockholders were indifferent. In the absence of Smith's financial help in the 1890s, Bowron believed, TCI might have failed. Smith's powerful voice on behalf of steel production in Birmingham helped to persuade the New York directors to go along with the local management in building a steelworks in 1897. Bowron does not, however, take into account the inhibiting effect that high railroad freight rates had on other southern industries. His own Birmingham neighbor, Governor Braxton B. Comer, built a successful political career on opposition to the railroads' high rates for finished goods. Indeed, most Birmingham businessmen and industrialists probably took Comer's view.[5]

Bowron is more willing than Woodward to accept the colonial nature of the South's economy as an inevitable consequence of the region's poverty. Woodward suggested that base motives were usually at work among the northern invaders. Although he was not involved in U.S. Steel's 1907 takeover of TCI, Bowron denied any monopolistic purpose on the part of the steel corporation. He viewed U.S. Steel's entry into Birmingham as a positive development because it brought abundant new capital to develop local resources. In his later years Bowron rejected the criticism that Birmingham's slow development owed to U.S. Steel's dominance, even though he was by then managing a competitor. Bowron spoke out for the Pittsburgh Plus pricing system, no doubt because his Gulf States Steel Corporation was the beneficiary of price supports. In the years just prior to World War I, he argued that Birmingham's economic growth was in fact very respectable. By then Bowron's was probably a minority view even among southern industrial promoters, and certainly it has been so in subsequent generations.

Bowron's view contradicts Gavin Wright's influential recent work, *Old South, New South*, which argued that outside ownership was not the root cause for the South's slow modernization. Wright embraced some of what Woodward called the "natural" economic difficulties—scarcity of capital, technology, and skilled labor—that Woodward himself thought of as merely "transitory barriers." Wright contended that technical problems in the southern industry were more nearly the cause of backwardness: its late beginning, the absence of technological expertise, and the poor quality of southern labor. Early in his career Bowron conceded that southern ironmakers were behind and slow to catch up, but he blamed much of their backwardness on the inadequate financial support given company operations by the New York directors. He was abundantly aware of his industry's slow technological progress, but that he also blamed on the ownership's shortsighted neglect of new technologies. He and others specifically presented the TCI board with opportunities to acquire new expertise, most of which were rejected in New York as too costly. Thus, the late development and the technological backwardness were actually results of the more fundamental problem of inadequate capital. As for labor, Bowron rarely complained about the quality of southern workers, though that might be attributed to his infrequent contact with production. Southern industrialists like Bowron complained about the disloyalty of their workers during strikes, but in normal times they characterized their work force—especially the black portion—as diligent, cooperative, and cheap.[6]

It is true, however, that Bowron would have agreed with Wright, and contradicted Woodward, on the benefits of Pittsburgh Plus. Wright argued that artificially high prices protected developing southern steel producers. But consumers of steel in the South—fabricators, machine shops, ship builders—were hurt by the relatively high price of steel. Lower-priced Birmingham steel surely would have made them more competitive, at least in the South. By 1920 most southern industrial promoters agreed with the point that Woodward and others later made about the negative impact of discriminatory pricing on the growth of new industries.[7]

Bowron's account of southern industrialization points to two main causes underlying the slow development. They represent the kind of "natural" economic difficulties that Woodward considered secondary causes, but they are different from the ones Wright emphasized. First, the shortage of capital for industrial investment was so dire that it is difficult to imagine any substantial modernization without outside ownership. The South suffered for many decades from the destruction of capital caused by the Civil War. After the war there were very few southerners with wealth even approaching the minimal level for iron development, and some among the few who had it—Henry DeBardeleben and Enoch Ensley, for example—were given to irresponsible speculation. Moreover, the belief that the South held great mineral riches was widely current in the 1870s and 1880s. It would have virtually defied logic for northern or European investment to avoid the region. Given the Civil War legacy of poverty and the surplus capital available among men knowledgeable about the South, it is difficult to imagine circumstances that could have prevented a colonialized economy. Bowron's autobiography leaves the strong impression that southern industrialists assumed that capital needs would have to be met outside the region.

Second, the southern iron industry had to depend on exporting its unfinished products because southern consumption of iron was so low. Relatively few foundries, machine shops, or other capital goods enterprises existed to use southern iron. Here again the burden of the past is very heavy. The region's economy had not historically consumed enough metal goods to support the level that regional iron production reached in the 1880s. The creation of a large iron-making capacity did not automatically precipitate greater local consumption. Some new industries emerged—iron pipe, most notably—but growth in iron consumption lagged far behind the increase in production. Estimates about the portion of southern production that was exported in the 1880s and 1890s were often over 80 percent. In the absence of a dynamic steel industry and other forward links from iron—developments that also depended on capital investment not available—exportation was the only viable alternative to iron producers. However commonplace that was in southern economic history, it presented many problems and few opportunities.

Thus, while he lends much support to the interpretations of southern economic history that emphasize the evils of colonialism, Bowron in fact attributes the South's slow industrial development to two more fundamental problems, inadequate capital and insufficient consumption. The source of those go back, of course, to the region's peculiar historical experience. Much of the South developed far later than the leading industrial centers in the North, and its original economic growth was driven overwhelmingly by the market for one agricultural crop. Capital formation for industry not only started later in the South, it had to compete with the often highly profitable option of plantation agriculture. Then the Civil War caused the destruction of the large majority of southern wealth, represented in slaves freed, securities lost, and land devalued. The agricultural alternative was no longer as attractive, but now there was little capital to develop industry and relatively weak consuming power to fuel economic growth. Outside ownership and export industries were the manifestations of basic economic problems embedded in the South's historical experience.

James Bowron's life provides a good vantage point for seeing how the iron and steel industry developed in the postwar South, but no historical figure understands fully the context in which his or her life occurs. Nor does any autobiographer explain completely that portion that is perceived. A brief overview of the history of iron and steel in the South will help to set the background for Bowron's narrative.

The industry had a long history in the region prior to Bowron's arrival. Iron forges appeared soon after the original settlement of many communities in or near the Appalachians. Major centers of iron making developed along the Cumberland River in Tennessee and Kentucky and in Richmond, Virginia. Louisville had a substantial iron foundry trade, much of it to serve steamboats on the Ohio River. Richmond's Tredegar Iron Works served Virginia's railroad-building effort and U.S. military ordnance. In the Old South, iron was made exclusively with charcoal, an expensive fuel but one that produced a high-quality metal. Southern iron production, however, grew rapidly only in the 1830s; it stagnated during the depression of the 1840s and regained momentum gradually in the 1850s. The region's iron consumption was limited largely to the needs of plantation agriculture, and much of that was met with iron imported from the North and abroad.[8]

The Civil War gave powerful new impetus for developing iron production. The Confederacy's huge demand for armaments spurred production in Richmond and caused the creation of new works in Selma, Alabama. There was a corollary push for coal and iron mining and for railroad building. Although the supply never came close to matching demand, the southern iron industry experienced unparalleled growth and modernization during the early war years and, in the judgment of many historians, performed well enough to supply adequate ordnance to the men in the field. Defeat, however, negated many of the industrial improvements instigated by the Confederacy. The invading Union army destroyed much of the iron-making capacity of Alabama and Georgia, including the necessary rail connections. One major exception to wartime destruction occurred in eastern Tennessee, where the early occupation of the Union army allowed the U.S. government to build a rolling mill at Chattanooga that ensured the safety of that city's industry. The presence of northern industrialists like John Fritz in Chattanooga at the end of the war gave that city and its surrounding region a head start in postwar iron making.[9]

The end of the war brought a great surge of interest in iron making as one means for a new southern economy. Whether they were reconstructed or not, many postwar southerners thought that the plantation economy had been fundamentally undermined by the end of slavery. They understood that iron was the most basic material of an industrial economy, and some believed that the ability to produce it would bring ipso facto a rapid industrialization. There emerged within months of the war's end urgent efforts to revitalize the Tredegar works and the Shelby and Brierfield works in Alabama. From the start, however, capital shortages handicapped the efforts of recovering southern ironmakers. Josiah Gorgas, the Confederate ordnance chief who took over the Brierfield works, had to mortgage the works to his wife to raise money to keep the company running. Problems of poor and expensive railroad service, inadequate but expensive labor, and unavailable equipment also contributed to Brierfield's failure in 1869.[10]

Northerners who during the war had discovered the South's iron-making potential invested in it afterward. John Thomas Wilder, a Union general in occupied Tennessee, established the Roane Iron Works at Rockwood in eastern Tennessee in 1867 with capital from his native Indiana. General Willard Warner got acquainted with Alabama's iron manufacturing while helping to destroy it for General Sherman's army and then in 1873 founded his own Tecumseh Iron Company in northeastern Alabama. Abram S. Hewitt, the prominent New Jersey iron manufacturer, said that Alabama was "unquestionably the most interesting [place] in the United States with reference to iron manufacture" and the "only place in the American continent where it is possible to make iron in competition with the cheap iron of England." He predicted that northern Alabama would be a "region of coke-made iron on a grander scale than has ever been witnessed on the habitable globe." Hewitt in fact took over the Chattanooga Rolling Mill built by the Union army and merged it with the Roane Works in 1870.[11]

Starting in 1871 some southerners, having recovered sufficiently from the war catastrophe, initiated new iron-making efforts. Arthur S. Colyar and his colleagues expanded the Tennessee Coal Company's operation at Tracy City to include a blast furnace. Daniel Pratt and Henry F. DeBardeleben used Pratt's fortune from cotton gins and textile manufacturing to begin the Eureka Iron Company near Birmingham. James Warner resurrected production at the Rising Fawn Furnace Company in northwest Georgia. To be sure, southern-born manufacturers did not depend altogether on local money. Virtually all the postwar Alabama operations had outside help.[12]

The English investment that brought James Bowron to Tennessee also began in the mid-1870s, marking the first major entry of foreign entrepreneurs. British investment in the South may be traced in part to the visit of Sir Isaac Lowthian Bell to America in 1874, when he was president of the British Iron and Steel Institute. A noted metallurgist and leading manufacturer at Middlesbrough in northeastern England, Bell wrote in 1875 that the close proximity of coal and iron in Alabama, Georgia, Tennessee, and West Virginia would "place several localities in those provinces in a position of equality with the most favored of those I have examined in Europe."[13]

Tennessee's Roane Company was the first successful southern effort to manufacture iron with coke, the hard carbon fuel made from processed bituminous coal. Coke was cheaper than charcoal; it already had replaced the wood fuel in northern furnaces. Making iron cheaply with coke was essential if southern iron was to compete in national markets. The initial achievement in eastern Tennessee in 1867 was followed in 1876 by a successful run at DeBardeleben's Eureka furnace, an experiment financed by the L&N Railroad. The Birmingham coke iron was especially promising because huge deposits of iron ore lay on the surface of a mountain not ten miles from a large field of high-carbon "coking" coal. Lowthian Bell had said that Birmingham's cheap production would "eventually dictate to the world what the price of iron should be." Whatever Birmingham's potential, Chattanooga had already used its head start to begin commercial sale of pig iron for the market and to initiate iron pipe production. It claimed the name of "Pittsburgh of the South." Its position as the center of the southern iron industry in the mid-1870s directed the attention of Bowron's English investors to eastern Tennessee.[14]

The southern iron industry suffered with virtually all capitalist enterprises during and after the panic of 1873. Even relatively strong organizations like the Tredegar works ceased operations, and most of the newer iron operations were substantially set back, if not ruined altogether. Only four of Alabama's approximately twenty iron furnaces operated during the hard years between 1874 and 1878. What was for decades called the "Great Depression" largely stopped industrial progress for most of a decade. The iron market looked up in 1880, showed higher prices for two years, and then plummeted again in 1882. One major by-product of the economic distress was the consolidation of small iron companies into larger, better-financed corporations. Such a consolidation in 1882 brought Bowron's English concern under the control of the Tennessee Coal, Iron and Railroad Company.[15]

The extended hard times depressed the spirits of even those who survived and caused some honest reflection on the prospects for industrialization in the South. Samuel Noble of Anniston wrote in 1883 that the history of iron making in Alabama since 1871 was "strewn with the wrecks of shattered hopes" of the men who built the furnaces, adding that the experience in Georgia and Tennessee had been no better. "It has been a weary struggle to make these enterprises pay; it has been [like] dragging an elephant." Willard Warner testified to a U.S. congressional hearing in 1883 that "our money has been in that business ten years . . . and we have not had any return; we have never had a dividend. . . . There has in Alabama since the war [been] more capital sunk . . . and lost than has been paid in dividends." Noble identified the main source of the industry's problem: "The great trouble is, we have [no] home market beyond the demand created by the iron furnaces themselves. The whole state of Alabama cannot take the product of a single blast furnace for a month. We depend entirely on the North and the great West to keep our furnaces going." In 1885 the president of the American Institute of Mining Engineers cautioned southern ironmakers assembled at Chattanooga that "notwithstanding all that Nature has done for the South . . . [it] has left a good deal to be done by skill and enterprise." Abundant resources close together, he said, did not necessarily mean cheap production costs and high profits. That was a message already clear to experienced industrialists.[16]

The iron market recovered in 1886, and a great boom of iron making then ensued in the South. Dozens of new companies were chartered and new towns sprang up—or at least got planned—to go with the new furnaces. The greatest activity took place in Alabama, where more than twenty towns were boomed as iron cities between 1885 and 1892. Even the Black Belt town of Montgomery planned an iron furnace. Many iron cities never in fact saw the furnace materialize, but new iron-making operations were started in Tuscaloosa, Gadsden, Sheffield, Ft. Payne, Talladega, and Decatur. By 1887 the center of southern iron making had moved from Chattanooga to Birmingham. There were, of course, iron boomtowns elsewhere: Scottish capitalists started iron making at Dayton, Tennessee, and English investors developed a steel-making operation at a place in Kentucky they confidently named Middlesborough. Virginia witnessed the most extensive growth in iron making outside Alabama; it would rank as the second largest iron-producing southern state in the years ahead.[17]

After Birmingham the most important of the iron boomtowns was Bessemer, just southwest of Birmingham, where Henry F. DeBardeleben, son-in-law of Daniel Pratt, built several new furnaces and laid out what he promised would be a large—and appropriately named—industrial city. After experiencing general failure with the Eureka Company in the early 1870s, DeBardeleben had enjoyed great success beginning in about 1880 with his Pratt Coal and Coke Company, only to sell out suddenly in 1881 when he thought his health was failing. The new DeBardeleben Coal and Iron Company, and his booming of Bessemer, by 1886 had put him back in the lead of Alabama's industrial development. With the aid of capital from England and Charleston, South Carolina, he soon would own or control 140,000 acres of Alabama mineral lands and be operating eight iron blast furnaces on his Bessemer properties.[18]

The iron boom that started in 1886 resulted in a massive increase in output. In Alabama alone, thirty-three new furnaces were built between 1885 and 1892, bringing the total number in that state to fifty-five. During the same years the annual production of iron in Alabama went from 203,000 to 915,000 tons. But during these years there would be little joy for any ironmaker. The price of iron began to drop in 1890 from the high levels of the late 1880s, and with it fell many of the new enterprises. Boom companies failed frequently after 1892, and, as had been the case in depressed times during the 1870s, the lucky stockholders were those whose company was taken over by one a little stronger. By the time the bottom of this new depression was reached in 1895, there were many fewer iron companies—and furnaces in blast—in Virginia, Tennessee, and Alabama.[19]

A major outcome of this contraction was the further concentration of the iron industry in Birmingham—and in the corporate hands of Tennessee Coal and Iron. The growth in production had glutted the market, and in 1892 southern ironmakers considered creating an iron pool to fix prices. But legal and political problems arising from the growing antitrust sentiment in the country suggested that a consolidation of the major companies was more practical. Their original goal was to create a single southern company; in the end only the two largest, TCI and DeBardeleben Coal and Iron, combined under TCI's corporate identity. Controlled by outsiders for most of its existence and dominated since 1880 by the stock manipulator John Inman, TCI after the merger became even more dependent on northern capital. Henry DeBardeleben's disastrous attempt to capture control of TCI in 1893 further tightened the grip of Wall Street on the southern iron industry. Now the fate of a basic industry, on which so much hope for regional growth and change rested, was largely in the hands of one board of directors in New York. The consolidation also put virtually the entire focus of the southern iron industry on Birmingham; even two of the next largest producers, the Sloss and Woodward companies, were centered in the city. Production in Tennessee and Georgia soon was relatively insignificant. It was no accident that in 1895 the Tennessee Company, and James Bowron, moved to Birmingham.[20]

By the early 1890s the more alert southern ironmakers recognized that steel was rapidly supplanting iron in the materials market, especially for rails. The nation's consumption of iron declined in real terms starting in 1893. The obvious need for southern ironmakers was to begin steel production. There were, however, fundamental technological problems with making steel from southern iron. The hematite mined on Birmingham's Red Mountain and the coke made from Alabama coal produced iron that was high in phosphorus and silicon, both undesirable for making steel by the Bessemer process, the first and still most common method. More promising for Alabama's iron was the basic open-hearth process, which relied on an acid-absorbent limestone furnace lining to remove phosphorus from iron. The open-hearth method usually depended on a certain portion of scrap steel to be added to each run, or "heat," of the furnace. The use of the basic open-hearth process was delayed during the 1880s because of a patent dispute, but in 1888 James Henderson made open-hearth steel at his small Birmingham works. Although technically a success, the Henderson experiment proved to be so violent that a second try was not possible.[21]

In 1889 Alfred M. Shook, a TCI executive momentarily out of the company's management, began a steel-making effort at the Southern Iron Company in Chattanooga. Shook had recruited a British metallurgist, Benjamin Talbot, to address the technological problems. Talbot developed a complicated "duplex" process by which molten iron was first treated to remove silicon and then put in the open hearth for final processing. The Talbot method presumably dispensed with the need for scrap steel, which was very scarce in the South. Northern steelworks used worn rails for scrap, but there was so little steel in use in the South on the railroads that scrap was an unavailable commodity. Shook and Talbot turned out steel in Chattanooga in 1890, but the Southern Iron Company was a commercial failure, apparently because Talbot's high production costs necessitated lower material costs than could be achieved in Chattanooga. This experience taught Shook and Bowron that the important task was to learn how to make steel in Birmingham, where the assembly costs were lowest. In the meantime Shook returned to the TCI management determined to move the company into steel production. In 1893 TCI applied the Talbot method in a pilot project in Birmingham, but the panic of 1893 and subsequent financial problems prevented further movement toward full-scale steel production.[22]

Bowron had been arguing for the beginning of steel production at TCI since at least 1888, when he attempted unsuccessfully to get Jacob Reese, one of the inventors of the basic open-hearth process, a hearing from the TCI board of directors. At the time the board was too consumed with the effort to boom the Ensley Land Company to listen to Reese. Had they acted on his offer to build a steelworks, steel production at TCI might have started a full decade earlier. Reese in all likelihood would have made the adaptation that Talbot ultimately implemented, and he might have done so during the prosperous days of 1888 and 1889. As it was, TCI's real effort toward steel making did not start until the company was struggling to cope with a severe depression and there was little capital free for technological development. Even after Shook, Bowron, and the other southern managers became adamant in the early 1890s that making steel was a company necessity, the TCI board resisted giving the financial support for a new steelworks. Only in 1897, when Milton Smith of the L&N issued warnings of economic disaster for Birmingham—and, incidentally, for the L&N—and threatened to take his financial support to another potential steelmaker, did TCI take definite steps toward building a steelworks. Even then the local managers, with Bowron in the lead, had to put up personal funds to underwrite the new plant. TCI's first run of steel came in November 1899.[23]

Bowron's autobiography makes clear that TCI's tardiness in making steel owed as much to the outside ownership's failure to see the need as it did to the technological problems with southern minerals. In the 1890s the TCI directors were governed primarily by their desire to push up the price of their stock, and to that end they demanded low costs. Any capital expenditure decreased the likelihood of TCI's showing immediate profits. Making steel, of course, represented a large expenditure. They reluctantly went along with erecting a steelworks only when virtually all the voices from the South insisted on it.[24]

The historical significance of TCI's late entry into steel making lies in the changing geography of demand for the product. One economist has presented evidence that the centers of steel demand in the United States in the 1880s and 1890s were in areas of relatively close proximity to Birmingham, primarily places with a great need for steel rails. The city's geographical advantage actually peaked in 1899. After that year the heaviest demand shifted northward toward Detroit and Chicago, with the advent of automobiles and tractors. In other words, Birmingham's greatest opportunity for growth as a steel center had passed prior to the time it realized the ability to make steel. Had TCI's ownership been committed to steel making in the 1880s, the company might have captured the benefits arising from its geographical advantage. As it was, Birmingham developed a steel capacity *after* its greatest potential had passed, and consequently its industrial growth was substantially less than it might have been.[25]

Efficient production eluded the company for the three years after the first run of steel, but success came finally in 1903 when a variation of Talbot's duplex process was applied. The same year the rail mill went into production, and rails soon became TCI's main product. But it still did not make a profit. The duplex process meant high production costs, and other start-up expenditures and rising wages left the company in the red through 1907, even as large sales of rails brought the company industrywide recognition.[26]

Despite the failure to make profits, TCI represented one of the more attractive steel concerns outside Morgan's giant U.S. Steel, created in 1900. John W. Gates, who had merged Illinois Steel into U.S. Steel but was himself left out of the management, began in 1904 to buy TCI shares in the hope of making it part of a rival to the Morgan company. Gates's move had the financial support of the brokerage house of Moore and Schley. In late 1905 Gates won control of TCI from the investor group led by James T. Woodward of the Hanover Bank. In the summer of 1907, however, the market for iron and steel fell drastically, and by November declining steel stock reputedly had Moore and Schley on the brink of failure. At that point, U.S. Steel took over TCI in the controversial deal sanctioned by President Theodore Roosevelt, who accepted the word of Morgan and other bankers that the takeover was necessary to avert the failure of Moore and Schley and a consequent Wall Street panic. For $35 million—truly a bargain price for 200,000 acres of mineral land, two dozen blast furnaces, a steelworks, and other equipment worth millions—the steel corporation got the southern industry. Later estimates would put the real value of the properties at closer to $1 billion. But as advantageous as the deal later seemed, Judge Elbert Gary and others at U.S. Steel doubted at the time that it was a benefit to their company because of TCI's history of losing money. After it took over and spent an initial $23.5 million to modernize TCI's plants, the steel corporation maintained that the high production costs largely offset Birmingham's low assembly costs. George G. Crawford, the young executive put in charge of TCI, dismissed in 1913 the "rosy pictures" of Birmingham's steel future but predicted that TCI would eventually become a "reasonably good business proposition."[27]

Though no longer working at TCI, Bowron believed that the takeover had an entirely positive impact on southern industry. U.S. Steel ensured abundant capital for TCI and, in Bowron's view, more enlightened management than the company recently had known. Hardly everyone in Birmingham agreed with him. Congressman Oscar Underwood, the banker W. P. G. Harding, and Senator John H. Bankhead believed that U.S. Steel's monopoly influence inhibited Birmingham's development. All Democrats favoring more business competition—Underwood attacked the takeover in his 1912 presidential campaign—these men wanted to see a rival company emerge. That probably accounted for Harding's determined commitment to save the bankrupt Gadsden steel company that Bowron took over in 1911. To the surprise and horror of many Republican businessmen, Bowron included, the Taft administration had instituted antitrust proceedings against U.S. Steel for the TCI takeover. In response, angry U.S. Steel executives delayed an expansion program until the government's suit was decided. In 1915 Richard Edmonds of the *Manufacturers' Record* blamed Birmingham's failure to develop a more advanced manufacturing on U.S. Steel's refusal to move ahead with expansion plans. Edmonds said that the slow development kept Birmingham enslaved as "hewers of wood and drawers of water" to the more advanced North. The company finally was cleared of the antitrust action by the U.S. Supreme Court in 1920, though its expansion in Birmingham had by then proceeded somewhat as a result of demand spurred by World War I.[28]

Meanwhile, the southern iron industry had stagnated, owing in large measure to the expansion of steel. But there were fundamental problems within the iron industry itself. From 1908 to 1912, the price of iron fell from $23 to about $12 per ton. The price fall hurt worse than it might have because of changes in the system of freight rates. Since the 1880s southern railroads had worked to set rates at a level to make southern products competitive in northern markets. They had succeeded by giving preferential rates for such southern commodities as cotton textiles and pig iron. Then in 1907, under pressure about rate disparities and with new powers granted by the Hepburn Act, the Interstate Commerce Commission set a flat maximum of $3.25 per ton for southern iron shipped North. The depression in the iron market led to a $1 per ton freight reduction in 1914.[29]

Freight rates were allowed to rise again with the increase of iron prices during the war, when the U.S. government's Railroad Administration ran the national roads. After the war, the Transportation Act of 1920 sanctioned both higher freight rates and a major railroad consolidation movement. Consolidation undermined the competition among northern railroads that had produced the preferential rates traditionally given in order to get the traffic in southern commodities. Acting to protect northern iron producers, northern railroads now refused to make cheap rates for southern products traveling above the Ohio River. The resulting higher freight rates effectively shut much southern iron out of northern markets after 1920. For the first time southern producers had to depend almost entirely on southern consumption. The Birmingham ironmakers were fortunate that the local cast-iron pipe and foundry industries had continued to expand and thus could absorb most of their merchant pig iron. Most other southern ironmakers were not so lucky; nearly all producers outside Birmingham had gone out of business by the mid-1930s.[30]

In the steel industry, the "Pittsburgh Plus" price-fixing mechanism allowed producers an umbrella of protection from rising freight rates. Under Pittsburgh Plus pricing, the entire American steel industry essentially agreed to a single Pittsburgh price for most steel products, rails being the notable exception. During the war years Pittsburgh Plus came under attack from many northern steel consumers who contended, quite rightly, that it gave an unfair advantage to producers in western Pennsylvania. Steel fabricators in the South who purchased steel made in Birmingham argued to the Federal Trade Commission (FTC) that Pittsburgh Plus effectively reduced the geographical area in which they could sell competitively. Bowron, however, spoke out in 1919 before the FTC in favor of Pittsburgh Plus, on the grounds that stabilized prices protected southern steel exporters. His Gulf States Steel, of course, received protected prices for the wire and nails it made.[31]

The FTC disallowed Pittsburgh Plus in 1924, but in its place came a "multiple basing point" pricing mechanism that still set Birmingham prices substantially above Pittsburgh's. The significant difference at that point, however, was that favorable freight rates were now much harder to get and southern steel was thus less competitive in northern markets. The change exposed southern steel goods to the problems that high freight rates presented to iron exporters. During the 1920s and especially in the 1930s when the Great Depression intensified competition, southern manufacturers and their political spokesmen would cry out against freight-rate "discrimination" by the North. The anger was warranted in the sense that the high freight rates were now the only cost holding back Birmingham steel. The availability of scrap steel now reduced production costs to some of the lowest in the industry, and in the 1930s discriminatory pricing was largely abandoned. But for the very high costs of transportation, TCI might have captured a much larger share of the steel market.[32]

U.S. Steel's poor management probably limited Birmingham's growth as much as did high transportation costs. In the 1920s and 1930s the corporation generally failed to supply its customers in the West with products made in Birmingham, even though lower transportation costs to the Pacific Coast should have dictated it. The corporation's subsidiaries in Pittsburgh and Chicago were favorably treated at the expense of TCI's growth. Moreover, the corporation was slow to expand TCI's product offerings. Besides rails and wire products, TCI produced mostly semifinished ingots and billets until a plate mill came on line to serve shipbuilding during World War I. A sheet mill was started in the mid-1920s. In the mid-1930s U.S. Steel's own management consultant criticized the company's failure to build a tin-plate mill in Birmingham. High consumption of tin plate by food processors in the South should have brought tin-plate production much earlier. Such mismanagement helped to undermine TCI's potential advantage and to perpetuate the reality of slow industrial growth.[33]

By the end of the 1930s the problem of inadequate capital had been overcome, and southern consumption of iron and steel had grown to a level sufficient to take most of the region's limited production. But that did not mean the South's industry now mirrored the North's. Indeed, the regional differences were often felt more acutely, as revealed in the public discussion of freight-rate and wage differentials. Colonialism remained a reality—one that received much public attention in the quest to discover the sources of poverty in the nation's "number one economic problem." Outside ownership, at least that of U.S. Steel, continued to inhibit the realization of the South's industrial potential despite the numerous signs of progress since World War I. The troubled history of southern industry still weighed on the region's economic prospects, and the burden sometimes seemed no lighter.

What follows is an abridged re-creation of Bowron's almost 2,000-page autobiography, dictated in sporadic installments from about 1915 through 1927. The original has been cut drastically and rearranged freely to lend thematic unity to Bowron's rigorously chronological manuscript, though the integrity of his sentences has been preserved. This version includes a few excerpts from his fifty-two-volume diary and some noteworthy portions of his scrapbooks and letters, which he intended as corollary texts to his autobiography. The spelling, punctuation, and capitalization of his autobiography have been made to conform to modern practice; material included from other sources has been used as in the original source. James Bowron had much to say about many things, and this is a mere sampling of the best of it.

James Bowron

Origins

James Bowron descended from a long line of northern Englishmen who had originally landed on the island with William the Conqueror. The Bowrons converted to Quakerism during England's Reformation, and in the eighteenth and nineteenth centuries the family apparently manifested the devout, industrious ways popularly associated with the Society of Friends. They ranked among the moderately prosperous members of the relatively large, and generally successful, Quaker community of northern Yorkshire and County Durham. James Bowron was educated at Ackworth School, a well-known Quaker preparatory academy near Leeds. Afterward, without benefit of collegiate education, he would go into his father's various industrial enterprises and ultimately try his hand in his own business. He quickly acquired firsthand knowledge of the chaotic commercial practices of mid-nineteenth-century business. He also gained valuable expertise in financing industrial corporations, knowledge that would serve him well throughout his long and eventful business career. Along the way, Bowron had a conversion experience in an evangelical meeting and adopted a kind of energetic, outward Christianity common in the late nineteenth century. As a young man he began to take on the heavy family responsibilities which would be such a central concern of his life.

t has been said that to train a man properly you should begin with his grandmother. In my case I can reach further backward. The original name was not Bowron but Bolron. The first Bolron, so far as we can gather, was a Norman soldier and follower of William the Conqueror. In Norman-French bol-ron or ronde means a round hill.

To avenge the loss of a Norman garrison at York, William swept northward through Northumbria with an army, laying waste the land. It is said that between York and Durham there was not one inhabited town, and for sixty miles and more the land was uncultivated. In 1085 the Domesday Book quotes a number of places in North Yorkshire, including the then name of Cotherstone as "waste." It would reasonably appear that as a reward for their services William made grants of land to his soldiers, and that in this way the Bolron family became settled on the banks of the River Tees at Cotherstone, and started a grist mill.

The only records that we can find in those distant centuries are the memoranda from the legal records which show the existence of our kinsmen. Thus, we find in A.D. 1227 a reference to Roger de Bolron and Thomas de Bolron. As is well known, the prefix "de" in French, like the German "von," is indicative of aristocracy. We note in 1251 reference to Thomas de Bolron as surety in a suit, showing that he must have been a man of some substance. In 1277 Peter de Bolron is recorded as the owner of lands in Bolron and Bowes. In 1279 John de Bolron was summoned as a juryman at York, and the son of Thomas de Bolron recorded as a witness.

In 1299 Thomas de Bolron is recorded as suing various people for trespassing and taking his land. In 1302 Stephen de Bolron and John de Bolron paid subsidies, according to the records of King Edward the First, to provide for a war against Scotland. When the army was defeated at Bannockburn, the flower of the Yorkshire knights, squires, and men-at-arms perished. The Scots followed the broken army into England, ransacked Yorkshire, and returned into Scotland leaving a cruel famine behind them. In 1308 we find Thomas de Bolron defendant in a land suit. In 1332 William de Bolron appears as plaintiff in a land suit, and John de Bolron as a witness. In 1410 John de Bolron, who appears to have been a chaplain, bought a house in York, and in 1415 was sued for cattle trespasses; and in this year the notable occurrence appears of Thomas de Bolron being present at the battle of Agincourt as a man-at-arms, and William de Bolron as an archer under the command of Lord Fitz Hugh.

Under English law a landowner has always stood with members of the learned professions as a legal esquire, entitled to precedence over the common people, who make their living by trade. Our ancestor, not being ashamed of his calling, assumed as his coat-of-arms the sails of his wind mill. And for the crest he made a pun upon the name. The village by this time had, or at a later time had, the name not of "Bolrun," but of "Boldrun." A pun upon the name Bold-run caused him to assume a springing greyhound as the crest of the family, for the greyhound is a bold runner. The motto attached to the crest is "Vigilans, agilis et fidelis." "Vigilant, active and faithful." No Bowron need feel ashamed of his crest and motto, and will do well to live up to it.

To interpose for a moment. The oldest son of John Bolron was John Bolron, Quaker missionary, born 1627, died 1704. He was one of the original Quakers, being converted at the age of twenty-six by the preaching of George Fox, the founder of the Society of Friends; and he [John Bolron] had the usual experience of persecution, as he preached himself. In 1656 he sailed to Barbados and hence to Surinam, Guiana, in South America, where he preached among the natives who treated him kindly. His return voyage to England occupied thirteen weeks, and some died from starvation on the voyage. He was imprisoned at various times in England for preaching, but lived to be "full of days," and died in peace in the same house in which he was born; and only a few days before his death preached, and sent word by his son to the meeting that his "days were almost spent." He died full of peace amongst his family at the age of seventy-seven.

His younger brother Henry Bolron was born in 1637, married 1669 to Mary Appleby; she died in 1708 and he in 1724. His oldest son Caleb Bowron was born in 1671 and married Ann Rains in 1695. At this point it is noted that the spelling of the name is changed to suit the dialectic pronunciation of the broad Yorkshire hills and dales. As a man might go into the field and call, "Lad gaw whoam and drive cowt i't field," meaning in plain English, "Lad go home and drive the colt into the field," so the Bowron is a phonetic spelling of the Yorkshire pronunciation of the seventeenth century. And, to tell the truth, I am rather sorry for it, for the name and the substance of a "bold runner" is rather attractive; but in this day a man may run the race that is set before him without his name being any handicap.

Amongst the children of Caleb Bowron we find Appleby Bowron, born 1700, who in 1725 married Mary Watson; of their children Caleb Bowron, born 1728, was married first to Margaret Simpson and later in 1766 to Hannah Fletcher. . . . Of their children I note my own grandfather, Joseph

Bowron, who was born in 1770. . . . Of his family of nine my father, James Bowron, was the sixth, being born in 1814. He married in 1840 Mary Hannah Moss, my mother, who was born in 1822.

It seems perhaps convenient to speak of my father at this point at some length, rather than interpose a long record in the midst of my own life. He was indeed a remarkable man. He was about my own size, heavily built, broad of chest, a man who bequeathed to me several invaluable traits, including the possession of an extremely retentive memory and the gift of easily acquiring foreign languages. When he was a young man he would take down the shutters at six o'clock in the morning at the country store, and put them up at ten o'clock at night. How many young men under such conditions would have become fairly fluent speakers of French, some knowledge of German, deeply versed in poetry—able to recite thousands of lines from memory—and would have developed an inventive genius both along mechanical and chemical lines? His invention of pressing fluid glass into curved and ornamental tiles for roofing was profitable to him as a glass manufacturer, and he was a co-patentee with his friend Dr. Robinson of several improvements in the manufacture of bleaching powder and alkali, and at the time of his death had secured patents on what, to my mind, would have been a distinct success, namely, the forging of steel car wheels in a die.

His indomitable industry and energy passes all praise. He set me an example which I have never forgotten. When I cleaned up his papers after his death I found notes for tens of thousands of dollars unpaid and long outlawed by death, or bankruptcy, or lapse of time. Truly he obeyed the scriptural injunction, "From him who would borrow of thee, turn not thou away." This, however, was hard both upon himself and upon his family, and as I develop the story of my own life I may have occasion to expatiate a little upon his life of financial difficulty, for he practically never knew anything else.

My mother tells me that I was born 3:00 P.M., November 18, 1844, and as she had not said anything to my father about it at dinner in the middle of the day, he was quite surprised when they sent down to the warehouse at the foot of the garden to suggest that he come up and see the new addition, without waiting until suppertime. I have not heard that there was any firing of cannon or flying of flags, or any other evidence of joy to the world, but it was a very important day for me. The last time I was in Stockton-on-Tees I saw the old home still standing intact. It was Number 2 Finkle Street, Number 1 being the only house between it and the River Tees; so that although I was born in the county of Durham, I was as near to being a Yorkshireman as the width of the river would permit. The house was three stories high, brick of course (I never saw a wooden house in England), and our nursery faced to the east at the back of the house on the second floor, and the window was guarded with iron bars to prevent us from climbing or falling out. There was a large old-fashioned roomy town lot with flower garden and central walk covered with vines, in the nature of a pergola, down the center of it, and at the foot of the garden stood the wholesale grocery house of Close, Bowron and Company.

I have a faint recollection of the joy of building blocks high enough on the floor for them to tumble over, but a keen and lively sense of injustice and distress when I was playing with a little woolly animal and brother Will took it from me and dropped it over on the inside of the fender in front of the nursery fire, and as neither of us was big enough to reach over the fender my toy was gone. My second sorrow was much more serious, and is a proof of the enduring quality of early memory. The death of my first brother Joe [came in] 1847. I could not possibly have been more than three. I missed my playmate and was told he had gone to Heaven. At that early age I associated Heaven in some way with the church. The Episcopal parish church was just two blocks away, with a square tower or steeple, and at each corner was a little wind vane. I used to stand and strain my eyes between the bars of the nursery window to see if he were not playing around there on top of the church tower. This is an interesting proof of the ability of a child under three to reason, and to associate ideas.

My mother was born in Sunderland, the daughter of Gilbert Moss and Hannah Laws. She came not of Quaker stock like my father, but was of sailor ancestry, one of her relatives having been lost at sea, master of a ship which never came home. She was a woman of about five feet and five inches in height, and within the time of my recollection rather portly, very dignified in her bearing, and thoroughly domesticated. She had fully adopted my father's Quaker simplicity. They took no part in what one might call social functions, but maintained a hospitable home, with a full measure of near visitation amongst friends. She was careful in looking after the regularity of our lives as to rising, retiring, hours of meals . . . so that the foundation was easily laid for the life of habitual system and precision which has supervened.

At some time or other the warehouse of Close, Bowron and Company burned down. It caught fire in the coffee roasting department. I do not know, but believe that in consequence of this the partnership was dissolved, and my father invested his share of the capital in the glass trade in South Shields, becoming the managing partner in the Tyne Tees Glass Company. This involved a removal from the banks of the Tees to the banks of the Tyne, and in 1852 our family moved bodily to Tynemouth, the romantic little watering place as it was then, with the remains of the priory commenced in 625 by the king of Northumberland, which gradually grew, although destroyed by the Danes.

Here at the early age of eight with brother Will, who was by this time twelve, I learned to row and to be at home in a boat upon the sea, helping the boatkeeper to haul boats in and push them out and to attend to his customers, for which we would be rewarded by the privilege of using them when business was slack. On arrival at Tynemouth Will and I were immediately enrolled as scholars at a private boarding and day school at Sunderland, kept by Joseph Special on Villiers Street. There were only about six or eight boarders, enough to make up one bedroom, and according to my recollection about thirty day scholars. Here from the age of eight to ten I was supposed to assimilate knowledge, but I assimilated a great deal more mischief than I did knowledge. The boys were not a nice class, and there was no supervision over them, and their ideas and conversation were very far from edifying. Our time here from a scholastic point of view was wasted. I know when I left there I was supposed to be able [to] work cube root, but I also know that I was not able to work long division, which is a pretty good proof of the shallowness of our studies. In fact, my belief is that [in] all the four years I spent from the ages of six to ten in so-called schools I learned about as much as I could have learned under proper systematic public school teaching in thirty days.

About this time I graduated out of frocks into sure enough trousers. This would seem strange reading to American boys, but up to the time of my leaving England in 1877, I had never seen a boy wearing a pair of short pants. No one up to that epoch in England ever wore knickerbockers, as they were called, except artists or gamekeepers, unless it was part of a regular shooting costume, supplemented by leather gaiters for traveling amongst the stubble. At the age of ten I was a little, delicate, timid child, wearing frocks with black ends about a foot long sewed onto my drawers so as to hang below the edge of the frock and look like sure enough trouser legs. In the absence of any special children's suits there was no go-between, and it was a question of graduating from the above into the regulation full length trousers. Great was the surprise and the congratulations showered upon me when I went back to school in the changed dress.

This seems to bring me to a momentous period of my life, the year 1854, when I went to school at Ackworth. I went there the first of November, 1854, as they would not receive boys until they were ten years of age, nor might they stay there after they were fifteen. My father had attended it in his day.

The school made a man of me physically, intellectually, and morally, and I owe to it and to the systematic and conscientious management of the Society of Friends an inestimable debt of gratitude. On my arrival I was placed at the bottom of the second grade, there being ten, numbering upwards from the bottom. I think my inability to work a long division sum put me in the second grade instead of the third. Our lives were most systematic. We rose at six in the summer, six-thirty in winter; gathered for evening scripture reading at eight o'clock, to bed at eight-fifteen; and all talking was required to cease at nine. The rules were iron clad, and they were maintained with a severity as hard as iron. If we did not know rule and discipline when we went there, we certainly did when we came out.

We had fifteen minutes after rising within which to dress and make our beds. If we were not out of the room fifteen minutes after the rising bell rang, the master on duty was there with his pencil and pocketbook to take our names for punishment. It was then our duty after leaving the room to go down to the cellars where there was a row of probably 100 washbasins to wash our faces and hands. Many boys used to skip this, naturally, as they would today if possible. Our first act was always to get the top of the head in the bowl, and the hair being wet, if a boy had a pocket comb he would make a mirror by putting his cap behind a pane of glass and divide his hair in front for an inch and a half. During my four years residence in the school I never saw but one boy use a hairbrush. We looked upon anything of that sort as dudish and effeminate, and wholly unworthy of our masculine standards.

Our breakfast consisted of a bowl of warm milk and a hunk of bread to each boy; our supper, a bowl of cold milk and a hunk of bread. Our dinner consisted of hot meat and boiled potatoes for the first course, and either bread pudding or apple pie for the second course. We could not get any more milk than was served to us in the bowl, but I think the quantity was sufficient as I never remember anyone needing more. We could have as much bread as we wanted by holding up the hand. At breakfast and supper we had our individual bowls of milk, but at dinner when water was served there was one large mug for six of us to drink from. That was all right, however, for microbes had not yet been discovered.

I confess that in the wintertime we did suffer for want of adequate warmth. The rooms were heated by large open fires, burning coal. There was some theoretical steam heating arrangement, but it did not amount to anything and I do not believe was in use. In wintertime when we dismissed from parade, after coming out from a meal, there was a wild helter-skelter rush for the two assembly rooms where alone the rank and file could go out of class hours. The first one to arrive there under the laws of the school could stretch out his arms in front of the fireplace and hold as much of the coveted space in front of the fire as he could stretch to for himself and his personal friends. The boy who was slow or unpopular had very little chance to get to the fire, bearing in mind there were only two fires for 180 boys, and perhaps six could be warmed comfortably at one time at each fire. For this reason I suffered very much. My lips cracked, and I suffered distressingly from chilblains on fingers and toes, and both my lips and all around the sides of my mouth were a mass of hard sores which I would keep licking, and they would continually crack worse and worse.

We worked every day at our lessons five days full, and until three o'clock on Saturday, and at least two hours on Sunday. We also worked eleven months in the year. We had no holidays at Christmas or at Easter, but one single month, from July 4th to August 4th. We studied twice as long as children of today, and consequently we made progress. Naturally we had not so very much playtime: half or three-quarters of an hour after breakfast, half an hour during the morning, an hour after dinner, and half or three-quarters of an hour before or after suppertime. Then on Saturday we had from three o'clock until suppertime.

Our method of study was not that which is commended today. We had one teacher for each grade, and it was his duty to teach every subject. There was not, as there would be today, a Latin master, a French master, a music master, or a teacher of mathematics. I started in . . . at the bottom of the second class, but at the first examination . . . I was elevated clean out of the second class and over the third into the fourth. I may say once and for all that I was at the top of every class in every grade during the whole time I was in school, with the exception of my writing, where I was at the bottom, for I wrote a little cramped and almost illegible fist. I liked the [fourth-grade] teacher and made excellent progress, so much so that [at] the following mid-summer examination, [it] being only eight months from the time I entered the school . . . I found to my amazement that I was vaulted over the fifth.

In my second year I had a very happy and successful time in the sixth grade under W. H. Longmaid. . . . I got along so well with Longmaid in the sixth, that at midterm I was moved into the seventh under William Tallack, who was an absentminded man and was not in touch with his scholars at all. I was duly promoted and went back to begin my third year in the eighth grade under William Pollard. [I] made about the usual systematic progress, being advanced in midterm to the ninth grade and J. W. Watson, another absentminded teacher, with whom we used to take some liberties. I went back for my fourth year, finding myself in the coveted and highest tenth grade, and there the work was much more difficult and progress slower. I found in some studies I had hard work to keep up with the others, and I had to work very hard to do it. But in what was called general knowledge I was always far advanced, and I never had the slightest difficulty in holding the top of the class in mental arithmetic.

We had a scriptural reading every night throughout the school year, the 180 boys on one side of the large reading room and the 120 girls on the other side. The teacher would read to us every night an extract from the life of some good old Quaker worthy, George Fox, John Woolman, or others, and afterwards a selected portion of the Bible to finish. On Sunday night the procedure was somewhat different. One teacher and one boy from our side and one teacher and one girl from the other side . . . had to read selected scripture portions. The readers were from the highest grades, and as I had a good voice and a clear enunciation, and have always known how to pronounce and emphasize my words, I was often selected. I became so accustomed as a lad of thirteen to sit there and face an audience of 300 and read aloud to that audience that I have never known the feeling of stage fright. I think it must be measurably due to this experience that throughout my life I have found it quite as easy to speak to 3,000 people as to 300, and would rather speak to 300 than to 30.

Having commenced my studies November 1, 1854, they were carried on until October 31, 1858, so that when I went back the last time it was only for a three months period, and that gave me the coveted position, with my last examination, of head of the school. I [was] either the youngest boy who ever attained the position or one of the youngest. The desk in the reading room for the two highest scholars was of polished rosewood instead of mahogany, and how proud I felt when I moved up to occupy a place there with my companion, William Johnson, a most studious, grand, thoughtful fellow, who gave his life as a missionary in Madagascar and was speared to death by the natives.

How little is it possible for us to foresee the future. My most intimate friend as a young boy in the lower grades was George Farrand, my most intimate friend in the tenth grade being William Johnson. So far as we three had any possible reason to suppose, there was no likelihood of any one of us ever going outside of England. Now today, George Farrand lies buried on a farmer's ranch in New Zealand and William Johnson at the Missionary Station in Madagascar, and I am here in Alabama! Should we not draw the lesson from this to be prepared to meet life and [its] developments anywhere, anyhow, any time, calmly, heroically, in the spirit of "delivering the goods" and giving the best we have?

The moral tone of the school was very good. There was a little tendency to what one might call "priggishness," a sort of imitation of the Pharisees. But in the main the school looked down upon everything that was mean or untrue or insincere or vulgar. There was no idea of cheating in our work. Such a thing would have been resented bitterly by the school at large. I recall with pleasure the visit of the great African missionary and explorer, the greatest of all, David Livingstone, to whom I listened with absorbing interest. Our hearts were much warmed toward missionary enterprise, and especially toward the circulation of the Bible. It is a mystery to me how out of our pennies so much was collected every year for the British and Foreign Bible Society. I think it got about 15 percent of my pocket money.

My mind seems to be naturally thoughtful, and I can well remember the impression produced by a sermon on the fifteenth chapter of John, "I am the vine, ye are the branches." On one rare happy occasion, having a visit from my father, when in accordance with custom I was allowed to go myself and invite any of my friends to take tea at the village inn, where we got buns and tea cakes and toast and felt ourselves millionaires, after the others had gone back and I could stay half an hour longer, I sat in front of the fire at my father's feet and thoughtfully looking ahead told him that I had about concluded that I would rather be a missionary. I was surprised and awed to see the teardrops standing in his eyes. The conversation, however, was not pursued further.

On October 31, 1858, having completed my four years, and having attained the headship of the school, I returned home very soundly grounded in elementary history, geography, arithmetic, and natural science, a fair knowledge of French, and a reasonable knowledge of Latin grammar, and as ignorant of the ways of the great world into which I was entering as a Hottentot. I started work without any interregnum the following day, November 1, 1858. My father took me to the office, and my uncle, Henry Briggs, who was the bookkeeper for the concern, looked at me contemptuously in my cheap school uniform and shoes with brass clasps. [Briggs, who] took snuff copiously, blew a resounding blast upon a huge bandanna hand-kerchief and addressed me: "Boy, are those Ackworth shoes?" I disliked him from that moment until the end of our acquaintance years afterward.

It is always difficult to decide what shall be the future of a boy when he leaves school. It was perhaps not so difficult for my father as it is for me. He had a business of his own, and he had no son in it. My brother Will, who had left school several years before me, was always of a restless tempera-ment. He had run away from school once, and yet later had run away from home and gone to sea. He made several voyages, but did not appear to settle, and when I left school arrangements were being completed by which . . . he was emigrating to New Zealand. This left me the only big boy at home.

An elderly Quaker who had been present at my final examination in the big meeting house . . . told [my father] that my readiness of speech in answering questions, and my evidently retentive memory, suggested a legal career, and he sent me some law books to read. But I could not take a legal course; the gate was barred. There were two ways to enter the profes-sion: the one to become the articled or apprenticed clerk to an attorney, and afterwards upon examination to be admitted to practice; the other to attend the law course either at Oxford, Cambridge, or London, keep the requisite number of terms, eat the requisite number of dinners, and then pass a stated examination, and so be admitted. England is not America and the traditions of caste and social status and privilege count heavily. A lawyer admitted through the attorney's clerkship would have [no] higher standing than a commissioned officer in the army who had worked up from the ranks as a "non-com." That was not to be thought of. The university career was the only reasonable gateway, and that was barred to me as a Quaker, and to all other dissenters, because the acceptance of the Thirty-nine Articles of the Church of England . . . was a condition precedent to matriculation.

If I had been born two years later I might never have seen America and would have probably been a successful barrister and in Parliament today. In 1860 the University Tests Abolition Act was passed, removing this religious requirement and opening the university to all without exception. I know that my powerful and well-trained memory, my ability to think upon my feet and to speak or write easily without embarrassment because of my audience, and my ability to debate earnestly would have made me beyond any question a successful lawyer. I am sure that I could have acquitted myself with greater success in that profession than I have been able to do in the humdrum busi-ness of sitting on the money box and driving creditors away from it. But the

Lord has given me greater success in life than I ever had any reason to anticipate, and I cannot repine at the conditions which forced me away from the law.

Under the circumstances, there seemed to be nothing else than that I should enter my father's office. My work began the day after I left school, and for a number of years was exceedingly uniform in character. It was my duty to walk a mile to town and back again . . . and six days a week I laid the letters in front of my father's plate when we sat down to breakfast at 8:00 A.M. After breakfast I went to the office, and it was my duty to copy letters in the old-fashioned way of the letter press, taking tissue copies and indexing the same; to go on errands of all sorts and kinds, remembering that in those days there [were] no telephones. For the first two years at the office I had no ambition. I was content to discharge the trivial duties of an office boy, spending a certain amount of the time in the works, naturally, watching the workmen making, preparing, packing, or loading our goods for shipment.

In 1856 the family [had] removed from South Shields back to Stockton-on-Tees, my father still retaining his interest in the glass works at South Shields, but also acquiring in that year an interest in the Glass Bottle Works at Stockton of Richard Price and Company. The glass which was made at South Shields was window glass, both crown and sheet. The competition of the Belgians had made the sheet glass trade unprofitable, and the works were shut down. Price sold out to my father.

With my present business knowledge it is easy for me to look back upon the situation and see that my father's business was very unsound. The profits were small and precarious, the wages paid being exceedingly high, and the business in the grasp of a domineering trades union. Ordinarily, unskilled labor at that time was worth sixty-five cents per day. Some of our skilled workmen made an average of $2.50, besides having certain guarantees and prerequisites. We had to furnish them with a house or an allowance for house rent, with coal, and with a certain amount of beer. Every time a crucible had to be put in [its] place, or moved, so many pints of beer would be given to that particular crew for the work. Needless to say that it was of a poor quality, pretty thin. But we had men who would drink as much as sixteen pints per day of it. It ran through them like water.

The class of customers was unsatisfactory. A certain amount was done direct from the factory to the brewers, wine merchants, manufacturers of soda water and lemonade, pickle manufacturers, people requiring preserve jars. But the great bulk of the business was done with merchants in London who would receive [a] shipload at the time of the bottles from us, dirty and sulfurous as they came out of the annealing kilns, and would wash them and thoroughly cleanse them, so that they should not spoil the beer or wine for which they were to be used, and then deliver them to the bottlers, who would buy beer for export in large quantities from the brewers and put up in bottled shape for exportation to the British colonies.

These bottle merchants in London, with hardly an exception, were people of small capital . . . used to making four months notes. As now, so then, the ultimate customers, people drowning in liquors, had a large percentage of commercial mortality. There [was] no adequate allowance made in the business for bad debts, not any allowance made in estimating profits for depreciation. The business was hollow and top heavy, and I can easily see how my father was embarrassed in carrying it on when I went in.

He took to himself a partner by the name of Charles Baily, who knew nothing at all about glass manufacture, but had been raised as an engineer in a southern county of England, and was supposed to be a practical man. Baily brought in some additional capital, and the business was changed as of January 1, 1859, from J. Bowron and Company to Bowron Baily and Company. In 1860 Bowron Baily and Company joined with a firm in London, the Hartley Bottle Company, William Watson being the managing representative. They formed together the Middlesbrough Bottle Company, Middlesbrough being four miles distant from Stockton. Each of them subscrib[ed] a part of the necessary capital.

I was transferred at this point from the Stockton office to Middlesbrough, going down on the train every morning, a mere ten- or fifteen-minute journey, or sometimes by preference taking the river steamer, a thirty-minute journey. It was my duty to keep the time, work up the payroll, and make the pay every Saturday afternoon; also to make out the invoices and bills-of-lading, and attend to the shipping end of the orders and see to their being discharged. I filled this position for about two years; at the end of that time, the business being found unprofitable the works were closed down, and I moved back to the Stockton office.

The business, as I have said, was unsound. The margins of profit were inadequate; the business was gouged by unreasonable trades union demands. But the greatest drawback was the unsoundness of the customers. The results were not satisfactory, and to keep things going it was necessary to renew a great proportion of the London merchants' acceptances when they matured due. To do this without exciting the animosity of the bank with which we did our business, J. Backhouse and Company, my father used to exchange some of the notes with others of his friends, taking from them notes which they were unable to discount, and so began, as nearly as I can recall, a system of unsound and vicious financiering, destined to break down my father both financially and physically.

I have often noticed in life how grace is given as, and how, and when it is needed. I can remember sitting one Sunday morning in stillness of a Quaker meeting, plunged in the deepest silent devotion and most earnestly committing myself to the favor and upbuilding of God. When I got to the office the next morning and saw the morning paper, I read that the glass works at South Shields had been totally destroyed by fire the previous Sunday morning, at the very time when I was sitting in the meeting. This brought about sudden results. There was an insurance of about $10,000 or $11,000, and when the fire insurance was collected from the North British Mercantile Company, which always treated us fairly, the check was paid in to our credit to J. Backhouse and Company, our bankers. They [then] quietly informed my father that we could close our account. As we had had an overdraft for a number of years, and the overdraft was now paid up by this insurance money, the account was not one that they cared to continue to carry. This at a stroke closed the principal avenue for discount of the customers' acceptance, which, as I have previously pointed out, were largely and increasingly renewed, owing to the inability of the customers to pay them.

This condition aggravated my father's partner, who had gradually been becoming more and more cantankerous, feeling that the business was not successful, and that he had made a mistake in putting his money into it. He began to make himself openly and manifestly disagreeable, never speaking except to find fault and more or less to recriminate and reproach my father, and to claim that the business was worthless when he came into it, and that we had never made any money, and that he wanted to get out. My father had no money with which to buy him out, however, and after considerable discussion of the situation it was finally determined to change the status of the business from that of a private partnership to a joint stock company.

Before proceeding with this . . . I should refer to a plan well conceived which failed by the merest touch to make my father rich. He conceived in his mind the idea of a consolidation of all the glass works on the East coast in Durham and North Yorkshire, so that we should have one London warehouse instead of half a dozen, and instead of cutting each other's prices we could maintain one uniform price there; consolidate our bank facilities and have some influence with our bankers; and to some extent select our own customers, and exact better terms of payment; and . . . be in better position to resist the arrogant domination of the trades union which ruled us with a rod of iron. The articles and memorandum of association, required by the English law, was signed, and the day was set for the signature which would have completed the proposition and would have made each of us rich.

On that morning my father woke up unable to speak, the right side of his face being paralyzed, his right eye and the right half of his mouth. He was the moving spirit [in the proposed glass manufacturers' association] and had handled all the negotiation, and the strain and pressure on his nervous system had brought this about. Today we know better how to treat facial paralysis, largely the result of albuminuria, but in those days knew nothing of such things, and could only fiddle with them with a little hand battery to . . . apply the current to the affected parts. The remedy was worthless.

In his absence, unable to travel, I was sent over to the meeting in Sunderland, for I was selected to be the secretary of the new company. When I got there I was shocked to be told by the leading manufacturer, John Candlish, a member of Parliament, that some questions had arisen which made them think it better to delay the signing of the papers. They never were signed and the whole thing broke down. If my father had been there, as usual, I have no doubt that his argument would have overcome any objection. The London manager of one of the companies concerned had been embezzling funds and knew that if this company were formed and all the London warehouses were consolidated into one and [closed] up their individual accounts, the defalcations would be discovered. So he raised some objection—I do not know what—which in my father's absence was sufficient to "sour the milk," and it all turned to clabber. The culprit was later detected, tried, and sent to prison, but in the meantime the damage had been done.

The failure of this enterprise had much to do with the development of the idea that we should convert the partnership into a limited liability stock company of our own, and the business was carefully valued and appraised, and a prospectus written. Efforts [were] made to obtain outside stockholders, but they were almost entirely futile. Mr. Baily's relatives subscribed for about twenty shares, the shares being $500 each. (As a matter of convenience I use American money at the rate of $5 for £1, to make the records easier for American readers.) We tried to induce our workmen to become interested and one share was taken by George Mustard, but he didn't like the flavor for he didn't pay more than the first $5 upon it. We tried to induce some of our customers to become stockholders by offering to give them a rebate of

2½ percent on all their purchases. This only had the effect of causing dis-satisfaction on the part of one or two customers who demanded the rebate anyhow, but would not take the stock.

Several of the parties failed to pay their bills which had been exchanged for ours, and suits began to be filed against the company and against my father personally. To avoid execution being levied upon his house, he exe-cuted a bill-of-sale to all his furniture to my grandmother, closed the home in South Stockton, and went to reside in a little watering place called Middle-on-Row, about fourteen miles higher up the River Tees. We were still residing in these furnished lodgings at this little rural village when I attained the dignified age of twenty-one and became a man to all legal effect.

At this time my father became interested with a Dr. Robinson in devel-oping certain chemical discoveries, and together they founded the Tyne Chemical Company, which constructed works at South Shields for the manufacture of sulfuric acid, sulfate of soda, baking powder, alkali, bicar-bonate of soda, and chlorate of potash. In this business they got some very good men interested and a fair amount of capital, but not sufficient as the plant was very expensive, requiring great quantities of lead for the acid chambers.

I was made auditor of the company, and it helped me considerably to expand my ideas of manufacturing books and accounts. I might say ad in-terim that in the year 1864, while my father was absent at Smedley's Hydro-pathic Institute at Matlock Bath, Derbyshire, I had without ever having received any instruction in the premises as to how to balance a set of double entry books, taken the half-yearly inventory, drawn off the trial balance, closed the books and sent him down a copy of the balance sheet. He was perfectly horrified on [its] receipt, for he had no idea that I knew how to balance a set of books—and for that matter I had no idea either until I did it. He was considerably wrought up, but after coming up and finding that it had been done correctly, except that I had failed to include one freight bill which had not been rendered, he spoke kindly about it. I was greatly en-couraged and felt that I really began to understand bookkeeping.

In 1864 his restless energy caused my father to start another enterprise which was extremely successful. He with four partners founded the Forcett Limestone Company, taking on royalty from J. Mittchel of Forcett Park an area of land underlaid by limestone suitable for a blast furnace flux. To get this to market it was necessary to build a railway. The Forcett Railway Com-pany was formed in compliance with English law. They had to build a bridge over the River Tees, and instead of getting rights-of-way for nothing, as people often do in the country, we paid at least $1,500 per acre for every foot of ground we occupied in going through six miles of farms. After the road was finished it was operated by the Stockton and Darlington Railway Company, afterward merged into the North Eastern Railway Company.

We made contracts for blast furnace stone for seven and fourteen years at a time with the Middlesbrough Companies, and I think it safe to say that the Limestone Company, with its small capital of about $30,000, paid something like from 20 to 40 percent per annum. The Railway paid either 4, 5, or 6 percent—I have forgotten which—and we endeavored to sell these shares as soon as it could be done without loss, so as to repay the borrowed money. I was made the auditor of both companies, the Railway Company and the Limestone Company, again enlarging my knowledge of accounting. In the year 1865 I began to feel my feet in the world by having my first individual speculation, which consisted in the purchase of one share of the North British Railway, and I was greatly elated to sell it out two or three months later at a profit of about $20.

The financial complications were so great, like a juggler trying to keep five balls in the air at one time, that my father's principal occupation had become meeting one note by swapping and discounting another. With a dozen different people in different towns to swap with where the paper would not be known and would not excite suspicion, things were ready for a crash. It was not very long before it came. My father had opened two different accounts in London. It was not supposed [that] anyone would have two different accounts. He was opening them for the sake of getting additional facilities for discounting bills. One day my Uncle Joseph in London, to whom my father sent a check to help him to meet a maturing note, took the same and presented it over the counter of the wrong bank. The cashier looked at it in amazement and demanded an explanation.

My father was telegraphed for to go to London, and the authorities of the bank said: "You are playing fast and loose with us; you have two different accounts; you must close this account immediately." This cut off one important avenue for discounts. I knew that he was in trouble . . . all kinds of trouble. I had become no mean financier myself—thanks to his tuition—and I pulled every string within twenty-four hours. To enable him to open another account elsewhere in London with prestige I sent him a whole list of stuff that I could get my hands on, checks and notes of various kinds, with a long letter for his information giving a general résumé of what was coming due that I had to protect at the glass works, and what paper we had under discount and where.

I was by this time entirely able to handle all of the business of the glass works, which Mr. Baily was supposed to be actively participating in, but was not. My father had removed in the summer of 1866 to Forest Hall, near Newcastle-on-Tyne. He was handling by this time the finances of the Tyne Chemical Company. I was in the habit of going over Saturday afternoon and spending Sunday, returning Monday morning, the journey requiring less than two hours. It was necessary for me to give [my father] information as to my financial surroundings which were no longer under his immediate supervision. [One] night my desk at the glass works office was broken open by Mr. Baily. He must have spent the whole night copying letters out of my copy letter press book, so as to get the whole file of my personal correspondence with my father. He took that and placed it in the hands of the manager of our bank.

I was promptly summoned [to the bank] the first thing the next morning, and to say that I had a time like a "bear on a hot iron" would be to put it mildly. The banker was furious beyond measure. The fact, however, that there were thousands of pounds sterling discounted with him, which would be useless if he would attack and push us to the wall, was our salvation. I put up the best face that I possibly could, extenuated much, explained some things, justified some things as being in the nature of what might be called credits drawn against existing assets. The same day I removed all the books of the company, except the payroll, from the office to my own lodgings.

At this time the panic of 1866 broke like a thunderclap. It was commenced by the suspension of the old established Quaker discount house of Overend, Gurney and Company of London, who failed for about $30 million. The panic was frightful. Within thirty days . . . many of the great London banks had closed their doors. Bears would sell down their stock on the stock exchange for the express purpose of discrediting the bank. As depositors saw the quotations going down they would become scared and draw out their money. The failure in the connection of the Agra and Mastermans Bank was one of the wickedest things ever known in this world. In the Agra bank were invested in its stock or on deposit the savings of thousands of English government officials, old army or navy men, colonial judges, administrators, and civil servants of every kind. The bank was perfectly solvent until its credit was slaughtered on the stock exchange, and instead of the widows and children of old Indian officers having a lifetime competency to depend upon, they had every dollar swept away from them and were called upon with hopeless and ruinous demands to pay up the remainder of the capital stock.

This awful catastrophe caused immediate legislation by the English Parliament, which passed a law forbidding the sale of any bank stock unless the number of the share certificate was stated on the sale memorandum. From that time on no one could sell bank stock unless he had it. The Bank of England rate was advanced within one week to 10 percent. Discounts, for the first time in my short business experience, were rigidly restricted and paper was scrutinized. There was no chance for any more kiting business. What were we to do?

We arranged to form a subsidiary company in London to take over the warehouse and stock of bottles belonging to our principal customer, and the bank agreed that the acceptances given for this purchase would be taken by them as legitimate business obligations, and that they would discount them and release a corresponding amount of other finance paper which they had in their hands. This was a big stroke, and I well remember how happy I felt traveling all night in a second-class carriage, lying full length on the wooden seat with a slight carpet cover on it, with the precious purchase money notes in my coat pocket.

The next step toward bringing order out of chaos came through the actions of Mr. Baily. I for years had been going to the post office and obtaining the mail myself, receiving it in a locked leather bag. He went to the post office and made the demand under the advice of his attorneys that the mail should be delivered to him. The post office authorities applied to the government in London for instructions and received a reply to continue to deliver it as they had heretofore delivered it. About this time a note came into my possession on behalf of the old firm of Bowron Baily and Company, which was in liquidation, and Mr. Baily in going through my desk at night as usual to see if I had left anything in the office found this and took possession of it, leaving a [memorandum] for me that, as I was not entitled to it and he was, he had taken it. This served as a peg on which I hung a circular, and I promptly printed one and mailed a copy to every customer, stating that as a sum of money had recently been collected in the office by one who was not the authorized secretary and treasurer of the company, it was expressly requested that all checks should be made payable to the order of the company and should be addressed to the company. Thus, having obtained the ratification of the post office for the delivery of the mail to myself, I was at liberty to shut him off.

In desperation he then took a step which caused his own downfall, for he called upon one of our city customers and collected a sum of about $150, and notified me that he had done so and to place it to the credit of the company in account with himself. As he had no legal authority to collect any money on the part of the company or to retain any part of it, this placed him in a very serious position, for such things are stringently construed under English law. Our attorneys promptly seized the occasion and notified his attorneys that criminal proceedings would be instituted against him for embezzlement. Realizing the mistake he had made, they then came down from a high horse, and instead of demanding the return of his paid-in capital of $12,500 they consented to accept $5,000 and quit, turning over all the interest he had in the company to my father. This we rejected and pushed the criminal proceedings, and in three or four days received the proposition to settle and get out for $2,500. We paid him out, restored the office from my lodgings back to the company's own buildings and works, and were clear of a traitor in the camp and snake in the grass.

Two developments occurred in the year 1865 affecting my whole life. The first one I might say commenced in 1864 with the formation of the Tees Amateur Boat Club. I had always been fond of rowing, and in the autumn of 1864 the first club races were held, and I was tried out as a substitute in one of the racing crews, and received to my surprise the warm commendation of the coach. I was not, however, a regular member and ineligible to compete. In 1865 I was, however, a full fledged member, and from that time until 1869 took part in every boat racing event on the River Tees with the most pronounced success. The regular systematic exercises of rowing single sculls, pairs, but more frequently fours in which I was usually the stroke, developed lung power and great muscular strength which has stood me in good service throughout my life.

The other event which tremendously influenced my life was my conversion one Sunday evening in the old Wesleyan Methodist Brunswich Chapel on Dovecote Street, Stockton, right opposite the Quaker meeting house. I had attended meeting as usual in the evening, for we would never have dreamed in our family of failing to attend any of the stated services. After it was over I went across the street into the after-meeting which was then commencing. As I listened to the fervid exhortation of a good pork butcher, who strewed his "h's" knee deep on the floor, I realized that my acceptance up to that time of Christ was purely intellectual, an act of the head and not of the heart.

I may as well go back a few months. A dear old man, whose memory I love and revere, John Dodshon, a wholesale grocer, was our regular preacher in the Stockton meeting. In the early part of the year under discussion, one of John Dodshon's daughters died, a young lady of about eighteen. That evening after the funeral he invited to his house about twenty or thirty of the younger people of the congregation, including myself. We sat down to tea together just as if it had been a social party, except that naturally there was a subdued air over the gathering. After tea he had Fred Williams and some-one else read several suitable selections, pointing out that death comes to young as well as to old, but that it must come to each and all, and that it was profoundly unwise to delay arranging for it. I was convinced. I felt that the argument was conclusive, and that I would become religious. I did not study upon it as being anything else than the effort of my own will, and did not realize until long afterward the beauty of the thought: "Not the labors of my hands can fulfill thy law's demands; Nothing in my hand I bring, simply to thy cross I cling." And so I went away that night feeling that I was a changed man, and that the religion of Christ was for me, for the future was a personal possession instead of a mere academic theory.

So, after rocking along in that way for several months, during which time I had commenced to attend the Young Men's Christian Association meet-ings, I came as before stated to the little simple after-meeting in the Meth-odist Church, and as I bowed over with hot tears falling on the ground, realizing that I had never grieved and wept because Jesus died for me, some-one came down the aisle of the church and said, "Better settle this matter in the vestry," and my companion R. M. Middleton, Jr., then bank clerk, subsequently steamship owner in West Hartlepool, England, went with me into the vestry. It may have seemed little to those good people who were there, half a dozen, but it has meant all the world to me, and maybe to many more than myself, that that night I realized with my heart as well as with my head that He had done it all and I had nothing to do but believe and live. If I were to pursue this line of thought I might write 1,000 pages upon it, but other references must come in from time to time, naturally, and I will leave it here simply as recorded fact of the most tremendous significance, coming in the same year with my attainment of legal manhood, and with my full physical entrance into the athletic competitions of the boat club.

My brother Joe had gone to school in Cheshire after he left Ackworth, and after he left there and came back home I noticed that he spoke after meeting one Sunday morning to a boy whom I did not know, who appeared to have been one of his school fellows. His name was Barrett. Serving on a committee one evening with Will Dodshon to look over the list of members of the meeting and to see that they were properly recorded, we came to the

Barrett name, and found seven sisters in a row. Will said to me, "There's a fine chance Jim for you to pick a wife." I had forgotten the remark and did not know which of the seven to speak to. One evening a young girl of about fifteen came over to the house to tea with her brother, who was Joe's school fellow, and I was introduced to her as Ada Barrett. That evening a tremendous rainstorm came up and when the open carriage was sent by the Barretts to bring the young people home, my mother allowed Will Barrett to go, but said she would take responsibility of keeping Ada all night and not exposing her to the rainstorm, as it was about three miles from our house to theirs. This seems a prophetic omen that she should have taken up habitation in the same house with me at our first meeting. The next day, after she had gone, my sister Kate, of whom I was intensely fond, deliberately suggested to me that she was a very nice girl, and wanted to know what I thought about it. I frankly said that I thought she was but that I could never be very much interested in any girl because I loved her [Kate] so much.

[In] 1867 Ada Barrett left school, being eighteen years old, and came home to stay, and I had the opportunity of seeing her at least in meeting every Sunday morning. American boys cannot realize how hard it was to make the acquaintance of a girl in England. The conventionalities of English society would not permit you to go to her house and ask for her. All you could do would be to visit the family. If you saw her, well and good. If you did not, you lost out. You talked with her in the presence of whoever might be in the room, from two to six people. If by any chance we would go to walk there would be at least three or four of us along, so that the intimate personal association or a tête-à-tête conversation was almost impossible.

In accordance with English etiquette, after talking to my mother about it, I wrote a formal letter to her father asking that I might be permitted to pay my addresses. He proceeded immediately to make inquiries about the city about me and was much interested in what my warm and kindly friends told him. He then invited himself to take tea with me at my lodging and told me that the inquiries he had made were satisfactory and if I could show him reasonable prospect of financial success in life he would not stand in the way. I then showed him the situation of the glass works and I made a clean breast of the vicious method of financing in the past, and the way in which I was wearing it down and getting out from under. I showed him the little pocket diary in which I noted for each day the amount and name of every note payable, as all notes are payable in England in London. The people living in the country must attend to them the day before maturity by making payment in their own city to a country correspondent of the London bank where the note is payable. I showed him that all my trade acceptances were entered in black ink, and all my finance bills were entered in red ink. I told him that I did not wish to get married as long as I had one entry in red ink in that book, and I kept that plan and promise and carried it out.

With this permission I went up on Wednesday night, the fourth of March, 1868, to see my girl. I went after her where she was playing one of Mendelssohn's songs and I felt pretty tongue-tied when I began to talk to her, and was thunderstruck when she gave me the answer "No." But something was said to allow me to suppose that it was still under consideration and I might come back the next week for my final answer. I went back the next week and spent the evening just in ordinary chitchat with the family, and when I started to go she went downstairs with me to the door. While I was putting on my hat and buttoning up my coat she hid behind some coats hanging there and peeped out at me. I said, "Why should you tantalize me this way; you know that you love me." And she admitted that she did.

The following Sunday I walked up after dinner to see her and took a pearl engagement ring in my pocket. I was headed off by her oldest sister, who said they thought Ada had acted hastily, and they were not by any means sure about it. I talked for a while with her, and she walked up and down on the lawn with her sister, and then we all had another talk heart to heart. Everything was straightened out and agreed upon and my ring accepted with much delight. The whole trouble was that there was another young man . . . A. J. Dorman, who afterwards became a millionaire iron manufacturer, head of the firm of Dorman Long and Company, Limited, and he was favored by the family, who thought he had superior prospects in life to my own, but I was the girl's favorite and in the main that counted more.

It would seem a suitable time here . . . to point out the profound influence upon my life of my identification with the Young Men's Christian Association. When I joined it in Stockton it had one little room next under the attic, at the top of a high flight of stairs at the back of a warehouse. We had one gaslight burning in a window to show where the place was, but no sign. But what we lacked in materials was made up in men. My great magnificent leader [was Thomas Whitwell,] who taught me first how to feather an oar in a boat, and who taught me first how to blow a note on the cornet. [He was] the captain of the volunteer fire brigade; the best swimmer in the city; six feet four inches high, homely as could be imagined in face, but lovely in heart; distinguished inventor of the firebrick stoves for blast furnaces. Rough, rugged, warmhearted Thomas Whitwell, a veritable giant in constructive enterprise [destined] to move on and upward in the world; the man who on desolate battlegrounds in France distributed Quaker relief to the victims of German rage and savagery.

We had . . . a devoted worthy druggist, W. B. Brayshay, who was president of the association, and who shocked me out of my senses one day by saying that as he would have some other engagement the following Friday night, I must take the Bible class for him. I told him that I had never done such a thing, and that I did not know how to do it. He said in reply that was the very reason I ought to do it, and that was the only way to learn. I have proved the truth of that statement now for nearly fifty years, and I shall say here that the only way that I know to learn the Bible is to teach it. Several of us connected with the YMCA began to chum together . . . and we began to make up crews on the river so that we might set the example of manly Christianity. A crew of four or five of us together . . . could make it hot for anybody in the racing proposition and hold our own with them, and then go from the shower bath straight to the YMCA meeting. Then nobody could turn up their noses and say that we were a set of "sissies."

So now, behold me from 1866 to 1869, inclusive, occupied with, first, the pulling of my company little by little out of the grasp of finance bills; second, building up a huge capital of strength by athletic exercises, rowing, swimming, and some little cricket and football; third, building myself up systematically into religious work, and by steady attendance upon all the YMCA meetings, and visitations with Whitwell to other towns to promote the association work there; fourth, the mellowing and softening of my own disposition by association, as a rule twice a week, never more, with my sweetheart, the engagement running from March, 1868, to June, 1870, before it was consummated.

In 1868 I cast my first vote for Mr. Gladstone, who was successful in the election and became prime minister of England upon the issue of the disestablishment of the Irish Church. It is hard for Americans to appreciate what it means to have a state church which, as in England the [Church of England], and in Scotland the Presbyterian, had a priority by law. I have already pointed out how this prevented my going to any universities. It certainly appealed to me as a Quaker that it was wrong that the Church [of England] should have any rights over the rest of the population, especially that we who were not members of it should be compelled to pay for it. On two different occasions church rates were levied upon my father which, as was usual amongst the Quakers, he refused to pay. The officers of the law took out some of his furniture under an execution and sold the same on the streets to help to pay the salary and expenses of some vicar who perhaps did not occupy his own pulpit, but hired some poor curate at one-fifth of his own receipts to maintain the services.

I gladly signed the petition requesting my friend Mr. [Joseph] Dodds, attorney at Stockton-on-Tees, to become the Liberal candidate. The Liberals won by a large majority; Mr. Gladstone was elected and a majority of the House of Commons in accord with his policy; and the Church [of England] in Ireland was disestablished. I always remained an ardent Liberal as long as I was in England, but I may say that after coming to this country I changed my views on English politics altogether and became a Conservative. I could not put up with the surrender by Mr. Gladstone to the Boers in South Africa, a mistake on his part which brought on the Boer War of 1899.

During these years we had had many opportunities of seeing the sterling worth and very high intelligence of Dr. George Lunge, and between 1868 and 1869, it was communicated to me that he was seeking the hand of my sister Kate, a beautiful young girl as she then was, foreshadowing the beautiful, brilliant woman that she has been throughout her entire life. I spoke favorably of him, greatly admired him, his ability as a chemist and as a linguist, speaking and writing four different languages.

I am sorry that I did not know and it did not occur to me to ask at that time his religious affiliation. I could not have consented to approve any marriage with a Unitarian, for to my mind the educated Unitarian cannot stand even on the same plane of recognition with the Jew. There is, of course, no difference of any importance between any of the sections of the Evangelical Church. Their differences are simply those of method and management, and as between the Congregationalists, Lutherans, Moravians, Christians, Baptists, Episcopalians, Presbyterians, Methodists, and Quakers, there is no considerable objection to intermarriage. But I entertain the most intense antipathy against any marriage between Protestants and Catholics, because of the right over the human conscience asserted by the Catholic hierarchy. And much more do I object to the tying up of a Christian believing in the Atonement of Christ for human sins with a Unitarian or a Jew regarding the Savior as a mere man. Where Christ does not come into the family, there cannot be, however tender that family may be, the same absolute peace and love and patience and tenderness, that we may look for where He is a resident partner.

In the summer of 1869 George and Kate were married at the Church of England of Forest Hall near Newcastle-on-Tyne. Ada and I participated in the wedding, celebrated after the English custom in the morning, for English wedding licenses were void unless celebrated before twelve o'clock noon. It is sad to think that after many years of married life, maintaining a position of distinction and honor, these two should have ultimately felt it necessary to separate. I only allude to that out of its chronological place to show how important it is that young men and women should marry in the Lord. As the scripture says, "How can two walk together except they be agreed?"

Although by 1870 I had succeeded wonderfully in getting the finance or accommodation bills in red off my diary, and was steadily working the affairs of the glass works into a normal and legitimate financial condition, the financial strain was still considerable, for the bad paper had been paid out but there was no accumulated working capital. It was with considerable difficulty, therefore, that I could see the way to organize finances so as to permit of my absence for a period of three weeks for the purpose of a wedding trip. The unexpected sale, however, to Portugal of a carload of bottles to be packed in bulk for Oporto put us in better financial condition than usual, and my father undertook to manage affairs during my absence, and on June 20, 1870, the greatest event up to that date in my life, excepting my personal acceptance of the loving Savior, was accomplished when I was married to Ada Louise Barrett at the Friends' Meeting House in Redcar, at 11:00 A.M.

The wedding in accordance with Quaker practices was very simple, dignified, and wholesome, a religious ceremony. In accordance with custom we two, the contracting parties, sat facing the audience in the raised seats usually occupied by the ministers. In the gallery immediately above sat two or three Friends, acknowledged as ministers. After the lapse in silence and decorum of a reasonable time we rose to our feet and I took Ada's hand and said to the company assembled: "I take this my friend, Ada Louise Barrett, to be my wife, promising through divine assistance to be unto her a faithful and loving husband until it shall please the Lord by death to separate us." Then she in turn repeated the same words, substituting my name for hers, and the word wife for husband. Then we sat down and another decent interval of silence ensued, after which someone in the ministers' gallery led in vocal prayer, and then someone else spoke for perhaps ten minutes words of wise counsel and sat down, and after a period of perhaps ten minutes of reverent silence and meditation, the officiating clerk wheeled a small table up in front of us on which was the large illuminated wedding certificate to be signed by us.

We settled in our own home and life began to settle into a very steady routine for me. I still went over to Newcastle or Tynemouth occasionally to see my father, and to assist him in the handling of his financial complications, which were thickening all the time with his various enterprises, and the mass of finance bills that he was keeping juggling in the air. As far as the glass works was concerned it was making a fair moderate profit, and I began to work steadily onto safer ground. I enlarged the operations of the glass works in several ways. We operated a branch warehouse in Liverpool, one in Glasgow, and a third in Dublin. I obtained the services of a man of about my own age, of remarkable energy, by the name of Horsley from Hartlepool and sent him to Dublin where he developed an extremely large and profitable business with E. and J. Burke, who bottled the famous Dublin or Guinness Stout for the colonies. We made money fast out of this business and soon got to a point where we could begin to pay dividends, greatly to the relief and comfort of my father, harassed as he was.

On May 25, 1871, the Lord blessed us with our first son, Charles Edward. I have always thought it proper to give my children two names, that they might select either one as a matter of preference as they grew older. I have been particular to select names that could be pronounced euphoniously, where the one name would slide into the other without a difficult aspiration, and until my last child I have drawn all of the names of my boys from the line of kings, Charles Edward representing not the Jacobite pretender of the Stuart family, but the separate lines of the Saxon Edwards, and the later Stuart family. This brought a new factor into our lives, and I can hardly think of anything in the whole world that is more intensely interesting than to watch the dawn of intelligence in a young child, evinced by an increasing responsiveness and appreciation.

On July 10, 1872, my daughter, Kathleen Mary, was born and on the 20th of September following my wife's cousin was coming down to take supper and spend the evening with us, and just as we were preparing to sit down to supper, the nursemaid ran in hastily upon us in tears and said the baby was dead. The dear little child in its sleep had turned partly on its face and was not strong enough to turn back, and had smothered in the pillow. Of course such a thing was a great shock to us. I knew nothing of what to do in such cases and was told I must go to the registrar to obtain a burial certificate, and I walked two miles for that purpose, and when I got there he looked at me in wonder when I told him I had no doctor's certificate of the cause of the death, and said he could grant no permit in its absence and that I must go to the chief of police and arrange for a coroner's inquest. It was two miles back to the station from which I had walked and about four miles to walk back to my home without waiting for the train, so I walked all the way home, and it was a sad walk. When I got there I went to the chief of police, and the formality of obtaining a jury and conducting the inquest did not occupy more than an hour, and the following day I had a sad lonely ride in a hack twelve miles to the Friends' Burying Ground at Stockton, as there was no burying ground at Redcar. I rode there alone with the little coffin in front of me, and there was no voice at the funeral except the few words which I could get out myself of resignation to the will of the Lord. These experiences are searching and not easy.

My family kept growing and my financial responsibilities with it. In 1873, on the 11th of December, my family was increased by the coming of Francis James, so that again we had two little ones to care for. My son Frederick William came to join us on January 7, 1875, and Arthur John came to keep him company on January 19, 1876.

Our expenses began to increase, but so did my income, for I was drawing now some little dividend on my stock in the glass works, as well as my salary. At the same time I developed a side or collateral business as a merchant. My brother Joe came back from Spain, but he left his heart there, and being deeply attached to a Spanish girl he was determined to return there as soon as possible. He ... returned to Spain to open an independent house of business there in his own name, but he was without capital, and again we committed a tremendous mistake which cost us both very dearly. We started, in other words, a partnership business, conducted at my end under the English name of J. Bowron and Company, and at the Spanish end under the name of Jose Bowron. I needed no capital for my end. I bought a little coal and sold it as a broker, at five or six cents a ton profit.

By far the larger part of my work was to sell the products which my brother shipped to me from Spain. In my own end of the business I never went into anything unless I could see a profit in it, however small, and I turned in nothing but profits to our joint partnership. But Joe had no capital; he was competing with established firms; and he could not buy to the same advantage that I could. He had not the same experience, and some of his deals were not profitable. He chartered several steamers on speculation, and after receipt of the cargoes in England the iron ore which he had shipped me, and which I had sold, did not come up to the guaranteed analysis, and we lost money on the transactions having to make allowances. Again he shipped esparto grass which did not come up to the standard and we lost money on the allowances. The losses, however, were not serious and we were about breaking even on our mercantile business, taking one thing with another, when several things began to go wrong.

It is better here to explain how business was done in Cartagena and some other Spanish cities, and perhaps is still done in some places in the world.

There was no bank there; there was no gold currency; and all transactions were either by the delivery of sacks of silver carried on men's backs, which was very inconvenient, or substantially by the different merchants carrying open running accounts with each other, and from time to time buying from or selling to each other drafts upon their various correspondents in other countries. Joe entered into the usual commercial method, and whenever he wanted money with which to buy a cargo of lead, or esparto grass, or iron ore, he simply sold in the open market his drafts on me for $1,000, $2,000, or $3,000 at the time, at sixty days after date. These drafts became quite a curiosity because in some cases they would be remitted from one city to another, perhaps from Cartagena to Madrid; from Madrid to Rome; thence to Zurich; perhaps to St. Petersburg; thence to Berlin; and thence to London. I have seen them passed through so many hands that there was no room for the endorsements on the back and additional lengths of black paper had to be pasted on to accommodate the successive endorsements.

The latter part of 1875, or the first part of 1876, I became practically overwhelmed by financial misfortune, arising out of my own lack of precaution, but not out of any act of mine. My dear brother Joe made additional heavy drafts upon me, because he purchased a stranded steamer about six miles from where he lived. She was in good condition and worth $150,000 if she could be got afloat. He and some of his men thought they could get her off, and he bought her for about $5,000 I think, and immediately commenced to buy equipment such as bags to be inflated with air and help float the vessel, timber with which to build a substantial bulkhead in the vessel to keep out the water or confine it to the forehold. Here again he made a great mistake because the salvage of wrecked vessels is a very highly specialized business, and I believe from what he wrote me and afterwards told me about the situation he would undoubtedly have succeeded if he had been willing to pay $10,000 or $20,000 to people making such work a specialty. He and his men from his ore mines and lumberyard worked on this steamer to a point where they got her afloat, and he sent me a cablegram to that effect that they had got her afloat. My pride and exultation that day were boundless, because outside my household furniture I did not possess $500 in the world. [I] thought that day that I was the joint owner of a $150,000 steamer. They were making preparations to get a tugboat to tow her around into the bay at Cartagena where she could go into dry dock for repairs, and whilst waiting a storm came up and the sea burst in the bulkhead they had made and down she went in a worse position than before, where they could not hope with their appliances to do anything further with her.

Over this unfortunate enterprise he had probably [invested] in the money [he] had paid out and the debts he had incurred for pumps and appliances $10,000 to $15,000. About this time a panic broke out in his town and the merchants there went down like a pack of cards striking against each other. I had to pay my own acceptances to them as they fell due, and in addition I had to take up out of the hands of my bank and pay the bills on other people which Joe had purchased and sent to me to cover his own drafts on me. It was hopeless. I would have been driven at that point into absolute bankruptcy but for the goodness of the Quakers. I applied to the Pease family [1] of Darlington, who designated Sir David Dale, managing director of the Consett Iron Works, to look into my matters, and I made a showdown. Upon stock in the glass works, the Pease family advanced $10,000. I should say this included the stock also belonging to my father which I had to pledge without his consent or knowledge, for he was in the United States and I had no means of communicating in a hurry or explanation of the situation. I had also pledged his life insurance policies (for all his matters were in my hands) with my bank in Middlesbrough to secure it for the overdraft caused by the dishonor of various and sundry drafts which had been remitted to me from Spain.

If any man ever paid dearly for leaping without looking I think I did for the next year and a half. Every day was a case of submitting meekly to bankers scolding and threatening and worrying me. Poor Joe did whatever he could at the other end to help the situation. The glass works of course was operating successfully, and my father wrote me a most touching letter back from America in which he said [I] had [as] much right to use his securities as I . . . had chiefly made them for him. I do not know that I was entitled to such a remark but was deeply touched by his kindness. The situation was almost unbearable.

America

English capitalists had a long history of investment in industrial and transportation enterprises in the United States. Some of it resulted from the historic connection with the former colonies, but in time most grew out of Englishmen's search for more lucrative returns than they could receive on their money at home. England was rich in capital; the U.S. economy often was starved for investment. English capital had financed much of the canal and railroad development in the United States prior to the Civil War, and its investments continued after the war. Between 1870 and 1875, British capitalists put £55 million into American railroads alone. Millions more went into industrial and land-development enterprises in the United States.[1]

Englishmen had long been interested in the economy of the South, which for many years was the main provider of cotton for the British textile industry. They were alert to industrial opportunities in the South as well. The English geologist Sir Charles Lyell had written enthusiastically in the late 1840s about the industrial potential that lay in the coal and iron deposits of the southern Appalachians. The interest grew after the war was over, helped along by promoters like General John Thomas Wilder, the Union cavalryman who took great interest in Tennessee's industrial potential while leading the occupying army at Chattanooga. After the war Wilder recruited English investors for enterprises in eastern Tennessee. English ironmakers had received incentive to invest in America when high U.S. tariffs on iron, starting in 1861, all but cut off the American market for British iron.

Among the Englishmen of Wilder's acquaintance was Lowthian Bell, who would write glowingly of the South's iron-making potential. The undeveloped resources of the region would, Bell said, "prove a match for any part of the world in the production of cheap iron."[2]

In northern England, a group of Quaker merchants, industrialists, and bankers moved to invest in southern iron making, no doubt encouraged by Bell's strong endorsement. This group included James Bowron's father and his father-in-law, though the largest investors were of the Pease family, probably the most important banking family in northeastern England. In what was a common pattern among Quaker businessmen, the Pease family had expanded from the wool trade into banking in the eighteenth century and then to manufacturing in the nineteenth. Edward Pease, grandfather to Bowron's associates, had been the primary financial backer for the Stockton and Darlington Railway, the first modern railroad in the world. The Bell family also supported the enterprise, and Thomas Whitwell, an industrialist and furnace technologist, took a leading role. Bowron's father became the general manager of an iron company that planned to develop the mineral resources on the Cumberland plateau in eastern Tennessee.[3]

James Bowron followed his father to America in 1877 to help with the new company, only to inherit all its responsibilities in a short time. He encountered extreme difficulties in starting an iron company in a backward region of a strange land. He soon realized that many of the vaunted natural advantages of Tennessee as an industrial center had been exaggerated—the coal was thin, the iron ore of relatively low content, the Tennessee River too shallow for barges. Bowron's task was made harder by the failure of his English sponsors to understand the peculiar demands of the new environment or to have confidence in the young Bowron's judgment. The death of his friend and supporter Whitwell in an industrial accident in August 1878 further weakened his position. The English company, which included among its investors some of the most knowledgeable iron and steel technologists in the world, failed abjectly to apply modern technology to its Tennessee enterprise. Bowron's account of the problems growing from absentee ownership of the company reveals much about the nature of economic colonialism in the postwar South.

ixing up as he did in his ceaseless task of exchanging accommodation paper, [my father] had met about 1869 or
1870 . . . two Americans: A. Mason of Boston and Edward A.
Quintard[4] of New York. They discussed in the presence of my father the
desire to find people in England who would become interested in developing
an immense tract of coal and iron land in West Virginia, the Gauley-
Kanawha district. My father discussed the matter with me, and I suggested
the possibility of arranging an English syndicate with the assistance of my
father-in-law, Mr. Barrett, managing director of the Norton Iron Company,
and my close personal friend Thomas Whitwell, . . . a successful ironmaster.
The idea took root, and I brought them all in contact. Several successful
ironmasters of the Middlesbrough district, including Henry Cochrane, E. F.
Jones, Joseph Dodds, M.P. for Stockton, and John Stephenson of the
Bowesfield Iron Works . . . joined together in a syndicate and agreed to purchase the large property alluded to upon the condition that we should send
out our own experts to examine the same and verify it. E. A. Quintard
[agreed] to pay their expenses if the report was not satisfactory.

This great property was offered to us on the basis . . . of about $1 per
acre. I have since been there and have seen a seam of coal so thick that the
standard locomotive was running with a train of standard loaded cars
through the drift entry. The coal must have been twelve or fifteen feet thick.
This property was offered to our syndicate on the basis of a printed paper
signed by Colonel Matthew Maury,[5] the state geologist of West Virginia. It
not only set forth the riches of the land in coal, but also a great vein of red
hematite iron ore, and great masses on the surface of kidney ore. All this
latter part was bunk, and any man with the title of state geologist should
have been put in the penitentiary for signing such a report, for there was not
then, and is not now, any known body of iron ore in West Virginia of commercial value, or at least in that district.

We sent out our experts, . . . a mining engineer and my brother Will, as a
metallurgical chemist. They cabled back their reports in code that the coal
was excellent, the iron bad, general prospects fair, and then returned, and
in conversation said that there was not enough iron on the property to make
a toothpick. Mr. Quintard was very manly about it. He paid the expenses of
the experts, and he said, "This property is a failure as to iron deposits, but
is worth all the money that was asked for it for [its] coal and timber, and we
can obtain and put into the operation of the syndicate . . . an iron property
in Old Virginia, two or three hundred miles away." We went back to our
syndicate with this report and the new proposal, but it was all in vain. One

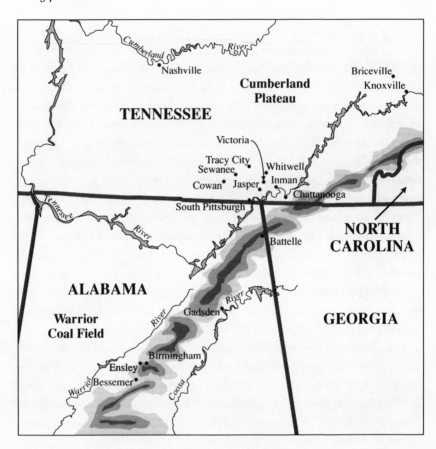

or two of the wealthy experienced men whom we had enlisted turned up their noses and said that this was a Yankee trick, that the first statements had been proved unfounded and grossly unreliable, and there was no guarantee of the later ones, and why should they believe in them? [They said] that they had something else to do but waste their time over it, and they were through.

This ended that transaction. But it put my father, who by this time was footloose on account of the failure and liquidation of the Tyne Chemical Company, in a position to devote his time to it, and he went out to the United States and spent about three months in looking into numerous proposals put before him by these promoters, not specially with an eye to iron and ore but anything. He came back again in 1871 loaded to the [gourds] with all sorts of propositions, [including] one from Senator J. P. Jones of Nevada to make and sell artificial ice machines in Europe. That was a brand new proposition at that time. Another was to sell the huge accumulation of guano from the Bat Cave in Kentucky. I think he had about twelve proposals to talk over with me when I met him at the ship's side in Liverpool. It is easy to understand, therefore, that after the death of my mother the following spring, and the liquidation of the Chemical Company, and the various Spanish companies having gone by the board in which he had been interested, and his glass works interests being thoroughly solidified under my own hand and requiring no attention from him, and his life being made a perfect burden to him of the most intolerable nature by the pressure of a large volume of finance or accommodation bills, he eagerly looked for relief to the great West. We did not cease talking about it, and it bore fruit.

A syndicate was formed consisting of William Barrett of Norton Iron Company; his cousin Henry Barrett of London, an iron founder; Thomas Whitwell; Daniel Adamson, an engineer of Lancashire; and perhaps another. They agreed to pay my father $5,000 and his traveling expenses to go over and acquire options on mineral lands with a view to forming a company to manufacture iron in [the United States], and thus get behind the [U.S.] tariff wall. It was represented that the machinery and equipment in this country, especially in the South, was of a most primitive character, and English ideas and equipment would make a very profitable venture. Accordingly he came to the United States and acquired options on nearly 100,000 acres of brown ore land in Cocke and Greene counties, Tennessee, and about 50,000 acres of coal land on the Cumberland Mountain plateau, facing onto the Sequatchie Valley, and a block of red ore land in Walden's Ridge on the Tennessee River. Of course, at $1 per acre either for coal land or brown ore land, one might say there was no risk, because the timber alone upon such land was worth more than that.

This land was not bought to hold and sell again but to develop. To develop these lands meant bringing products together, paying transportation, and investing large capital for manufacturing. After getting these options Thomas Whitwell himself, accompanied by Charles L. Bell, a son of . . . Isaac Lowthian Bell, . . . went over to America and rode around over these properties with my father, and then back to England full of enthusiasm. [They] sought to enlist the aid of the millionaire family of Pease of Darlington, who were leading Quakers in the north of England. A meeting was held in Bell Brothers office in Middlesbrough, and Thomas Whitwell quoted a remark as coming from General John Thomas Wilder of Chattanooga, and to our surprise Mr. Bell said, "General Wilder is in the next room. Let us have him in." He being full, like any ordinary American booster, of the

James Bowron at about the time he migrated to America (courtesy of James French)

enthusiasm of his own stock, blew up like a volcano promising all sorts and kinds of things that would happen to us in the way of good luck if we would come in and develop these resources. He convinced the two members of the Pease family, Edwin Lucas Pease and Henry Fell Pease, and they told Thomas Whitwell that they would join in the enterprise.

That cinched it. The Southern States Coal, Iron and Land Company was formed, of which I was made the secretary, which in England also means treasurer, although they do not use that title.

Newcastle [England] *Daily Chronicle*, November 28, 1876:
Within the last two or three years a great deal has been done, or projected, by capitalists in parts of the United Kingdom to develop the remarkable resources of the United States. A number of companies are now established on the other side of the Atlantic, the origin of which has been largely, if not entirely, due to English capital and enterprise. . . .

Probably a more important project than . . . any of the kind originated within recent years . . . is that which was launched some time ago in the Cleveland[6] district, and bears the name of the Southern States Coal, Iron, and Land Company, limited. This concern has been floated by a small syndicate, composed of North of England ironmasters and their personal friends, and if it realizes anything like the full expectations of its promoters, it will result in the establishment in the State of Tennessee of another and perhaps a still greater Cleveland, by the application of capital withdrawn from, if not actually and wholly acquired in the district of that name on the banks of the Tees. . . .

It is quite impossible to foresee to what ultimate issue these comparatively small beginnings may lead. . . . The company have acquired 52,000 acres of coal land, which is being connected with the railway at Jasper, by a branch line and tramway five miles long. Here the coal seams cropping out horizontally to day, are five in number, and vary from two to twelve feet in thickness, dipping to the face twelve feet to the mile, and without any "fault" except where intersected by ravines and water courses, which have cut down through them, they have been proved to extend over the whole of the property. The lowest seam is about 700 feet above the bottom of the valley, so that the coal will be mined entirely by drift ways, and the expense of sinking shafts will be avoided. With reference to the iron ore lands acquired by the company, it is stated that "they comprise about 114,000 acres, of which about 84,000 acres are on the French Broad River which runs into the Tennessee. They contain extremely large deposits of brown hematite and also specular iron ores, which are disposed vertically, varying from 80 feet to 240 feet thick, measured on a bared outcrop across the deposit; one deposit intersected by the railway was traced for nine miles, on a varying elevation of 600 feet above the line. These ores range from 42 to 60 per cent of metallic iron, they are all free from sulphur, low in phosphorus, and suitable for making car wheels. Several of the ores are sufficiently pure for the manufacture of steel; and there is also close at hand a large deposit of rich manganese, available for the furnaces or convertors. This property being intersected by both rail and river, there is easy transit for the ore down to the company's furnaces. The distance is about 210 miles by rail, or 300 by water. These distances in England would seem long, but are as nothing in America, where manufacturers carry ore from Iron Mountain, Missouri, to Pennsylvania, a distance of 1,000 miles, against stream. The cost of water transport, down stream, is very low; and by rail or water, the iron ore can be delivered at Battle Creek on very reasonable terms."

Fire bricks and lumps are made on the ground from the fire clay underlying the coal, and hence the furnaces, coke ovens, heating stoves, . . . will be constructed with great economy, and a new source of profit and revenue will arise from the sale of the bricks, which are here worth from £10 to £15 per thousand. Apart from the manufacture of iron, exceptionally large profits are expected to be made. Coals can be sent down to Charleston or Savannah, at a good profit, the company's coal estates being nearest to the Atlantic sea board. Being only half a mile from the railway, the manganese can be sent down to the same ports, whence, as ballasting in cotton ships, it can be sent to Liverpool, leaving a good profit at present prices. Lead and baryta[7] also exist on the estate, and the company are already working the latter; and it is of some importance to add that, unlike the settlement which Dickens has made memorable in Martin Chuzzlewit, the climate is healthy and bracing, the mean elevation being about 1,500 feet above sea level, while the soil is so fertile that a Swiss colony are already growing upon it corn, peach, and apple orchards.

In the pride of the English race, we had thought we have everything better than the Americans, and that we must send out to this country English equipment and machinery for the Southern States Coal, Iron and Land

Company, and also English management throughout. We advertised for different men and selected H. C. Amos to come to this country as treasurer. He was selected from 202 applicants, and turned in testimonials from a great well-known contractor of international reputation, which we had subsequent reason to believe were forged. He claimed ability as a financier and to install every variety of accounting in a strange country. He was sent out under a five-year contract with the directors, paying his traveling expenses and that of his family and furniture.

We selected George Spence of the Coltness Iron Company as our mining engineer. He was not a man having had a technical education and was somewhat illiterate, but had occupied a leading position with his company in Scotland. There he had nothing to originate, was surrounded with familiar conditions, and merely had to keep doing as a manager what he had done through many years as a working miner. He was selected from about forty-five applicants. We sent out A. Woodward, known to some of our people from Teesside as a blast furnace manager. This position was not advertised. We sent out one of our stockholders who had two shares of stock and applied for the position, Thomas Newton, from cooperative stores, as the manager of our commissary department. With whole England to select from it could hardly be imagined that it was within the broadest of human chance that all of these appointments should not be bad only, but very bad.

If we had had the very best men available my father would have had considerable difficulty in organizing a company on a profitable basis. As I later ascertained the ore in Walden's Ridge, it ran rapidly down from 28 percent metallic iron to below 20 percent, the rest being lime and too lean to justify operating as a regular ore on which to base a furnace burden. The brown ores in Cocke and Greene counties [were] rich in iron but high in phosphorus, and had been bought with the same stupendous ignorance of American conditions that permitted it to be supposed that we could load these ores onto wooden barges built out of timber on our own lands and float them down the French Broad River to South Pittsburgh, where they would discharge the ore for the blast furnaces and take on board cargoes of coal from our Sequatchie Valley mines and go on down to New Orleans where the coal would be sold and the barges broken up and sold for lumber. The only difficulties in the way of carrying out this scheme were that in the first place there was not enough water in the French Broad near the ore deposits to float a barge except after a freshet, and in the second place there was a perpendicular fall at one point in the river of eight or ten feet which would be impassable at any stage of the river.

It was only after I got to America that I found out that there was only reliable draft above Knoxville for steamers drawing two feet of water at certain times of the year. In the next place the river was not navigable then and is hardly so yet below South Pittsburgh on account of the Muscle Shoals. And in the next place, the program could not have been carried out because the Sequatchie Valley coal was too soft to bear shipment, only one-third of it passing over the screen at the foot of the mountain, and there would have been no sale for slack coal if it had been sent to New Orleans.

Yet, we actually raised more than $700,000 in cash in England to carry out the enterprise to bring these brown and red ores together and smelt them in South Pittsburgh with coke to be made from our own coal in the Sequatchie Valley. Our company was formed of about 150 stockholders, of whom all but two or three were Quakers, the money being subscribed by them upon faith of the knowledge and representations of Thomas Whitwell and of the two Peases.

We began to get reports, and this thing seemed to be wrong, and that thing seemed to be wrong, and finally we sent out a very smart auditor from Price Waterhouse Company of London, and he wrote us back the most alarming letter after he had been in this country a few days that the accounts were perfectly hopeless, being a mass of muddle and contradiction and discrepancies and apparent embezzlements. My father had three men's work on his hands and was relying very much on his chosen staff. Mr. Amos in his absence was building himself a $10,000 house to live in, and exercising authority in other things in the most idiotic way, such as ordering a carload of coffee for a little mining and manufacturing village in its early beginning, when to buy a couple of bags at a time would have been sufficient. I have never been able to decide whether the man was mad or a fool, or a downright thief and swindler; he was all of them.

The receipt of this letter changed my entire outlook in life. The directors held a consultation and asked me if I would leave England and accept the position of assistant general manager, my father having the title of general manager. It did not take me in my own heart two minutes to decide. I knew what it would mean to my wife to leave her family and country and go away from civilization into the backwoods, but I also knew that my own life was simply unbearable as I was then living it. The dreadful financial complications into which Joe's unfortunate ventures had drawn me were clearing up all too slowly for my various creditors, and I had to take drastic steps to end it. I am quite sure that my helpmate and comrade realized this, and that her tender heart bled for my mental sufferings. The only unkind word that I ever heard her utter in her life was an expression of indignation against Joe for pulling me into so much trouble. But if he had succeeded I would have shared equally with him. He was one of the noblest men I ever knew, and his misfortunes and mine never made the slightest shadow between us for one moment of time.

Under the conditions it was obvious what the answer had to be. We went through the formality of consulting the Barrett family at Norton, bearing in mind my wife's father and his cousin were two of the seven directors who had made the proposal to me, and of course with her father one of the moving powers in it, it could not be otherwise than accepted, although the whole family looked upon it as a temporary measure, and that we would certainly return at the end of the five-year engagement.

When I rose the first morning out I was disposed to feel that I had left behind me a life of trouble and responsibility, and care, and distress; and that my future was bright and full of hope. I had a five-year contract at £1,000 per annum. The position was one of dignity, being the one of assistant general manager, which meant more than it would if translated into American terms. In England there is no president of a company, and my father, who was general manager, occupied a position of authority equivalent to that of president, and I equivalent to that of vice-president. I knew that the persons connected with the enterprise were not working well together or rendering adequate services, and that there was not sufficient money fully to carry out the plans. But I had no reason at that time to doubt the full ultimate success of the enterprise, and indeed believed with all my heart that it would be the greatest kind of success.

We arrived in New York August 25, 1877, and were met by my father, who took us to the Metropolitan Hotel . . . where I was interested for the first time in seeing the pompous carriage of the Negro headwaiter in the dining room. The folks were interested in strange foods, such as corn-on-cob, cantaloupes, tomatoes. We left for the South . . . arriving [at] Bridgeport, Alabama, early August 29. To the great interest and amusement of the family [we] went up on a section hand push-car, arriving [at] South Pittsburgh, our future home. We went to my father's house until the one we were to live in . . . was prepared for us.

I note from my father's diary that on October 7, 1877, up at Whitwell he had a sharp attack of chills, and was confined to bed. On November 19 he arrived New York and was taken to the house of Mr. W. W. Mann, with whom he had negotiations relative to some promotion syndicates. He wrote to me of his illness, which was in fact malignant yellow jaundice. He was always of a bilious tendency and type, and living the life which he did for many years of indescribable financial worry and strain, and confronted with countless difficulties in the enterprise he was attempting to handle without any adequate support from his associates, and being exposed as he was to a much hotter climate than that of which he was a native, it is not surprising that he should, although of powerful constitution and physique, have succumbed to liver trouble. His heart had been out of order for years with pronounced regurgitation, causing attacks which had to be treated with nitrite of amyl, and we had always expected that heart disease would bring about his end. But it was to be otherwise. On November 26 Mr. Bayne, our New York banker, wired me that my father was extremely ill, and I started the first train thereafter, arriving New York on November 29, . . . taking my sister Amy with me. We never left him from that time, and when I first saw him I judged that his case was hopeless.

At 7:50 P.M. November 30, 1877, whilst peacefully sleeping, apparently, he rose to a sitting position in bed with an inarticulate gurgle, and as I threw my arms around him to support him, he was dead. The shock to me was appalling, but I was in the very height of my strength, both physical and mental and nervous, and I simply commenced immediately to take the necessary steps, cabling to absent members of the family in Europe and to Thomas Whitwell, who cabled answer "First Peter 5:6, 7." ["Humble yourselves therefore under the mighty hand of God, that he may exalt you in due time: casting all your care upon him; for he careth for you."] A splendid passage and one which then and subsequently has been of the most infinite comfort to me.

On December 3 I received a cable appointing me as acting general manager in my father's place, and on the same day I started for the South with his body. The interment took place in the corner of the cemetery owned by the company at South Pittsburgh, the service being conducted in the machine shop (for there was no church building) by Bishop Charles Quintard.[8]

I may say that it took me years to clean up my father's estate, which was so very heavily involved, but I felt how much I owed to him and to the family, and with all my knowledge of his affairs I was the only one who could have done it. I did handle that matter with skill and success, cutting down his liabilities boldly, defiantly, refusing to admit them in various cases where I thought he had been defrauded, and compromising them in other directions.

I was able to divide out on a basis of about $4,300 per head the net value of my father's estate, this being after liquidation of debts and expenses approximately $17,000. In cleaning up his papers I found from $30,000 to $50,000 of different parties' notes, many years overdue, representing the result of his kindness and friendship.

Every conceivable person that my father had had financial dealings with when I came to this country seems to have been either a failure, a fake, a crook, or something else equally undesirable. He certainly never distrusted any man, or he must have realized as I was compelled to do after him the generally rotten character of the people who surrounded him like so many parasites.

[For example], our "banker," L. P. Bayne of New York. This fine-looking old man with high hair combed straight upright from his forehead, always telling me what a great man my father was, had thousands of dollars of the company's money in his possession. They were supposed to be attached by the suit of a disgruntled man in Georgia who had offered to sell us land with certain guarantees of quality which we found to be absurdly absent, and he alleged breach of contract and attached these funds. They were hung up in Bayne's hands, some $17,000 or $18,000, for about three years, and I afterwards learned that the attachment suit was obviously collusive and might have been dismissed at any time within an hour or two by giving bond.

Bayne sold our drafts on the English office; these drafts were made at sixty days date, £500 or £1,000 each. The plan was that Whitwell or other directors would sell enough stock when they knew the money was wanted to meet the draft at its maturity. Bayne used to write a letter every two or three weeks to the South Pittsburgh office that it was difficult to sell sterling drafts, and to let him have one or two and plenty of time, so that he might always have them on hand to utilize an opportunity. I afterwards found that far from selling them and placing the proceeds to our credit, he would sell them all right to the firm of Balzer and Lichtenstein and hold back the money for his own use until he got the next sterling draft from us, and then he would place to our credit the proceeds of the former one. Indeed he would sometimes overdraw his account with Balzer and Lichtenstein, telling them that we were overdrawing our account with him in advance of sending on sterling. His business was conducted on a fraudulent basis from first to last. I thought he was my father's best friend in America. I did not suspect evil until it was thrust upon me in later years.

With at least 30,000 acres of coal land facing on the Sequatchie Valley, Cumberland Mountain plateau, in which to locate a satisfactory mine, Mr.

Spence had made the most unfortunate selection that was possible. So far as I know there was never one single drill hole put down from the top to test the thickness of the seam, although the cover was not more than from 75 to 100 feet, and the drilling would have been relatively cheap. The Sequatchie Valley forks at Victoria, the little valley running up into the heart of the mountain. Entries could have been driven from either side, after having proved the thickness of the coal, and [they could] have developed a large tonnage to one gathering station. The formation of the little Sequatchie Valley was due to anticlinal disturbances which had broken the strata, and [Spence should] have naturally been on guard against laying out his money and jeopardizing the entire success of the operation by locating in a disturbed neighborhood, instead of going further up either the main or little Sequatchie Valley to get into the solid and undisturbed condition.

The consequence was that Mr. Spence opened up an acreage of coal ranging from five or six inches in thickness to sometimes three feet. As a general proposition it would scarcely average more than from two feet to two feet six inches. In addition to this, the coal having to be lowered into the valley about 1,000 feet vertically, he arranged an inclined plane, and instead of having it straight so that the man in charge of the drum at the head of the incline could see his trip all the way down, he actually put a right angle in it. At this right angle he made a change in grade so that when the first trip was run the rope very naturally jumped from the guides thirty feet up into the air and went off of its own accord, into the woods at its side. This threw the descending car off the track. It ran over and cut the other length of rope which was bringing up the empty car from the bottom, and everything was chaos.

He built the coke ovens at the foot of the incline with limestone rock instead of sandstone, and when it got thoroughly heated it became partially burnt to lime, descending to cause it to swell, and the ovens went to pieces. He laid these ovens off at a right angle to the side tracks on the railroad, so that each car [was] required to be turned on a turntable to get it in, and was pushed up empty by nearly a dozen men to get it in front of the coke yards. Everything else that he did was in line therewith.

When the first kiln of so-called firebricks came out and I, who knew nothing about the manufacture of bricks, asked him why they were so red, he told me he supposed it was because the kiln had been covered over with red bricks to keep the heat in! I knew that firebricks ought to be white, and did not know until I began to investigate and learn the business that it was because there was more than 2 percent of iron in the clay from which they were made. That [was why] these bricks were red. There was something very dreadfully wrong about this business. The samples of fire clay supposed to underlie the coal had been sent to us in England, six or seven of them, and analyzed by one of the highest professional chemists in the country, showing the clay was suitable for the production of the best quality of fire-bricks. Someone, somewhere, somehow, changed the samples. No such clay as the samples sent to us existed then or exists now in the state of Tennessee, and the clay which we had underlying our coal was simple rubbish.

I first made my hand felt in connection with the blast furnace engineer, Mr. Woodward of Middlesbrough. There was nothing for him to do as the blast furnace construction was stopped for want of money, under orders from the board, and no work was proceeding except the development of the coal and coke, firebrick works at Victoria, and baryta at Whitwell. As we decided to push the coke oven work and were short of a draftsman, and Woodward had nothing on earth to do, I asked him to prepare a drawing in connection therewith, which he refused to do on the ground that his contract called for services as a blast furnace manager, and coke oven drawings had nothing to do with his duties. On the spot I gave him written notice of suspension, which was approved by the general manager, and notwithstanding his two-year contract he went back to England, and I got rid of one deadhead and his expenses.

I found on my arrival that Mr. Amos, the treasurer of the company, had already gone—he had been suspended by my father—and accounts were then being formulated showing that he had embezzled money. He had obtained goods from the store without payment. He had wrongfully expended the company's money without authority in such items as starting to build himself a billiard room paved with mosaic tiles.

On February 4, 1878, I received a cable from the home office to stop work on the furnace. This of course meant insufficient funds. The company never had enough money, but kept selling stock by private solicitation as fast as Thomas Whitwell could find someone who had £1,000 to spare. This confined us to the sale of coal and baryta and was depressing. The following day for example I measured very carefully the working places in Victoria mine, finding the coal fifteen inches in the main entry and an average of eighteen inches in other headings. Then Mr. Spence admitted that unless the coal thickened up the mine could not be profitably worked.

The company's store . . . was under the care of a stockholder by the name of Thomas Newton. I think this man was honest and well meaning, but he was eccentric to such a point that it is doubtful whether he was entirely of sound mind, and was certainly not truthful. He had been in England the manager of some cooperative store, and that was why he had been selected for the job. I found that notwithstanding the extremely stringent condition of our finances they were carrying a stock of about $21,000, including such goods as gilt mirrors and expensive furniture, for which there could not be any possible demand amongst the workmen in South Pittsburgh. In other words, his stock was what might be called a dead stock, and it was not earning more than 1 percent per annum after deducting working cost. I learned from a diary of his which he inadvertently dropped in the streets that he was in the habit of wearing clothes, shoes, [and] hats out of the store over Sunday, putting them back in stock.

I also learned later that [Newton] was responsible for writing to England some slanderous letters concerning myself and possibly other people, alleging that in the purchase . . . of the neighboring Battle Creek colliery there had been secret commissions passing. When confronted with this charge he denied originating it and attempted to put it on another man who promptly denounced him as a liar and kicked him along the road. The situation was ridiculous, and I dealt with it roughly and quickly. The stock was taken off our hands by Block, Lazard and Geismar of Chattanooga, three Jews, at what it stood on our inventory so that we lost no money by it, and they agreed to pay us a commission. In this way I got the benefit of $20,000 restored to our working capital, and turned a dead proposition into one that was producing revenue. Mr. Newton expostulated but went back to England, being the second one sent out by the directors whom I had fired.

On March 4 I received a cable to stop the colliery until the blast furnace was ready. This put me in a very bad shape, for the furnace was already stopped at this time under instruction. I went up the following day and discharged all the miners who were not under fixed agreement, and the next day received cable to employ the men who were under agreement in working the lower seam. The only trouble about this was that the lower seam had never yet been located and only had a theoretical existence. Even if it had been located it would have required months of preparation to open it up, drive narrow work and headings, and provide a connection with the incline and separate winding drum, and other arrangements for handling the coal down the mountain. I might as well have been told to mine coal in the mountains of the moon.

Such an episode shows the absurdity of trying to run the details of a business in another country thousands of miles away. Up to the present our enterprise had been tied to the apron strings of our directors in England; all the plans were drawn in England, machinery made there, officials employed there. As nearly as possible they were reducing us in this country to automatons. If they had been as wise men as they were both rich and good, they would have realized that an enterprise in a new country under different geological and metallurgical conditions, with difference in laws, customs, climate, money, machinery, and everything else, should be entrusted to men in whom they had confidence both as to skill and integrity, and who were familiar with the conditions under which the business must be carried on.

Spence, having at last many months after the promised date started his coal crushing and washing machinery, everything a confused mess and muddle . . . I took upon myself one of the hardest duties that up to that time had ever fallen to my lot, and told Mr. Spence, a man ten or twelve years older than myself, that I was perfectly satisfied of his incompetency. Bear in mind that he had been raised from the position of a working miner to that of mine foreman or manager of one of the largest companies in Scotland, and that I had a year prior to this date known nothing whatever about coal mine management. But I had learned enough in one year to show me that Mr. Spence might have been perfectly competent to conduct operations with which he was familiar in Scotland, but that he was absolutely unable to conduct them in a new country under novel conditions that required technical knowledge. The interview was painful, but I was firm, because it was a matter of duty.

After a couple of days consideration he asked me for five weeks leave of absence to go to England and see the directors, and offered to give up his seven-year agreement of which one year was then completed and to take half a year's salary and cancel the remainder of the agreement. I gave him the leave of absence and I wrote to the directors recommending a settlement with him upon that basis, and he left the next day. This was the third of the English experts that I had fired.

The next day I succeeded in arresting Mr. Amos, who . . . escap[ed] either on straw bond or some collusion or bribery of the officials, and I think he went far enough away this time to avoid being caught. And so ended the last of the special experts sent out from England.

On September 9, 1878, our family was enlarged with another son and as was natural under the circumstances he was called after my great departed friend Thomas Whitwell. On October 16 we were shocked and deeply grieved at the death of our splendid little boy Frank, who was about six years old, a manly, hearty, and very handsome fellow. The local doctor said that he died from typhus, which I do not believe, as that is a disease of either hunger or dirt, and he was not exposed to either one or the other. Our water was only well water in the town, and I am convinced that it was not typhus but typhoid, and if we had known anything of modern medical practice the life of this splendid little fellow might have been saved.

Edith Ellen, called Nellie, Bowron's seventh child, was born in November 1879. She died in June 1881 after a brief illness.

The carpenter, who was the only undertaker in the village, had cut his foot with an ax and could not work, and I had to make the necessary measurements myself for a coffin. It struck me then what unusual experiences are thrust upon one in pioneer work. Her death was designated congestion of the lungs. I suppose we would call it pneumonia now. I remember with interest an incident in her life. The floor of the room had been varnished, and the little tot was toddling around with a duster in her hand imitating older people and undertaking to dust the chairs off, and she was perplexed at the floor being sticky, hardly able to talk, partly by words and partly by gestures and looks inquiring as to what was the matter, and pointing to her feet. On June 25 we laid the little one to rest in our corner of the cemetery beside Frank and my father.

Tennessee Coal and Railroad Company had originally been developed in the 1850s by Nashville capitalists interested in increasing their city's supply of coal. They had learned in the 1840s of substantial deposits of coal on the Cumberland plateau to the east and south of Nashville. In 1852 they persuaded the New York financier Samuel F. Tracy and other northerners to invest in the company, and they built a railroad and developed coal operations at Tracy City near Sewanee. Over the next few years the company succeeded in getting substantial coal production, if not in making a profit. Although managed locally by Tennesseans, the company was owned largely by outsiders; ten of the twelve company directors in 1860 resided in New York.[9]
Over the objection of the Yankee directors, the Confederacy seized the com-

pany's works in 1861. Arthur S. Colyar, a shrewd lawyer from the Tracy City area, ran the company and produced coal with slave labor until eastern Tennessee fell to the Union army in 1862. Much of the company's property was destroyed or damaged during the war.

Colyar regained control of the company after the war and, using his myriad political and financial contacts, made it a major industrial concern in Tennessee. In 1870 the company secured its first lease of state convicts. Thereafter it would depend heavily on unfree labor in its coal operations. The convict lease, however, created a substantial financial liability for the company, and in 1876 Colyar lost control of the management to three men—Thomas O'Connor, William Morrow, and William H. Cherry—who held what was in effect the state's franchise on convict labor. Like Colyar, all three were well connected in Tennessee's Redeemer politics. O'Connor was especially influential and, until his death in a shootout on a Knoxville street in 1882, was the most powerful of the Tennesseans in the management. O'Connor pushed for the company's initial unsuccessful effort at iron making at Tracy City in 1873. A second furnace would be built at nearby Sewanee in 1880, and the company's name changed to the Tennessee Coal, Iron and Railroad Company. The company, like so many industrial corporations in the United States, fell on hard times after the 1873 panic and experienced great difficulty in recovering during the mid- and late 1870s. The TCI management made several overtures to Bowron, offering to sell a major, even controlling, interest in the company in an effort to raise needed money.

The company's financial problems eventually led its managers to seek help from a fellow Tennessean on Wall Street. John Hamilton Inman, who had fought for the Confederacy as a teenager, emerged as a dominant force in the company in 1880. Inman had moved to New York within months of Appomattox and embarked on a career as a cotton broker. He formed Inman, Swann and Company in 1870, helped to organize the New York Cotton Exchange, and was reputed to be a multimillionaire by 1875. As he grew wealthy, Inman speculated more and more in railroad and industrial stocks. He would ~ain national notoriety in 1893 for his unscrupulous manipulation of the R imond Terminal Railroad, which failed at that time partly because of Inma ; mismanagement.[10] His role in TCI's development, as portrayed by James B vron, was no less opportunistic. Inman's two main allies in the TCI managen nt would be two other Tennesseans who, like him, had joined the Confeder e army at age sixteen: Nathaniel Baxter, a Nashville lawyer and banker, and Alfred M. Shook, the Sewanee-based company manager.

On March 23, 1878, . . . Major Thomas O'Connor of Knoxville and Nashville . . . asked me whether we would entertain a proposal to buy the property of the Tennessee Coal and Railroad Company at Tracy City. I made a promise to visit the mines with him and carried this out March 28 and 29. No proposition was made to me at that time as to the price at which we might acquire the property. I visited Nashville, and Major O'Connor had me spend the morning at the penitentiary operated by his firm. At this time I met Dr. William Morrow, the then president of the Tennessee Coal and Railroad Company, and Mr. Nat Baxter, president of the First National Bank [of Nashville]. On April 30 O'Connor visited South Pittsburgh and said he would retain his fourth interest in the Tennessee Coal and Railroad Company if we would buy the interests of William H. Cherry and Alfred M. Shook.

They were very much in earnest about our buying them out. This subject was resumed in Nashville on July 12 when I spent the entire day with the four partners discussing the terms of the purchase. We had been told in an unofficial way that we could buy a half interest in the Tracy City property for $200,000, but no definite official statement had been made, as we were endeavoring to familiarize ourselves on each side with the value of the other's property. There is no reasonable doubt I think but that if it had been otherwise we would in a short time have come together and would have absorbed the Tennessee Coal and Railroad Company, but on August 5, 1878, I received the shocking news by cable of a serious accident to our chairman, Thomas Whitwell, followed the next day by a cable that he was dead.

On April 12, 1879, Major O'Connor came to South Pittsburgh to urge me to buy the interest in his firm, the penitentiary lease, and the Tracy City property of Colonel Shook, who owed to O'Connor and Morrow $30,000, and would take $20,000 clear and step out. This interest within the then ensuing two or three years was worth at least $500,000, perhaps $750,000. If our directors had authorized me to accept it, what a different tale there would have been to tell. We would have taken in the Tennessee Coal and Railroad Company instead of being taken in by it later on. There was opportunity knocking at the door.

Authority was given to proceed upon an agreed schedule with the construction of the blast furnace and its equipment [at South Pittsburgh]. Here, however, our friends in England made a grave error. They had not enough money, and yet the entire plan was laid out for two furnaces. The bridge and stock elevator, the stock house, main gas flue, railroad tracks, engine house, and many other parts of the layout [were] pushed to completion, tying up much money without a chance of any return upon it until the starting of the second furnace. If this had been avoided we would have had money enough to complete the first furnace a year earlier than we did.

It had become so perfectly obvious that, owing to the extreme thinness and variability of our own coal, we would not have an output sufficient to keep the furnace supplied with coke. We finally made a contract with the Tennessee Coal and Railroad Company on October 10 for five years for 30,000 tons per annum. This was to cost us $2.80 per ton on cars at Cowan Station, they to wash the coal as per the Stutz washer which we were to make and furnish. This was to be coupled with an option on the property.

Mr. W. Thomlinson arrived on a visit, he having been in Mr. Whitwell's office, and having been selected by him as the English secretary after I came to this country. He had been sent out really as a special expert, and if I may use the word "detective," to see how we were spending money and what there was still to do and how much capital it was yet necessary for them to raise in England to see us through. He requested us to stop the operation of our coke ovens although we were showing a profit on the coke, and also to stop [one] hot blast stove, and start the furnace with three [stoves]. He informed me that the directors were prepared to offer £10,000 upon mortgage of the company's property for completion of the work.

On June 13, 1879, the many misunderstandings between the board in England and myself began to come to a head, and I received a letter violently censorial. My friend Thomas Whitwell [was] succeeded as chairman by my father-in-law William Barrett, with whom his cousin, Henry Barrett, would naturally vote, but they were only two out of six, and the company was ruled by Henry and E. Lucas Pease of Darlington, two very rich men. On receipt of this letter I wrote the board offering to resign, to which letter I never received any reply or acknowledgment. It was simply ignored. About this time, I subsequently learned, my assistant Mr. Pechin commenced to carry on a private correspondence with the directors in England, making some direct charges and other insinuations as to my mismanagement. Better an open enemy than a perfidious friend.

Pechin was a man at that time of forty-three, ten years my senior. He had been a lawyer until thirty-three years of age, had no technical knowledge anymore than I had, and had no knowledge of general information, drawing, or chemistry. But he was sharp and shrewd and very quick in observation, and an extremely good mixer. He had . . . spent several years with the Dunbar Furnace Company in Pennsylvania, and had made a study of the coal and iron fields and blast furnaces of the Hocking Valley in Ohio. He had evidently come [in February 1878] at the request of our people in England to look around.

In September 1879 Mr. Pechin addressed to me notifying his intended resignation, the secret of which was that from private and underhand[ed] correspondence with the board he was endeavoring and expecting to obtain my position and to supplant me. Nothing is easier than destructive criticism. He knew and the board knew that I had absolutely no information of a technical character when I was appointed to my position. That I would make and did make many mistakes goes without saying, but I do not know that I made any of a serious character. The greatest ground for complaint was that I resold some of the Tracy City coke and afterwards found that we needed it ourselves, and that our furnace was often stopped for coke. The answer to this is fairly obvious: the coke was resold at a tolerably good profit when we were extremely dissatisfied with the quality [our ovens] were supplying us. But the failure of the ovens which Spence had built before my arrival, and the calamitous failure of the coal mine to supply an adequate amount of coal, together handicapped our own fuel production in a way that was not contemplated.

They also criticized my sale of too much pig iron on a rising market, thus losing the advantage of the high prices which prevailed for six or seven months. These sales were largely made before the furnace started and when we hoped for a production of nearly 100 tons per day. But built on English plans suitable for English material, [they] got a commencing figure of 45 tons, gradually working up to about 70. If the furnace had been built on American lines with American equipment, it would have given a larger tonnage and we would not have been oversold.

The errors that I can see that I did make were that I allowed myself, in my distress as to our own lack of revenue, to be diverted to examining and recommending to the directors several things which they turned down, . . . such as the buying of [a] boiler plate rolling mill, . . . paying in stock, and moving it to South Pittsburgh. The iron we made would not have been suitable for it. In the main I can look back with my present knowledge upon the record of my activities and see that I worked with prodigious activity both with body and mind, swathed about with red tape, handicapped by shortage of money, by ignorant officials, by a lack of teamwork and of loyalty, people working against each other for individual advantage and going behind my back to the directors, who to a certain extent neither treated me with consideration nor with frankness. I admit that they were justified in irritation because I was not enthusiastic about getting up sets of cost accounts. I was not familiar with them at that time. It hardly seems, however, that there was sufficient in the situation to justify their listening to a scheming and intriguing lawyer, a man who by his personal habits and conversation as an avowed skeptic was helping to demoralize some of the younger men upon whose personal character a good deal depended.

On October 17, 1879, Major O'Connor definitely offered us one-fourth interest in the Tracy City property for $65,000, he already owning one-fourth, agreeing that he would buy another fourth and give us power of attorney to vote his stock for ten years, the payments to be made easy. As an alternative to this, he offered us a one-third interest in the company for $100,000, his party still to retain control. I need not repeat that the acceptance of this proposition would have placed us in control of a profitable business which was supplying the fuel requirements of the Nashville, Chattanooga, and St. Louis Railroad Company, and which had a profitable contract for convict labor ([which] was free from strikes), which owned its own supply of rolling stock, and would have made us entirely free on questions of quantity and quality of fuel. It would have been infinitely better for the directors to accept this proposition than to devote further funds to the completion of the second blast furnace from which we had neither the coke nor the ore in sight. So my errors were of far less importance than their own.

In January 1880 the directors figuratively cut their own throats and cabled me rejecting the pending offers of [the] Tracy [property], but on the contrary instructing me to buy the bricks and material for the second blast furnace. How it could have been said of them in the language of the prayer book that "they did those things which they ought not to have done, and they had left undone those things which they ought to have done." In my personal opinion this action on their part settled the outcome of the Southern States Coal, Iron and Land Company.

I received the official copies of the resolution from the board asking on what terms I should resign my position. It was bad enough to be in a little country town in a strange land, thousands of miles from my family and friends, and to have closed out all my business relations in England. At this moment I had no place to go, no one to appeal to for help, a family of young and helpless children on my hands, and only a few hundred dollars of assets outside of my immediate furniture. The outlook was not pleasant. I knew that I had done right and was still doing right and that their action was unjustifiable, and I stood firm on my contract and declined to offer any terms for its cancellation.

In April Pechin arrived again so as to be on hand for his installation in my position, evidently having private arrangements with the board of directors. He advised that a "committee" was on its way. In May Mr. Ramwell, the English attorney of the company from Bolton, Lancashire, who was also a director, arrived together with Mr. Thomlinson, the former secretary of the company who had made a visit the year before. He made me the proposal of $5,000 to cancel my engagement. I promptly declined it but offered to accept $10,000 cash, as I thought with that amount I might possibly buy an interest in some current going business in the district where I could employ my time. He then stated that he was not authorized to pay that amount. He put in several days together with Mr. Thomlinson and myself examining the property of the company at every point, the entire visit occupying nine days.

During this time Mr. Ramwell, a trained and skillful investigator with a keen legal mind, was making every possible inquiry about me and my management, and about Mr. Pechin and his ability, and also as to the personal character and reputation of each of us. These inquiries were made in Nashville and Chattanooga for the most part. Foreseeing that these questions would come up, I addressed a letter to a number of prominent people who had business relations with us, and who knew somewhat of my management, saying to them that questions had arisen with my board of directors which might perhaps involve my leaving the company, and asking them to favor me with a letter stating frankly their opinion of my work and how it showed up among American businessmen. In reply to this I received strong letters of endorsement.

The letters were interesting in themselves, and a strong representation of the effect produced in the community by the integrity and unremitting industry with which I had pursued my duties, and they were pleased to accord to me a high degree of intelligence. If they had known of one-fourth part of my difficulties they would probably have spoken even more highly. I do not know of course whom Mr. Ramwell interviewed and what was said to him by Mr. Pechin's friends, whoever they might have been. As the result of his investigation Mr. Ramwell withdrew his request for my resignation, declined to negotiate with me, and stated he would take the responsibility as having power of attorney from the board to confirm me in my position. I think he paid Mr. Pechin's expenses for the month that he had been hanging around Chattanooga and sent him away.

The directors found they had run up to the end of their money raised by the second issue of stock, and cabled us to draw no more drafts upon them for construction purposes. We had nothing to show for the additional money raised except a second blast furnace partially completed. If that money had been put into the acquisition of controlling interest in the Tennessee Coal and Railroad Company their fortunes would have been in sight. On consultation we found we needed at least $30,000 to finish the furnace. We decided to stop both the baryta works and the firebrick works, sell out all stocks there, discharge men, and concentrate our operations.

I had a most interesting visit from Sidney Gilchrist Thomas, the generally recognized inventor of the basic Bessemer and basic open-hearth steel-making process, which is called the Thomas process on the continent of Europe. He stayed with me two days and went into calculations as to the necessary money needed to finish our second blast furnace, open up the new Whitwell colliery, [and] provide the necessary incline and coke ovens, and made his own estimate of the savings to accrue to us, figuring up $4.34 per ton of pig iron. This included having local autonomy in managing things on the spot, rather than from England. His head was level. He talked about finding this money and also, subject to other negotiations that he had pending, of our having a basic steel plant there. He left me feeling greatly encouraged, for I had never lost hope and expectation of making a success of the business in which my father had laid down his life. Unfortunately it came to naught. The health of Mr. Thomas was then failing, and . . . he died. This ended all hopes of our spreading out at South Pittsburgh, for we had no special friends in this country and our directors were too rich to want to work and too jealous to allow anyone else to do the work, and they by this time were trying to find some way to get rid of the responsibility.

On September 19, 1881, Messrs. Edwin L. Pease, chairman of the company, and Francis Greg, a cotton spinner of Lancashire who was also a director of the company, arrived on a visit. Of course they came to my house as all visitors of distinction had to. We little thought when we took them in that the visit would be extended to three months. After a week we went to New York together and [on] September 28 commenced negotiations with O'Connor at the office of Mr. John H. Inman, a wealthy cotton broker.

The following day [Inman] suggested a merger of the two companies on the basis of each company's stock being put in at par, which I objected to strenuously as our stocks represented as all English stocks do actual cash value paid in dollar for dollar, and I knew their stock had been swelled recently from about $300,000 to $1,750,000, so that it would have been a most unfair proposition. I should here point out that during the year 1881 they had built the Sewanee furnace at Cowan without ever putting a dollar into it of their own money. The furnace was built for $124,600, an extremely cheap outfit. This money was raised by the sale of $100,000 bonds to the Nashville, Chattanooga and St. Louis Railway, drawing by way of overdraft $24,600 from the [First] National Bank of Nashville. Nathaniel Baxter, the president of the bank, [had] also become a director of the Tennessee Company and [was] being slated for its presidency, this for the sake of financial help and local influence.

At the next meeting we proposed that they should buy our company, taking over all our assets and liabilities, and giving us their stock on a basis of dollar for dollar. Our English visitors then went with me to Philadelphia to confer with our Quaker friends there and get their ideas as to the standing of the Nashville and New York parties, and were entirely satisfied when I gave them the list of directors.

Inman came down from New York accompanied by Major O'Connor and Mr. Baxter, and my house was full to overflowing. The visitors went away and on October 31 made us an offer to pay $700,000 for our property in the shape of $300,000 of bonds and $400,000 [in] 6 percent preference stock of their own company. I fiercely resisted this offer and the directors declined it. The directors . . . [later] accepted their offer to give us fifty cents on the dollar in their stock, subject of course to our existing bonds which were held in England and by our friends in Philadelphia. The Tennessee Company, however, was to furnish the money to pay off these bonds at their maturity.

After several days discussion between the lawyers an agreement was finally executed . . . giving the Tennessee Company the right . . . to purchase our property for about $700,000 of their bonds out of an issue of $1 million, to be secured upon the property itself, they to assume the American assets and liabilities, and the Southern States Company going into liquidation to retain and liquidate the English liabilities and assets.

Mr. Pease I never saw again, as he sailed the next day for England, and subsequently broke his neck by a fall from his horse whilst fox hunting. I was very much amused at a later date when Mr. Baxter was discussing the negotiations. Mr. Pease, to overawe Baxter and Inman with a sense of the wealth of our people and himself in particular, had been discussing fox hunting, horses, [and] dogs, no doubt thinking he had made a great impression, and that Mr. Inman would come down a notch and not hold his head so high in bargaining. But Inman that evening said, "Baxter, if these men care so much for horses and dogs, do you not think we ought to get the best of them in a trade?" And they certainly did! During the course of these negotiations it had become apparent that the firebrick in the first furnace was getting into bad condition, and that it would be proper to blow it out for relining and blow in the second furnace in its place. The directors would not permit me to do this as they thought it would have an injurious effect on the trade. On the other hand that second furnace when it was started averaged about 100 tons per day against the average of 70 which we were getting out of the old one. If we had blown it in and got this result it would have greatly improved our status.

On January 12, 1882, President James C. Warner and General Manager A. M. Shook [of the Tennessee Company] arrived and instructed various developments: the completion of the second furnace in every respect; the opening up of the limestone quarry and the building of workmen's houses; also the starting of all the ovens which had been finished but not lighted. [They] expressed their desire to lease out the brick works to someone else. As a matter of policy they decided to concentrate and cut off what they called outside things. This is good business for a small concern which cannot find money enough to make its auxiliaries complete.

Baxter and Shook ... without any inquiry on my part or solicitation ... offered me the position of secretary and treasurer, to assist the president in the Nashville office of the company, at a salary of $3,000 per annum. This was a great comedown from $7,500, but as he told me they were only paying their president $4,200 and their general manager $4,000, and they left it to me as to whether $3,000 was not relatively a fair compensation for the office. I was compelled to admit that it was. I have never in my life asked for any situation whatever. Every position and office, whether paid or unpaid, has been tendered to as unsolicited throughout my entire life.

I look back upon my life in South Pittsburgh with nothing in the nature of self reproach. I saved money whilst I was there; paid off balances of debt left in England; contributed out of my own pocket toward my father's liabilities in recognition of his generosity, liquidated his assets to advantage; ... detected various forms of wrongdoing and brought the offender to book; successfully met and overcame intrigue and treachery; and as far as I can see it I did my whole duty as a man, and have nothing to regret concerning the place except that it broke with its inevitable hardships the health and strength of my wife. The little place is beautiful, and I have always loved it and shall always love it for the sake of those who lie there.

Nashville

Bowron's early years with TCI would be some of the most difficult of his life. The new job kept him in the United States, where he knew great opportunities existed, but it was in reality a step down from his position as chief operating officer for the English company. His new employers, though usually closer at hand, did not always manifest more wisdom. As a TCI officer, he took on some responsibility for the convict-lease system, which he knew to be highly controversial, even if he did not readily admit its inhumanity. The convict lease gave TCI a great advantage in relations with industrial labor, as Arthur Colyar later testified: "For some time after we began the convict labor system we found that we were right in calculating that the free laborers would be loath to enter upon a strike when they saw that the company was amply provided with convict labor." By the early 1880s, TCI and convict-leasing had become virtually synonymous in Tennessee, and accusations of brutality and corruption were made against the company in highly public fashion. In 1885 the Nashville *Banner* would accuse TCI of payoffs to secure an exclusive lease, an allegation soon affirmed by those who received large amounts of money not to bid for the lease. At the same time, reformers began to investigate the health conditions of Tennessee's leased convicts and reported awful rates of illness and death.[1]

Bowron's beginning with TCI in 1882 coincided with the start of another recession in the iron industry. All southern ironmakers suffered and many companies failed. Low iron prices resulting from a worldwide glut were the obvious problem, but men like Samuel Noble of Anniston had already seen the basic difficulty of building an iron industry in a part of the country with so little demand for pig iron—the raw, unfinished product. What was needed in the South, Noble and James Bowron knew, were tool and machinery shops and plants that manufactured finished goods from iron. Even after he moved to Nashville to work for TCI, Bowron would spend much energy and money attempting to develop those "forward-linkage" industries for his beloved South Pittsburgh. He would be instrumental in starting cast-iron pipe manufacturing in South Pittsburgh, an effort that first involved him in what would become the South's main "finished" iron product.

The effort to build up satellite industries brought to South Pittsburgh many potential new investors, men like John S. Perry of New York and William D. "Pig-Iron" Kelley, the Pennsylvania congressman and industrialist. Perry started a stove works in South Pittsburgh, in which Kelley's son was an officer and the senior Kelley probably an investor. Both men were imbued with the "New South" spirit, which heralded an industrializing region fully reconciled with the North—indeed, a region wholly different from the Old South. Like Henry Grady of the Atlanta *Constitution*, Henry Watterson of the Louisville *Courier-Journal*, and Richard Edmonds of Baltimore's *Manufacturers' Record*, Perry and Kelley celebrated the great natural advantages for industry in the South. Characteristic of New South promoters, Perry emphasized the positive capabilities of blacks as industrial workers. Kelley noted more realistically the problems with labor recruitment in the South, though he tried to sound positive about the likely success of securing an effective work force. On the other hand, Kelley was hardly the optimistic booster when he discussed the neglect of South Pittsburgh's development by TCI, whose corporate concerns by 1886 were turning southward toward Alabama. James Bowron was far more committed to South Pittsburgh's development than anyone else at TCI, and in time it would become clear that he was a more constant friend than the Yankee boosters Perry and Kelley.[2]

Increasing the southern consumption of iron would prove to be a difficult and sometimes failed proposition, as Bowron's experience in South Pittsburgh showed. Southern ironmakers would continue to export the vast majority of their iron to northern manufacturers. The necessity to compete in northern markets required cheap and flexible freight rates—indeed, rates that appeared to many other shippers as preferential to the "long-hauled" southern iron. Midwestern opposition to long-haul and short-haul differentials led to the passage of the Interstate Commerce Act in 1887, which granted the federal government some power to regulate railroad rates, presumably on a more equitable basis. As an articulate southern ironmaker and one who understood the national and international markets, Bowron stepped forward to speak to the newly formed Interstate Commerce Commission against any increase in the long-haul rate for iron.[3]

As he confronted the myriad of business problems presented him by TCI and his South Pittsburgh investments, Bowron had to deal with the greatest crisis of his life, the death of his devoted and diligent wife Ada. Ada had given birth to eight children in eleven years and had suffered the loss of three of them. The physical and emotional costs of childbearing, combined with the hardships of emigration and a virtual frontier existence, finally broke her health in early 1883. James Bowron was left with five small children and little means, other than his own energy, to cope with the burgeoning responsibility. Partly as a matter of practicality, he almost immediately began looking for a replacement for Ada. He found, according to his own description, a woman of equal tenderness and bounteous love—with, in fact, the same Christian character and name.

I began my Nashville life under circumstances of both hope and regret. Regret for the loss of identity with the enterprise formulated by my father and for which, however successful it might become under another name, his family would never receive the same credit. Regret at stepping down from a position of chief importance to one much less so, and at greatly reduced salary. Regret at leaving workmen and associates whom I had come to regard as friends. I did not appreciate the fact that a much larger field was going to open before me in which I would be able to receive and give more help, instruction, and benefit than ever before. These feelings were checked by hope of becoming a factor in the development of an important enterprise with greater financial and political backing. These hopes were realized. I also felt that it would be a distinct advantage to my wife and family to move from a little country village to an important city where all the conditions of life would insure greater comfort, education, and benefits at large. These hopes were realized to some extent.

On August 10, 1882, my family arrived in Nashville. We moved into 502 South Summer Street ... and that night I thought I would go crazy. No sooner had we put out the lights than countless millions ... of mosquitoes in this old empty dreary house sang delirious songs of triumph over us. My wife managed to protect the baby with a piece of curtain, and we fought it out the best way we could. By degrees we got our furniture there and got reasonably settled down. [We] brought with us one of our servants from South Pittsburgh who had been with us for years. To add to the trials ... the servant was declared by the doctor to be ill with typho-malarial fever, and ordered to return home to South Pittsburgh immediately ... leaving us helpless. I mention these things to show the accumulated strain which was going to break down my wife in the very near future. On September 22 my dear wife developed illness and was compelled to take to bed. Dr. Atchison pronounced it yellow jaundice, an ailment well known to arise as the result of worry, care, and strain, together with adverse climatic conditions and malaria. This illness continued for about two weeks, and materially reduced her strength.

On January 3, 1883, we had some callers, and my wife sat with them in a cold drawing room before supper. I took them back to their hotel after supper, finding to my consternation on my return home that she had been seized with violent pain. I went to the nearest telephone and called the doctor, who came out and pronounced it pleuropneumonia, and gave me instructions to go downtown and get leeches from the nearest drugstore and apply them, which reduced the inflammation but at the same time reduced her strength. I do not think it was the best treatment for such a case. I was up all night with her on that night and the next, and on January 5 I telegraphed to my sister Amy, who was in west Tennessee. She arrived during the night to take up the nursing.

[My wife] said to me as the days went by that she felt that she could never endure another illness, as she was "draining the very dregs of life." On the evening of January 8 she was feeling much better and free from pain, and beginning to take nutriment, and spoke of my sister's careful nursing. [She] referred to Dickens's story "Barnaby Rudge," which I had been reading aloud to her for a couple of weeks in the evenings prior to her illness, expressing the hope that I would soon be able to recommence as she was so much interested in the story. She had a very peaceful night, but the next morning after I had left her in good spirits thinking that she was recovering nicely, the doctor telephoned me ... to come home immediately. [He] told me that her strength was inadequate to cough up the mucus which the irritation in the lung was discharging, and that it was accumulating and shutting off the action of the lungs. She was growing weaker every hour from the effects of carbonized blood.

In desperation he administered emetics, thinking that it might expel the phlegm which she could not cough up. At 2:00 P.M. she addressed my sister, saying, "Stay, take care of my babies." About 4:00 P.M., "Jamie, come and kiss me," and "Simply to thy cross I cling." At 4:30, twice, "Asleep in Jesus." Then "Goodnight." Later I asked her if she was conscious, if she knew me, if she had peace, peace with Jesus. Being past the power of speech she nodded her assent several times, as also [she did] to my suggestions that she would soon be beyond pain and with our beloved children in Heaven. After patiently without tear or groan enduring much pain, she passed away at 6:45 P.M., so ending twelve and a half years of a loving and lovely partnership at the early age of thirty-four.

At this time Charlie was eleven and a half years of age, the only one of the children old enough to realize the tragedy of the home, and he suggested that he thought he would get a knife and cut his throat. It was better if it had to be that they should be so young that they did not realize their loss, and I am sorry that I do not know any way in which I can convey to her children any adequate description of their mother. All that I can say is that she was slightly above middle height, medium weight, quick and active in her movements, of a cheerful, sunny disposition, and of most remarkable patience and unselfishness. She was always the one to do or to bear something that someone else might be spared. Quick in sympathy, friendly in demeanor. Our means were not such as to enable us to give parties either in England or in South Pittsburgh, but in the latter place especially we entertained innumerable people at our home, some of them staying for weeks, and in one case for months, entailing a great deal of drudgery upon her for which she never received the recompense. I am greatly reminded of her character in the precious namesake that she left behind her, and I can pay my daughter Ada no higher compliment than to say that in her conceptions of duty and her tender and devoted character she greatly resembles her mother.

For myself I had risen that morning without the slightest dream of the tragedy, the greatest in my life, that was hanging over me and ready to occur. I was shocked beyond measure, but the dear Lord has said, "My grace is sufficient for thee: for my strength is made perfect in weakness." I was perfectly calm and went down to the office very promptly the next morning, first to see the undertaker and make the necessary arrangements and to telegraph to South Pittsburgh to prepare a grave in our family lot. When my friends went out to the house to comfort me they found I was not there and came back to the office in amazement where they found me . . . making out the payroll. My sister Amy offered to stay and take charge of my household until I could make other arrangements.

On January 12, after prayer at the house by myself, I went with Charlie and two or three friends to the railroad station, and Charlie and I took the body of our loved one to South Pittsburgh. The [Anglican] service was read by Alfred Craven, an Englishman in our employment, and I personally had grace and strength to deliver a sermon, prayer, and benediction, using the text, "The sting of death is sin," pointing out that where sin had been pardoned there was no longer the sting in death. I stayed with my brother Will, who was living in South Pittsburgh, and he and his wife offered to take the baby Ada and raise her, which was very kind, but I preferred to hold my family intact.

On September 27, 1883, I went for the first time with my sister to call on a young lady, and this was done deliberately. I had always up to the time of my wife's removal felt that one was married once and for all, and that any second marriage was a species of infidelity to the first. I think if I had had no family of young children on my hands that probably this would, or at least might have continued to be, my frame of mind. But as it was I had five children left on my hands ranging from eleven and a half years down to eight months, and had no female relative within a thousand miles except my sister Amy, whose husband had no fixed place of abode but was traveling from place to place conducting skating rinks, and depending very much on his wife to assist him in handling and popularizing the business with the young ladies of the towns where he went. The skating craze at that time was playing out for the second time. It has since sprung up for a third lifetime, but it was going down and he was having a hard time making a living, and resented her absence with me as militating against his own success. I have no doubt he was right.

I realized that the housekeeper I had engaged was a lady of absolutely cold disposition, apparently selfish, considering her own comfort and caring little if anything for my little ones, and that I could not count upon the continued presence of my sister. I began to consider the matter very seriously and thoughtfully in the light of the Lord's personal message that in Heaven there is neither marrying nor giving in marriage, but that we shall be as the angels of God there. The more I thought about this the more I felt that as we would be brothers and sisters together in Christ, there was really nothing except a question of sentiment to prevent a second marriage, and that situated as I was with a large family of young children they had a right to a mother's care, and I began with this in mind to look at every young woman that I met with the idea that she might possibly become my wife, and to weigh her qualifications. It will be seen that it took me some time to weigh them all, not because they were too heavy, but because they were too light.

My sister pointed out many matters of grievous complaint that were obvious to her trained and skillful eye as the result of three months experience with my housekeeper. She was extremely dissatisfied with conditions in which she found matters, and said she would stay indefinitely and manage my household and that I might dismiss the lady, which I did the following day, giving her of course suitable notice.

I changed my mind, as all wise people do sometimes. I had thought it was useless for me to qualify as an American citizen where my vote could be offset by that of an ignorant Negro. But a man said to me that if that were so it was the more necessary and imperative that I should qualify, and that all educated and intelligent persons should do so. I felt that he was right and on April 25, 1883, filed my declaration of intention to become an American citizen.

On October 7, 1885, I became a citizen of the United States and got my naturalization papers from the court in Nashville. I cannot say that it has helped me very much for I have been in the minority all my life. In England as a nonconformist instead of [Anglican]. In this country as a Republican in Tennessee and Alabama. But I am glad to say that does not bother me in any way. So long as I vote as I think best and discharge my conscience I feel clear of responsibility. On October 8 I cast my first vote, for the reform party as against machine politicians in the municipal election. We elected some of our candidates, but on the whole I think the old crowd counted the victory.

My diary for the previous five years [1877–82] resembles that of a blast furnace superintendent, but for the coming four or five years resembles more that of a YMCA secretary or a traveling evangelist. Every evening practically was put in at some church or another, playing, singing, or making addresses, taking midweek services, going to various towns in the interest of YMCA work, helping to raise funds there, making many addresses, some in churches, in halls, and on the public streets.

The first evening that I was in Nashville I went to the YMCA and put in my application for membership. The next evening I attended a revival service at the Cumberland Presbyterian Church. Oddly enough [the visiting preacher, E. P. Hammond] picked me out and requested me to address the audience briefly, which I did without hesitation. The following evening, sitting at the organ waiting for the meeting to open, I somewhat timidly ventured to play a well-known hymn and sing a solo, and was immediately pounced upon by the pastor . . . and required during the remainder of the meeting for the next two weeks to sing several times. In this way I became known immediately to what one may call the religious life of Nashville.

On November 1, 1882, a meeting was held at Monteagle on the Cumberland plateau . . . at which was formed the Monteagle Sunday School Assembly. Our company gave $5,000 in money and 100 acres of mountain surface land, retaining the mineral rights. It was understood that the Sunday school forces of the states of Tennessee, Georgia, Alabama, and Mississippi were going to combine to make a success of whichever point might be selected for the location of the assembly. After the decision of the locating committee in favor of Monteagle, the charter was signed, I being one of the five charter members, and [I] was elected the first treasurer of the assembly and the secretary of the executive committee. This became a very great factor in my life.

In 1885 I attended the international YMCA convention in Atlanta, and as a member of the international committee, to which I was that day reelected for six years, I made many additional friends. The same day the Tennessee delegation expressed the earnest desire that I should become chairman of the Tennessee state work. At that time I was present at an affecting interview with Henry Grady, who became a national figure as a journalist and orator. With tears running over his face he dedicated himself to the promotion of YMCA work and started the campaign for the large new building for the Atlanta association, which up to that time was being conducted over a Chinese laundry—no doubt in accordance with the axiom that "cleanliness comes next to godliness."

[That year] I presided over a mass meeting at the gospel tent held in the interest of the YMCA building fund, where Sam P. Jones [the evangelist] preached on the text "Withhold not good from them to whom it is due when it is in the power of thine hand to do it." We had had a previous gathering of the board of directors with him an hour before the meeting, at which each one there stated what he would give, and one or two of our friends had also mentioned the amounts they would give. These were held back so to speak, and announced at suitable moments to keep the interest from flagging, and the active members of the association mingled with the mass of people, offering them pledge cards and pencils, and from time to time holding up a hand to attract attention and announcing to the platform any important subscription, to which Jones would respond, "All right brother, keep on fishing in that pool." In the course of about forty minutes we gathered up a total of $22,500.

In July 1884 I [had] preached at the Monteagle Assembly a sermon which my dear wife says she still remembers in which I denounced all forms of untruth including false hair and painted faces. This was the summer when I saw Miss Adah S. Cunningham for the first time. I heard my friend Professor Wharton address the assembled crowd and say that everyone had to accept without hesitation whatever duty was laid upon him and that there must be no hanging back. I thought that everyone who went to Monteagle was some learned person or experienced worker in religious or sociological work and that it would require someone fearfully high up to teach them. The first name that was called by the professor was Miss Adah S. Cunningham, and I wondered who and what she could be, and I saw the young lady step out promptly and go and take her place with the young children. I did not forget her, or the occasion, but the acquaintance scarcely ripened at that time.

In June 1886, having received letters speaking of my sister Gertrude's illness, Amy left to be with her. I realized that without either sister or house-keeper my little folks at home during my absence . . . had no one but the Negro servants to take care of them, and this further emphasized my desire to make some more permanent domestic relationship.

At Monteagle in August 1886 I spent my evenings either attending lectures or walking out to the bluff with Miss Adah Cunningham, laying deliberate siege to her, although I doubt whether she had yet realized it. On Sunday, August 22, 1886, I tried to make hay whilst the sun was shining and as it was a fine day walked with Miss Cunningham to the table rock, went to church together, and walked somewhere afterwards.

She has never told me yet what induced her to give me the preference over the different people whom I know were calling upon her at that time and to declare to climb into the rolling chariot of life beside me and share my fate. I saw her teaching and controlling with the assistance of two helpers about 150 children at the mission school in North Nashville. I thought then . . . that if she could manage 150 she could probably manage my five, of whom one was a dear little girl who did not need any management, and would probably make a better job of it than I could with the four boys. Her natural sprightliness and remarkable capacity for making friends with everybody, which makes her today the most popular woman in her church and in the YMCA, have always given her a grasp upon the hearts of children.

It is not everyone, however, by any means who is willing to step into a position surrounded by the responsibility and care incidental to a ready-made family. By this time I had a decent salary, but I was not by any means a rich man. My whole estimated assets in life that year according to my books which I started January 1, 1886, amounted to less than $30,000, but out of this amount subsequent knowledge shows that about $16,000 was bad, so that the assets I then had really panned out about $13,000, and I had a salary of $5,000. This was none too much with five children growing up. I do not think she ever considered the financial side of it. I was grateful to her then and have been ever since for her willingness to take me on trust without our really having been sufficiently . . . associated to reasonably justify such an action on her part. I think in this matter as in so many others, however, we were directly guided and our conclusions directed by the Lord, as it had been a matter of constant personal prayer on my part that I should be guided aright in this matter. We are both of us willing to accept it as of His leading.

It is interesting to carry the mind back to the preparation for the stock-holders meeting of April 1882, when at the desk space rented me in the unfurnished room upstairs over the bank, without even a gas jet, I attempted the night before the meeting to blend together into one harmonious balance sheet, by the light of a tallow candle stuck in the neck of a bottle, the separate statements of the Tracy City and Cowan divisions, made out as they were on entirely different bases. It was a hard job and James Warner [president of TCI] was not very well pleased with the result.

The coal mines at Tracy City had been running separately under the name of Tennessee Coal, Iron and Railroad Company, and the blast furnace at Cowan under that of the Sewanee Furnace Company, each keeping its own accounts entirely. My plan of accounting was to keep all capital accounts at the main office in Nashville, and allow the working accounts and the personal accounts to be kept at the different divisions. Instead of their keeping separate banking accounts in different names and drawing checks upon them, we would keep one consolidated account in the name of the general company upon which we would check in Nashville. I also drew out various blanks upon which information as to the daily operations would be sent to the central office, so that we might be advised as to the status of their operations. All this hurt the dignity of Edward Doud, the manager . . . of the Sewanee Furnace Company. He felt that I was intruding on his business and [he] wrote me an offensive letter, which I naturally referred to my president, with the result that at the next directors meeting his resignation was accepted. After this they all settled down harmoniously into my working plans.

John Inman arrived from New York, and with the assistance of Messrs. Warner, Baxter, O'Connor, and the general bookkeeper at the bank, [he] went through my books for the first three months, to see whether I was keeping them correctly and that none of the company's money was sticking to my fingers. This was amusing to me. None of the directors subsequently ever troubled to do this, but have been content to leave it to professional auditors. I note at this time that we were borrowing money for the company from Mr. Inman at 9 percent per annum—6 percent on the loan and 1½ percent each time that the six-months note was renewed. This was certainly profitable business for the lender.

During July 1883 TCI became the new lessee of the state penitentiary, agreeing to pay $101,000 per annum for six years from the first of January next. I might write a good deal on the subject of convict labor, but will condense it. It is proper that the convict should work and earn his own living. It is impossible for him to work without competing with free labor. The suggestion that he be taken out of the mines and put on the public roads to avoid competition is ridiculous. He is doing the work which a free man might do quite as much on the road as in the mines. It is much easier to guard him from escape in the mines than on the road where if he should escape he terrorizes women and children working or living on the adjacent farms.

The coal industry is a basic industry, and a necessity of civilization. It is not right that it should be placed under the control, arbitrary and inconsiderate, of union leaders. It is highly proper that the convicts should be worked in the mines in the production of fuel to be either used by the state or sold by it at the current market prices, not below them. The lease system is wrong as it used to be conducted, where the cupidity or inhumanity of the lessees might permit the convict to be overworked or underfed, or abused. Where he stays, however, in the custody of the state officials, who regulate his work, provide his food and clothing, decide when he is sick, and protect him from any imposition, they are not selling him but the fruit . . . of his fair and honest labor.

In the case of the Tennessee Company, unfortunately, we contracted to pay a lump sum and had to make what we could out of the mine. We could not work them all in our mines, and therefore some were subleased in the main penitentiary to Cherry, O'Connor and Company, and later some to the Knoxville Iron Company to work at Coal Creek, in east Tennessee. In the main penitentiary these men were taught to build wagons, involving the use of woodworking machinery, blacksmithing, planing, et cetera, so that when they should go out from prison they would have one or more honest trades at which they could make an honest living, and would not have an excuse to steal.

BOWRON DIARY, March 11, 1878:
Shook . . . invited me to see Tracy City mines. He had convicts working over 100 bush[els] per day. [He] gave them [a] bonus of five [cents] . . . [every] sixteen bush[els] . . . [of] extra work beyond their task.

March 29, 1878:
We visited convicts at [Tracy City] stockade . . . saw their breakfast, coffee, bacon, corn bread. Two hundred eighty eight [were] there and four sick. [They get] tobacco every Sunday. Some [sentenced to] twenty years for horse stealing.

April 16, 1878:
All morning at [Nashville] penitentiary with [Thomas] O'Connor. They make wagons, ploughs, staves, kettles. Everything [is] very systematic, clean, busy. They make two thousand dollars worth of goods per day.

In 1885 TCI came under harsh criticism from reformers who believed the lease system was inhumane and corrupt.

Chattanooga Times, January 18, 1885:
SHAME ON OUR STATE
THE AWFUL CONDITION OF THE STATE CONVICTS
THE BRANCH PRISONS CONVERTED INTO CHARNEL HOUSES — OUR STATE THE MURDERESS OF ITS OWN CHILDREN — AN AWFUL CONDITION OF AFFAIRS.

The following able and exhaustive article was prepared by Dr. P. D. Sims, of this city, and will be found to contain much matter of interest and importance: . . .

The earliest report that I have been able to find is that for the two years ending December 1, 1880. In this the Warden says:

Number of convicts on hand Dec. 1, 1878	1,153
Number on hand Dec. 1, 1880	1,211
Number died in the two years	135
Number escaped	83
There were in the main prison at date of report	663
In branch prison at Tracy mines	302
In branch prison at Ensley farm	139
In branch prison at Coal Creek mines	112
In branch prison at Spence's farm	25

Analyzing the report, I find that the death rate for the entire prison population for the two years taking the population at its maximum which makes it most favorable, was fifty four per thousand per annum.

The white death rate was thirty two per thousand per annum; the colored, sixty five per thousand per annum; the death rate in main prison at Nashville was forty per thousand per annum; the death rate for branch prisons in aggregate was seventy one per thousand per annum.

There is a significant disinclination manifested on the part of the wardens of the Tennessee Penitentiary to thus analyze their mortuary reports. This one endeavors to soothe the nervous sensitivities of his colaborers, by stating that "all the officers have done their utmost to mitigate the unfavorable conditions, and their success is shown by the small death rate and little sickness in the prison, which will compare favorably with any prison in the United States." The good Lord pity the standard of comparison! He must, however, have drawn the comparison between his rate of mortality inside the main prison, which was fifty four per thousand per annum, and that in the branches, which was seventy one, instead of comparing, as he says, with other State prisons of the United States. The annual report of the Commissioners and Warden of the State prison of Massachusetts for the year ending October 1, 1883, . . . shows a prison population of six hundred fifty; deaths for the year, seven; rate of mortality ten and seven tenths per thousand per annum, and no escapes.

The number reported killed outright in the Branch at Tracy mines is within a fraction of this rate of mortality, to say nothing of those that die of disease, and those reported as "blanked"—as a suspicious cause of death in a leased prison. . . . We are forced to the conclusion that by this system of prison management, society is less protected, criminals are less reformed, criminally inclined are less deterred, and a far larger per cent of convicts die from their punishment. . . .

But one solitary consideration commends it. It brings a revenue to the State—it is self sustaining. This is the argument that is in some way tacked on or interpolated into every report submitted in reference to it, and they might well add "it is self perpetuating," for it is simply a school where men and women and boys are trained and educated by association with each other, in the mysteries and methods and science of crime, and exasperated to a fierce enmity to society by the inhumanity of their treatment. Nor is it alone upon the crime class that the evil effects of the system fall. When that idea of monetary gain as palliation or concomitant of an evil has once taken possession of a people they lose sight of all better and higher considerations of the subject. It blinds the judgment and dwarfs all the finer sentiments of humanity. Crime becomes one of the available assets of the State, and greed a ruling sentiment of her nature. The more criminals the more revenue, and the less the poor oppressed tax payer has to contribute to the support of the government. There are the considerations that urge the perpetuity of this hurtful and demoralizing system.

On October 1, 1886, I had a meeting with a gentleman which was very important in its aftereffect upon my life, George E. Downing of Chattanooga. I learned from him that he had withdrawn from the Chattanooga Foundry and Pipe Works, and he was thinking of starting a new plant somewhere. I urged that South Pittsburgh was the place for it, and he agreed to meet Colonel Shook and myself there the following week. Mr. Downing came to South Pittsburgh, met Colonel Shook and myself, and also Mr. Duncan and his associates in the management of the new city company, and it was a time of great activity. Downing agreed to start a cast-iron pipe company at once, and the others present agreed to start a bank immediately. I subscribed as a charter member to each. The stock in the pipe works was all eagerly taken, everyone anticipating much success. The company was organized and the presidency offered to me, but I declined to avoid injuring TCI with its customers. They then made me vice-president.

On November 22 I [met] Mr. John S. Perry, who came down . . . from New York. [He] represented the Perry Stove Company of that city, which had operated a large stove foundry with convict labor at Sing Sing. They were contemplating the opening of a Southern branch and competition was fierce between Birmingham, Anniston, Chattanooga, and South Pittsburgh, and other places. They arrived in a drenching rain and Mr. Perry was very uncomfortable, and afterwards said . . . he hoped God would forgive him if he were so foolish as to locate there. The next day however I had him out upon the slag pile explaining to him the general outlook and special advantages of South Pittsburgh, and a steamboat came majestically sailing past on the broad Tennessee River, and that turned the scale in our favor and he decided to locate there. It was a poor day's work for me personally as will appear later. I am sorry that I ever heard of him.

John S. Perry statement in Albany, New York, *Journal*, December 29, 1886:

A sojourn from time to time of several months in the South during the past four years, a careful observation of its condition and a somewhat extensive acquaintance with its leading men, among whom I might name governors, ex-governors, and ex-Confederate officers (some of whom spilled their blood and left their mangled limbs upon the battle-field where they gallantly fought for an idea), as well as with numerous people in the humbler walks of life, have given me some right to speak of the bearing of Southern people towards their Northern brethren, concerning which I am often interrogated. If any one entertains the idea that there is any feeling of hostility or even coldness towards the people of this section, a personal acquaintance with the South would instantly remove it. During all my intercourse with the people of Kentucky, Tennessee, Georgia, Alabama and other States, not one word of bitterness has ever fallen upon my ear, nor have I ever heard a regret expressed that slavery had been abolished. On the contrary, all appear happy and thankful that they are freed from the incubus which so long repressed their energies and retarded their growth.

In every case and under all circumstances my observation has been that Northern men who brought capital, brains or muscle, and who were willing to work, for idleness is now at a discount there, were received with cordiality and even enthusiasm. The wonderfully eloquent and graphic speech made by Mr. H. W. Grady, of Atlanta, Georgia, at the New England dinner in New York last week, should be read and reread by everyone who rejoices in unity, or who has any lingering doubt of the good faith of Southern people. . . .

South Pittsburgh . . . was settled ten years since by an English company who, after a long study of the country, decided it was the best place in the world to make iron, and proceeded to erect two large furnaces in the complete and perfect manner in which Englishmen generally do their work. . . .

I gave considerable attention to the question of skilled negro labor and found it very interesting. I saw there men at work in foundries, machine shops, plow works, rolling and nail mills, wrought-iron pipe works, forges and wood-working establishments of different kinds and found the work to be uniformly good and approved by their employers, and further that for the same work these men were receiving as good wages as white men in the North, less the difference in the cost of living. The negroes in the South can be made available for almost any kind of mechanical work, and at the same time elevated and improved. They are with us in increasing numbers, and it is a public duty to hire them to better their condition.

William D. Kelley, *The Old South and the New*, 1888:
In perfect confidence that no risks of loss of reputation is thereby incurred, I declare that South Pittsburgh, Tennessee, will be a prosperous industrial center, whose trade in coal, coke, iron, and advanced manufactures produced therefrom, with the lower Mississippi, will vie with that of its prototype, Pittsburgh, in my own State, and that it will also be the seat of a great local commerce, as it is the predestined enterpot for a number of valleys, each of which is remarkable for salubrity, fertility, and the value of its mineral resources. . . .

Had the English company, as I shall speak of the founders of the place, been spared, there would, I am confident, now be twelve or fifteen thousand prosperous people in South Pittsburgh, and a large diversity of employment open to new-comers. . . .

But, since the consolidation of that company with the Tennessee Coal, Iron, and Railroad Company, little care has been bestowed upon the town of South Pittsburgh. . . . The streets were not macadamized; those running from west to east have been washed into deep gullies, and in many places the curb-stones that had been carefully set have fallen into the road-bed; and the town site, as I first saw it in November last, indicated continuing neglect and dilapidation rather than progress toward a notable future. . . .

The number of homes for working people that had been commenced on the 13th of May, when I left, was plainly inadequate to the demand for such buildings that will disclose itself from day to day as the great industrial works, which are nearly completed, employ workmen and start their machinery. In my judgment, they do not use too harsh or significant a phrase who say the supply of such houses is shamefully and mysteriously inadequate, especially as a hundred of them would be only a convenience to the heads of the establishments whose success will build up the town, and a means of comfort and health to their employes [*sic*], but must have been a source of profit to the company upon whose lands they ought to have been built. . . .

These unfortunate facts are alluded to because, having undertaken to speak on the subject, I accept it as a duty to assure all who may read these letters that the agricultural and mineral resources of South Pittsburgh are so great, and her location so admirable, that no such mistakes as have been permitted to occur . . . can permanently impair the prospects even of that company, or do more than inconvenience for a brief time parties who may seek the advantage of cheap coking coal and iron of the highest quality, especially for foundry purposes, at a natural seat of commercial distribution.

It is the perception of the inexhaustible value of these resources that has induced a number of experienced men to abandon established locations and stake their fortunes in the erection of more extensive works at South Pittsburgh. Among the establishments to which I allude are the Perry Stove Company, the buildings of which cover about six of the ten acres acquired by the company along the railroad, and in which the requisite machinery is now being erected. As Mr. John S. Perry, the projector of this company, has for more than thirty years been a manufacturer of stoves at Albany and Sing Sing, I need hardly add that this machinery is of the best quality and of the most recent conception. As an illustration of the fact that there is a New South, a truth which is sometimes disputed by those who too profoundly revere the memories of the Old South, and as also illustrative of the difficulties business men who go there must encounter if they require skilled hands, and cannot induce trained workmen to accompany them to a new and distant home,

I insert at length the following advertisement, together with a statement of the means by which its circulation was accomplished.

5 0 0 MEN WANTED!

———

STOP AND READ

———

THE PERRY STOVE MANUFACTURING CO.,
SOUTH PITTSBURGH, TENN.,
Will open their
MAMMOTH STOVE FOUNDRY
during the month of June, giving an opportunity to 500 young
and middle-aged men and boys from the farm, mill, and
shop to learn the trade of
moulders, mounters, polishers, nickel platers, car-
penters, pattern finishers, etc., etc.

They have engaged 50 of the best mechanics to teach those who want to learn. Early application should be made at the office of the company to secure the opportunity of your life. Liberal wages paid while learning the trade.

———

ALL WAGES PAID EVERY SATURDAY NIGHT.

———

CHAS. W. RICHARDS, Manager.

There is no district or city in the South from which the number of skilled workmen needed in the departments named in this advertisement could be drawn; and, as mechanics who are well employed and contented with their surrounding could hardly be induced by any ordinary temptation to go so far from home as pioneers, unskilled workmen must be employed and trained. Mr. Richards informed me that, by offering special inducements, he had succeeded in engaging fifty competent men, who were well known to him, as foremen and teachers. The question that now troubled him was how to get the raw hands for them to teach. There are, in this part of Tennessee, no towns upon the walls of which placards can be posted, nor do any advertising sheets, even in the form of weekly papers, circulate among the mountain woodsmen and old-time poor white cotton-growers, from which classes his recruits must be expected. To secure the circulation of his advertisement he took advantage of the fact that a circus was making its annual tour of the Sequachee Valley and surrounding country, and employed a man to . . . accompany it for several days, and distribute handbills containing the advertisement in each town to which it should go. The device was a success, for before leaving South Pittsburgh I saw a number of young men call in person, and was permitted to look over a bundle of letters from others, pleading for the opportunity to escape from their past unremunerative employment in the service of King Cotton and become skilled hands at stove-making, on the terms proposed by the Perry Company. It is only in a new country that such an advertisement could be required, and that such promises as it holds out would be regarded as a favor by thousands of people. I therefore reiterate the assertion that I introduce this advertisement in proof of the fact that there is a New South, whose poor people are, thanks to a diversification of employments, to be more fortunate, and to enjoy more of the comforts and luxuries of life than those of their class ever enjoyed during the life to the Old South, with its single industry.

On February 18, 1887, we had a meeting with Jesse R. Norton from Ironton, Ohio, who offered to move his equipment from that point and open at South Pittsburgh a hoe and tool company for the production of shovels, picks, et cetera. This was a misfortune for me. I went into it, of course, becoming a director, helping to organize it on the principle that every new industry made the others more valuable. He, however, developed like some other men in this world a liking for the cup that does not cheer, but still inebriates. His business went to the bad and was closed out two years later at a loss to me of $1,180, besides interest on the money which I had had tied up in it.

Having [early in 1890] invested nearly $7,000 in the purchase of additional stock in the stove works at South Pittsburgh on the strength of the cost accounts shown by the manager, Charles W. Richards, I was informed to my disgust [in December] that the cost accounts might vary from $5 to $7 per ton from the reports made. This was the first intimation I had of what turned out to be gross and culpable negligence almost amounting to fraud. On February 10, 1891, I agreed with the president of the stove works that manager Richards's salary should be reduced because of the many evidences of incapacity, and it was reduced from $5,000 to $3,000. [The next year] an assignment [of bankruptcy] was made. Thus ended that chapter in which thanks largely to my investments on false and semifraudulent cost accounts I made an aggregate loss of about $12,117. Even on the $4,000 bonds that I took and paid for to help the concern if possible to a new life . . . I only got $30.10 dividend on the final windup! It was a lamentable experience for a hardworking man who had no money to lose except out of his salary, and his family needed all of that.

In April 1887 I was [asked] to go to Mobile and appear before the Interstate Commerce Commission. This was something entirely new. It was just formed and traveling around the country getting information as to existing conditions upon which to predicate its action in controlling railroad rates. A great deal was being said about the inequality of [freight] rates. Large cities and long hauls were favored as against smaller places and shorter hauls. The southern pig iron manufacturers were afraid that we were going to be confronted with rates to Cincinnati, Chicago, [and other northern places] equal to the sum or aggregate of all the intervening local rates.

For some reason best known to themselves the manufacturers . . . put me up as the star witness. Because I have a strong, clear voice, and am not afraid to speak out in public what I think, and am fairly well at home in the witness chair, my evidence attracted a great deal of attention, and two columns of it were telegraphed by the Associated Press to New York papers.

Bowron's testimony, in part:[4]
There was then and still is a large surplus of loaded cars coming south over those going north. This surplus has been greatly decreased of late by the shipment of pig iron north. . . . The fact that there was so much surplus of empty cars going north was quite an element in inducing railroads to give us low rates of freight and of entering into these contracts with us. . . .

We have been placed on the basis of the most favored customer, and we have had many concessions made us. There were clauses by which rates of transportation on iron have been made contingent upon the value of the iron in the market. . . .

[From Nashville] to Columbia, Tenn., a local rate would be charged, but to competitive points like Louisville, St. Louis, et cetera, a [lower] rate would be charged. This was a matter beyond our control. The entire consumption of iron in the Southern States would not keep one half of our works in operation. . . .

[Judge Thomas M.] Cooley[5]—Do I understand that sixteen million have been actually invested in lands and property by your company?

Bowron—Yes, sir.

Cooley—Has the stock been subject to changes in the market?

Bowron—Yes. It is listed in Wall Street. It went up to 116. Today it is not more than 45. This was the result of a readjustment, bringing in new works and bringing in other stock. The highest quotation after the reorganization was 54. Since then there has been a steady decline. There is no special reason for this except the general stagnation in the iron business. We have not yet shut down any of our business because we have a hope that the [Interstate Commerce Act] will not be enforced.

Cooley—Do you think the stagnation has been caused by the enforcement of law as to the roads north of the Ohio?

Bowron—Most emphatically I do. . . .

Cooley—As I understand you as to your business, you expect to be crippled by this act, but not by any over product of the trade?

Bowron—I know that if I could say I would deliver iron for three months or for six months at St. Louis or Detroit at the same freight, I know we could sell from 30,000 to 50,000 tons inside of the next 20 days. We have competitors in New York and New England, in Eastern Pennsylvania, in Scotland, this much as to the East; and in Missouri, at St. Louis, in Michigan, etc. These are the leading competitors. . . .

Cooley—Is it because of these contracts with the railroads that you are able to put your products into these competing markets?

Bowron—Yes, sir.

Cooley—Do the manufacturers in Michigan, Pennsylvania, etc., regard this as just? Is it the tendency to drive them out of the business?

Bowron—Legislation is designed to produce the greatest good for the greatest number. Whatever their opinion, the consumers up there [outnumber by] fifty to one of the manufacturers, and the consumers would hold up their hands and bless the Commission which should help them to get the cheap iron they need for every kind of industry.

Cooley—Are not these advantages you ask for at the expense of some other industry of the same sort?

Bowron—I think not. The life of our iron works is of a limited duration. All in the East of late have been established with a view of the risk, and I submit that the enforcement of local rate is to put a wall around each State, a policy which might be equally applied to each county and prove at length to be a preventive of true intercourse. . . .

[William R.] Morrison[6]—How much freight does your Scotch competitor pay?

Bowron—I have known the freight from Glasgow to New York to be twenty-five cents a ton. The usual freight is $1.75. This is about a standard rate. It costs me $2 more to get to New York than it does the Glasgow man.

The outcome of the ICC concern about southern freight differentials was to allow the railroads and the iron producers to fix a sliding scale for rates, on which the railroads' tariff went up or down with the price fluctuations of the iron market. Then in 1897, in the case of ICC v. Alabama Midland Railway, the U.S. Supreme Court ruled in effect that the federal judiciary could overrule the ICC's findings. The effect of this decision was that the railroads, by appealing any adverse ICC ruling to a friendly judge, continued to determine their rates. The issue would, however, resurface after the turn of the century when the ICC gained new authority with the 1906 Hepburn Act.

On June 14, 1887, I attended to business as usual until 4:00 P.M., everything being arranged and no occasion for hurry or flurry, and going to my room at the Maxwell House to dress, I was married at 6:00 P.M. at the First Presbyterian Church, Nashville. Someone had blundered in the matter of the key to the organ, and they could not get into it to play for some minutes, so Adah and I sat in the carriage together in front of the church until we were informed that it was all O.K. The ceremony was quiet and simple, the church being well filled with our friends. I have laughed since at Dr. Jere Witherspoon, who performed the ceremony. He was the beloved pastor of the church. He says that when he asked me the momentous question I swelled out my chest and answered "I will" in a voice that could be heard out in Church Street. It must be remembered that I had been accustomed to public speaking in churches and elsewhere and always made it a point to have my voice carry into the furthest corner.

My bride looked very pretty and sweet in her white dress ornamented with green fern leaves, green and white having always been my favorite combination, and the one I selected as our club colors in my old rowing days. This was a most momentous day both for myself and my children. The soundness of the union and the propriety of it is perhaps best shown by the fact that whilst we have been blessed with a second family to grow up beside and behind the first one, there has never been the slightest shade or shadow of discrimination between them, and my children of the first family who were too young to have remembered their mother have never known or seen any difference between their own treatment and that received by their brothers and sisters who came later.

Boom

In 1886, the first year of the big iron boom, the management of TCI began a corporate roller-coaster ride as various investors fought for control of the company. William Duncan, a Nashville investment banker and former member of the board of directors, began to acquire stock and proxies soon after TCI was listed on the New York Stock Exchange in late 1885. By April 1886 he had gained effective control of the company from John Inman and made himself president. Duncan's most fateful action was to remove Alfred M. Shook as general manager. After his ouster Shook made a strategic alliance with a Birmingham ironmaker, Thomas T. Hillman, who had lost power in a similar corporate struggle in the Pratt Coal and Iron Company of Birmingham. The Pratt Company, Henry DeBardeleben's original creation, had consolidated most of the developed mineral land in the Birmingham area, a large portion of the area's coke production, and two blast furnaces. Shook and Hillman planned first a takeover of the Pratt Company—relying heavily on John Inman's financial power—and then the merger of the Pratt Company with TCI.[1]

The dual mission was accomplished on September 28, 1886, with several important results. First, Inman and others used the opportunity to take huge stock bonuses for themselves, thus creating liabilities that would burden the company in the years ahead. Second, TCI's center of operations would soon be shifted from Tennessee to Birmingham, though the corporate offices stayed in Nashville for the time being. Third, TCI's major preoccupation for the several years after October 1886 would be the building of four furnaces and a new industrial town near Birmingham, called "Ensley" in honor of Enoch Ensley, the Pratt Company president. The creation of the Ensley works on such a grand scale clearly overreached the company's financial ability—especially given the stock bonuses—and would cause big problems when the boom ended. Fourth, William Duncan lost his dominant position in the TCI boardroom to John Inman. Alfred Shook was brought back as general manager, and Nathaniel Baxter functioned as Inman's chief local representative, gaining the office of TCI president in 1887.[2]

After the takeover of Pratt Coal and Iron in 1886, TCI created a subsidiary, the Ensley Land Company, on the basis of $10 million of watered stock, which the company held in exchange for about 4,000 acres of land. Much of the Ensley Land Company stock was then distributed among TCI stockholders. Enoch Ensley and his close ally H. G. Bond, a land speculator later indicted for fraud and embezzlement in connection with a failed iron company development in Decatur, Alabama, were more interested in booming the land company than in iron production, though few in the TCI management resisted the temptation to speculate in land.[3]

In April 1889 Duncan recaptured control of TCI from Inman. Perhaps distracted because of his manipulations of the Richmond Terminal Railroad, Inman was caught unaware by Duncan's second takeover effort, but he appeared to accept his defeat in the TCI boardroom with relative equanimity. Duncan installed the old Redeemer governor of Tennessee, John C. Brown, as TCI president. When Brown suddenly died after a few months, the New York Republican politician Thomas C. Platt assumed the office of TCI president. Almost as gifted at stock manipulation as he was at politics, Platt immediately pushed the TCI stock upward by means of the "washed quotation," in which the stock's market value was raised artificially high by Platt's repeated buying and selling of his own stock. It worked well through 1889, but danger lurked in the person of John Inman. Angry because Platt had sued him in December 1889 charging past mismanagement of the company, Inman secretly plotted his revenge, first by helping to push the stock up and then by executing "bear" raids on it. The drama played out in early 1890, much to the detriment of Thomas Platt.[4]

These changes in TCI's management in the end worked to diminish the standing of James Bowron, though at times it would appear that they benefitted him. Had he not been so essential in the management of the company's finances, Bowron probably would not have survived. He began in about 1886 to comment on the chaotic, and sometimes foolish, manner in which the company was directed. He disapproved of the TCI board's general in-attention to production and to technological advances, especially steel mak-ing, failures which he attributed to their disregard of the company's real work. He saw this as another example of the costly burden of outside owner-ship, for the preoccupation with "bulling" the stock was one cause of TCI's long delay in making steel. Bowron, who himself did not engage in land speculation, believed that Enoch Ensley and H. G. Bond were altogether irresponsible in the effort to divert company resources to land development. Bowron also believed that the top management was utterly dishonest in its accounting practices. He objected strongly to the company's bribery of pub-lic officials to secure convict labor. Usually helpless to correct mistakes, however, Bowron persisted out of personal necessity as well as loyalty to the company whose potential he thought was so great.

On March 28, 1886, I was shown a telegram from William M. Duncan, a Nashville stockbroker, to his partner in Nashville that the "New York stockholders were my friends and would stand up for me." I had not the slightest idea what the telegram meant, nor had the gentleman who showed it to me, but in a very few days it developed.

Duncan returned from New York and told me that the [large] stock-holders were dissatisfied with the action of Messrs. Warner and Shook in selling their stock in the company and intended to leave them off the board. [He said] that I should be made general manager in place of Colonel Shook. As this was restoring me in a measure to my former position which I had occupied with the Southern States Coal and Iron Company, and would per-mit me to resume residence in my own house at South Pittsburgh, I was naturally very much elated—especially so as Colonel Shook was a rich man and it was not hurting him in any way to be left out. [But] Colonel Shook was a very warm personal friend of President J. W. Thomas of the Nashville, Chattanooga and St. Louis Railroad, and . . . on April 11 President Thomas wrote the company a letter demanding that we pay the railroad its freight bills in cash every month instead of by notes at four months as heretofore.

I assumed my duties April 12 as general manager in the most active and vigorous manner that I knew how. From this time on I led a life of the most intense activity, habitually leaving Nashville early Monday morning as a rule for Tracy City, going down Tuesday afternoon to the Cowan blast furnace, riding over Wednesday on the coke train from that point to South Pittsburgh, going up the valley visiting the Inman ore mines, sleeping perhaps at Jasper, thence by train or hand car or horseback to Victoria coal mine and coke ovens, back to South Pittsburgh on the train or by hand car, and leaving there Saturday morning for Nashville.

On September 18 I heard of the resignation of my colleague Leslie Warner as treasurer of the company. He no doubt had advance information of the impending changes which I did not know of. On September 28 the office was full of caucuses which were secret and to which I was not invited. I was informed by Mr. Duncan an hour before the general meeting [on September 29] that I was not to be reelected as general manager, but that I might if I wished be elected treasurer of the new company at the same salary ($5,000), my work being in the office at Nashville. I felt very much hurt at this, although it ultimately worked out probably all right. I resigned my office as general manager and my position as director and was elected as treasurer. The consolidation of the Pratt Coal and Iron Company was agreed to, thus placing under our control the Alice furnaces in Birmingham, the Pratt Mines, [and] the Linn Iron Works.

Fortunes were easily made in those days. It was not deemed improper for directors to trade with a company without advertisement or public [notice]. In November 1886 John Inman bought $500,000 of our bonds at par with $500,000 of stock as a bonus. I have since seen that stock down as low as ten cents on the dollar and as high as $1.19. The same day one of our Nashville directors[5] bought $200,000 of bonds with $100,000 stock bonus. The bonds . . . were very soon at par, and the bonus stock was all profit. On April 1, 1887, I wrote my report as secretary and treasurer, which was approved by Thomas T. Hillman but objected to by Messrs. Baxter and Shook as showing the stockholders too much of the company's business, more especially as to the cost of refunding the old bonds. We were at least $100,000 short of necessary funds for the completion of the Ensley furnaces. In the recapitalization of the company, ample provision had been made for private fortunes, but not sufficient for the completion of the works which had to earn the interest upon the various bonds.

After a visit from Mr. Inman, Nat Baxter proposed that we should raise funds for the present to complete the Ensley furnaces by the notes of the company for $25,000, each being endorsed by himself, Colonel Shook, Mr. Hillman, and myself, and discounted by Mr. Inman. I never could see

Nathaniel Baxter, president of Tennessee Coal and Iron (from Ethel Armes, *The Story of Coal and Iron in Alabama* [Birmingham: Birmingham Chamber of Commerce, 1910])

the propriety of such an arrangement as Mr. Inman's interests in the company were vastly greater than mine, but it was a case of having to do so or have a pretty cold shoulder turned towards me. I had a wife and five children to support and needed my position and salary, [and] therefore I did as they wished, in consequence of which I was recognized as a director and elected as one. Mr. Inman went away saying that my work was very "efficient."

We received dismal reports from Birmingham of total lack of system amongst the officers (all of whom . . . we had taken over from the Pratt Company) and a prevalence of internal jealousies, each man wanting to get ahead of the other. Mr. Baxter was very much annoyed at the magnitude of our capital expenditure at Pratt Mines, and insisted that it would wreck the company, and that he would resign first. But he did not, and he never intended to resign. He should have restricted the expenditure instead of letting all the operating officials spend money and make requisitions on me which had to remain weeks and months in many cases unpaid, leaving me to carry the odium of the delay.

BOWRON DIARY, February 22, 1888:
Duncan returned from New York. Says lethargy in our stock is owing to the repeated delays in starting new furnaces.

February 27, 1888:
McCormack[6] back from Ensley. Says Hargreaves [the furnace builder] still looks to middle of March for a start. . . . Great apparent waste all around everywhere at Pratt Mines. Lack of system and prevalence of internal jealousies.

March 14, 1888:
Baxter says capital account must[,] shall be closed. If it is to go on spending money, it shall be under some other president.
He wants impossible mixture of accounts but seems finally contented that he cannot do better than accept mine. Desires several changes in them which I make reluctantly, as [they] tend[ed] to withhold information.

Baxter's fertile mind proposed that we should buy $1 million worth of common stock at 30, as it was down that day to 25 on the open market. We should [then] clothe it with an 8 percent preference dividend and offer it back pro rata as a privilege to our stockholders at 85 (this was later changed to 90). That was to give us $600,000, less a commission to the underwriters. Out of that we were to repay the $200,000 borrowed from Inman on the notes of the directors, and have $400,000 available towards finishing our furnaces. This scheme was ultimately carried out. Our Nashville attorney . . . said it was absolutely illegal without the assent of every individual stockholder, but Ed Baxter, the Louisville and Nashville Railroad attorney,[7] quoted a railroad act which permitted the issue of preference stock by a railroad company on sixty days' notice, and a three-fourth's vote in favor at a special meeting of the stockholders. As the Tennessee Coal, Iron and Railroad Company had the railroad power included in its charter from the state, it was construed by us as legalizing the issue, and this was actually carried out in the then near future. The common stock was not paying any dividend, and it cost us $80,000 per annum to pay the preferred dividend on the $1 million of preferred stock. So this was paying $80,000 per annum for the use of $600,000 . . . or 13⅓ percent [interest]. Without this it is hard to see how the Ensley furnaces could ever have been finished and started up.

Inman . . . complained about my reports of the earnings. It is needless to say that these reports were always so far as I could make them accurate in the highest degree. I was not always allowed to make them correct. Profits were estimated, not upon the basis of the pig iron shipped to market, but on the tonnage actually produced by the furnaces. This was a most improper and unsound method from an accountant's standpoint. It permitted the president at any time to advance prices $.50 or $1.00 per ton, which meant that at the end of the month I would be required to estimate the earnings of the company on the difference between the cost of production and the inventory price, that is to say, the nominal selling price. Profits might be and sometimes were estimated, particularly in subsequent years, which never were earned and had to come off again.

Mr. Inman's complaint, however, seems to have been that he wanted me to take off the exact amount of coupon interest paid each month, and when I took off a larger amount than the coupons in that month, he claimed that I was falsifying the report. As a matter of fact, I was doing what every prudent accountant will do and making an average deduction for every month in the year so as to avoid radical changes as between the months when there were heavy coupons maturities and other months when there were not. Where coupons might mature February 1 or April 1, I would insist upon showing as a liability of the company [on the previous] December 31 the proportion of interest which had accrued up to that date, so that the books might be a true exhibit of the liabilities of the company. I had a good deal of argument with my superior official.

I knew that I was right and would not give way about it, but it was extremely disagreeable for me to have such a fight to make. [In response to Inman's complaint] Mr. Baxter remonstrated by wire . . . saying that I had promised to send "corrected" returns. This was an absolute falsehood, as I never sent any that were incorrect and could not have promised to send corrected ones. He, also, inspecting my accounts prepared for the stock-holders' meeting, insisted upon several changes in them which I made very reluctantly as [they tended] to withhold information from the stockholders.

In May 1888 I had a long conversation with Mr. Jacob Reese.[8] None of us knew much about making steel. I knew it would take a great deal of money and that we had none. No one in the North had any confidence at all in our ability or the suitability of our materials, or would put up any money for the purpose. Reese stated to me that we could convert Birmingham pig iron into [steel] ingots for $8 per ton and that the works with 250 tons daily capacity could be built for $600,000. He was not far wrong on either of these estimates. On January 17, 1889, Reese proposed to form a company to take all our product of Ensley pig iron for conversion by his duplex process into rails at Ensley. It might have been done sooner.

I was told that Colonel Ensley and Judge H. G. Bond insisted that we should endorse the notes of the Ensley Land Company to the extent of $150,000 that they might spend the money making streets, building [a] hotel, so as to make the property salable for lots. I insisted that we had no legal authority to endorse their notes, and that as the treasurer of the company I was positively opposed to it.

The proposal carried by three against one for endorsement of the bonds of the Ensley Land Company, five directors present refusing to vote, and our general counsel stating such action would be illegal. I asked for instructions and was specifically ordered not to enter the resolution on the minute book until its legality was approved by counsel. This was contrary to my ways of doing business. The following day Jacob Reese left for Pittsburgh, having waited two days in the hope of getting an interview with our board as to the establishment of a steelworks at Ensley—a plain case of neglecting the substance for the shadow.

The president and general manager insisted that we would be paying dividends by July and that our stock then at 37 would go anywhere from 60 to 70, and I bought 1,000 shares. I had no right to speculate in any such way or on any such wild guess. I knew quite as much about the prospects of dividends as they did. The company was not then within ten years of paying dividends. On March 8 I sold 500 of my 1,000 shares at 4 points profit, just in time, for the next day there was a panic in Paris and the stock dropped to the buying point. Our stock was worth just as much the day of the panic in Paris as it was the day before. Stock quotations are most inconsistent.

We were surprised to learn that the proxies in New York were being contested against the administration, and William Duncan of Nashville had already obtained control of a large mass of them, just as he did in 1886. He telegraphed that his warfare was against Mr. Inman alone and not against the management. Inman wired Baxter [on March 25] recommending him to retire. I closed out my stock at the same price I bought it. Baxter urged me to stay with the company and not follow him into retirement as he knew I could not afford it. Practically every officer was changed except myself, retained at the same salary as secretary and treasurer. Former governor John C. Brown of Tennessee was elected president, as he was then leaving the Texas Pacific Railway. The general management of the company was divided between Colonel James L. Gaines for Tennessee and Judge Bond for Alabama.

We went around to all the different works accompanied by the new directors. We were also to have new sales agents, Naylor and Company . . . they having lent Duncan the money with which to control the stock at the election. From this time forward the entire policy, controlled practically by Judge Bond, was to make sales of iron with reference to speculation rather than as heretofore to cover the requirements of our customers and to give them satisfaction.

Governor Brown, a sick man, arrived from Texas to assume his position as our new president, and to my great perplexity started a private secretary to make a list of all the checks which he signed. It appeared that, familiar only with railroad accounts where the net revenue of the company is the difference between receipts and disbursements, the good man supposed that our statement of revenue would be made up in the same way. He was greatly surprised when I explained to him the complexity of industrial manufacturing accounts and how the profits or losses were entirely unrelated to receipts or expenditures. He was satisfied with everything that I said and treated me most kindly.

Governor Brown further requested that I would engage a secretary to take clerical work off my hands and free my time to visit the works frequently and keep in close touch with the executives, saying also that if they could have spared me from the finances I would have been put in charge as general manager. This was complimentary and encouraging, but it did not get me the general manager's salary. At all events I felt so much pleased with the outlook, being backed by a new and enthusiastic crowd, and with the above sentiments on the part of the new president, that I went the limit in borrowing money on my pipe works stock and buying additional TCI [stock], as Inman and friends were "bearing"[9] it in New York.

To my perfect consternation Governor Brown died most suddenly. I felt this not only as an official, but as a personal loss. United States Senator Thomas C. Platt of New York was elected president in place of Governor Brown. This was not because he knew anything at all about the production of coal and iron, but because he had a great many political followers and friends who would naturally buy any stock that he, Mr. Platt, might recommend. In other words, the company was being run not to obtain results but to put up the stock.

Judge Bond informed us that he was busy patenting a process to make Bessemer steel at a cost of seven cents per ton over pig iron. I never learned whether this patent was completed or not. I did learn that his scheme was to blow some powder in through the tuyeres into the blast furnace. His schemes were wonderful. He had another one later on by which after dipping pigs of iron into some liquid they were to be so strengthened as to withstand thirty or forty blows with a sledgehammer without breaking.

On September 15 Duncan wired from New York earnestly advising purchases, and I bought 1,000 shares from 47½ to 49½. On November 18 our stock which I had bought at an average of about 48 rose as high as 86. If I had sold my 1,000 shares I would have had $38,000 and would have been practically independent. But rightly or wrongly, I have always been so absolutely loyal to my chief that I was not willing to take such action, because I knew that Duncan and his associates were doing their very best to put up and keep up the price. It was a one-sided loyalty, however, because leaving for New York I found on November 26 that Bond was entirely in control of the sales situation and was describing me to Mr. Platt as a "chronic bear." They between them set the prices of iron so high that we could not sell any.

Duncan admitted the errors of the sales committee in fixing prices above my views. On account of Bond's representation of my bearish views they had put the making of prices into the hands of a special committee to consist of Bond and Duncan and myself. This might have worked out all right but for the fact that Bond assumed to correspond with Naylor's direct from Birmingham and to make prices with which we in the general office at Nashville were wholly unacquainted.

On December 3 I closed the year by selling 300 shares of my TCI stock from 80 to 85. If I had sold it all out I would have been a richer and happier man. I balanced my books to show that I had made a profit of $45,574 that year, nearly all of which was in TCI stock, but the misfortune of the situation was that this was assuming it to be worth 80 per share, the prevailing figure at the end of the year. It was another case of counting the chickens before they are hatched, as was very apparent when the stock came down the next year with a crash.

On January 2, 1890, President Platt and R. A. Alger, ex-secretary of war and Michigan millionaire, were [in Birmingham] with Bond and Duncan, but never came to the office. Duncan notified me to sell iron at my own discretion regardless of the sales committee and that he would uphold me. The party then left for Tennessee without having entered the company's office. Bond [later] wired Platt and Duncan that a combination was being formed at Birmingham to put up prices. They at once notified me to suspend selling. The following day . . . we were embarrassed for money, iron piling up and sales not being made. To my mind it is highly culpable to destroy the valuable sales connection between a producer and consuming customers for the sake for speculation on the market. It was hard for me to manage under such conditions.

On February 19 our stock began to drop from 82 to 76, the following day to 70, the next day to 67. All of us left February 22 for New York, sleepers full, a cold irksome ride in a smoking car to Louisville. On the way I had a very full heart-to-heart conversation with Mr. Duncan. I [had been] told . . . that Bond was intriguing against me. I told [Duncan] that my ability and experience entitled me to confidence and not to be ignored in favor of a visionary speculator like Bond. He said he had seen me treated with discourtesy, but he tried to avoid offending Bond, who had helped him greatly on Wall Street in getting control. But [he said] that he would remove him out of my path when it should be necessary. This was a sort of deathbed repentance. On February 25, [with] Duncan saying Bond was a traitor, I resumed charge of iron sales without form or ceremony.

On March 13 our stock broke to 47, hurting me still further, as I had bought some in New York the previous week at 57½. Duncan was worried and told me he was rattled and must lean on me. Platt and Bond said they would raise all the money we wanted, but they did not raise a dollar for us, and on March 15 I sold half the stock I was carrying at 48, unable to bear the nervous strain any longer. This was the price at which I had bought it the previous autumn, paying 6 percent interest in the meantime, receiving no dividends. Again it shows the folly, the supreme folly, of . . . a man with young children jeopardizing his home and furniture and prospects by such reckless plunging. The intense financial anxiety brought about by such conditions was enough to lead to a physical breakup. It has killed many a man, and it is a marvel that it did not kill me.

On March 18 I sold out the balance of my common stock at 44¼ and lost more money, and the next day it went back to 51 and the following day to 54, Mr. Platt being supposed to have secured control. Instead of Bond being fired out of the company as Duncan had promised he should be within twenty-four hours, Bond told me that Platt's friends . . . had bought 10,000 shares when Inman was bearing the stock, and that Platt now controlled things without Duncan's help. This did not look as if I was going to get any relief from Bond's vexatious policy.

On May 30 I sold about 26,000 tons of iron at advanced prices, being unable to get any reply from Bond as to his acquiescence, or otherwise, but on his own responsibility without consulting me he wired Naylor in New York to stop all sales. Thus the company's interests were battered around like a shuttlecock.

BOWRON DIARY, September 12, 1890:
Money very stringent. Birmingham bank cannot provide currency for the payrolls. Chicago broker refuses discounts of paper. Sloss company wants to give note instead of cash. Florence furnace cannot pay note, wants renewal. Anniston [Pipe Works] fails to pay. Everybody dunning us. Nobody paying anything.

September 13, 1890:
Knountz[10] refuses further discounts unless larger balance is kept. Naylor declines to handle paper for us. Money tight as a drum.

December 18, 1890:
Noble's note protested. Knountz refuses discounts. Cameron demands specie. Southern Iron Company, Citico, Lady Ensley Furnace all fail to pay their accounts. Almost impossible to manage.

Up to this time, we had always played fast and loose with the [First] National Bank of which Mr. Baxter was president. He was not at this time president of the TCI Company, so . . . [on] September 18 J. P. Williams, cashier [at the First National Bank], said they could not allow overdrafts or pay our notes unless we provided the funds. This compelled me to refuse all kinds of payments from the works as the money had to go for the payment of notes. On October 10 our 8 percent preferred stock sold down to 80. There was quite an idea that the company was about to break up.

On November 10 there was a new panic in New York arising from the failure of Baring Brothers in London. TCI stock dropped to 33, the Louis-

ville and Nashville Railroad's stock to 69. On November 18 the financial
situation tightened to a point where the First National Bank of Nashville
declined to discount any of our customers' paper. At the same time I protested to Duncan against his son's firm standing us off with notes for coal
where we were ordered to pay the freight for their accommodation. In reply
he showed me a letter which he was writing to Mr. Platt tendering his resignation. The Platt-Bond party were handling the company's business in his
opinion against the company's best interests. At this time I heard that my old
associates, Baxter and Shook, had taken advantage of the panic to buy considerable blocks of stock at very low prices, which suggested possible
changes in the near future.

On December 3 . . . Mr. Platt put through the directors' meeting a resolution abolishing the sales committee, dismissing the executive committee,
and removing the office of the secretary and treasurer from Nashville to New
York. This dreadfully disconcerted the Nashville party, Duncan, Baxter,
Shook, and others, as Mr. Platt . . . unfamiliar with its business or with the
iron trade, was entirely under the domination of Judge Bond, a speculative
boomer equally unfamiliar with the trade and ready to make any arrangements that would boost the stock.

Returning to Nashville I was confronted with the action of the First
National Bank, which demanded immediate payment of its $70,000 loan, in
view of the impending removal of the financial office of the company to New
York. Mr. Baxter offered me the position of vice-president, treasurer, or
general manager of the Southern Iron Company if I decided to leave the
TCI. Under these circumstances, negotiations were thick and fast. I was
equally friendly with all local parties in Nashville. Duncan, who had originally put Baxter out of office, offered his resignation as vice-president for
Baxter to come in again, and so bring the powerful aid of Mr. Inman in New
York, who in turn could influence Mr. Platt. This negotiation was followed
by the demand of the Nashville, Chattanooga, and St. Louis Railway for
cash settlements of their freights instead of settling by four-month notes. So
it became apparent that the removal of the financial office to New York
would entail the provision of considerable money by those who were in sympathy with such a move.

In December I continued as the medium for negotiation, being asked to
obtain three directors' resignations for Inman, Baxter, and Shook to fill
them. After a couple of weeks of most intimate and confidential negotiation
as between one man and another, on the last day of the year my negotiations

were crowned with success, three vacancies being provided on the board, Baxter and Thomas Hillman elected vice-presidents, [and] Inman director. The removal of the treasurer's office was rescinded, and the control of the business remained vested in Nashville.

By 1888, when Jacob Reese had attempted unsuccessfully to argue that TCI should go into steel production, Bowron was completely convinced of the necessity for steel production. Perhaps even more than Bowron, Alfred Shook believed that southern ironmakers had to start converting their iron to steel. During his exile from TCI in the late 1880s, Shook organized the Southern Iron Company at Chattanooga and recruited Benjamin Talbot, an English metallurgical chemist, who succeeded in producing steel by combining the basic open-hearth method with a process to remove the high silicon content of southern iron. While technically successful, their effort did not prove profitable as a business enterprise because of high production costs. Men like Bowron and Shook understood how inextricably tied the technological and business problems were. They recognized that their main task lay in persuading the TCI board of directors of the importance of initiating steel production in Birmingham. In 1890 Bowron explained the significance of the Southern Iron Company's work to the Nashville American:

The large product of southern pig iron has of necessity for several years been sent to distant States to the extent of 75 or 80 per cent of the whole. This has been and still is a great drawback, as the labor employed in the manufacture of pig iron is largely unskilled, and this crude material is shipped to the North or East where skilled labor is employed to work it up into 1,000 varying forms, which are returned to the South as the ultimate consumers. The people of the South have thus paid the freight both ways.

The most important step towards emancipation from this undesirable situation has been taken within the past year by the adoption, both in Chattanooga and Birmingham, of the basic open-hearth process for the production of steel. The manufacture of steel in large quantities has been practically confined to the owners of the Bessemer works in the North, as we have had no ores in the South suitable for the production of iron which could be converted into steel by the old, or acid

Alfred Montgomery Shook, Tennessee Coal and Iron executive and developer of steel making (courtesy of Birmingham Public Library Archives)

Bessemer process. Our ores are so high in phosphorus as to prevent the adoption of this process. . . .

To the Southern Iron Company, with headquarters in our own city, managed by southern men, who have provided the energy, the brains, and the money, belongs the credit of practically demonstrating the advantage to our section of the basic open-hearth. . . .

The analysis of the steel which has been made by this company was submitted week before last to enlightened critics on the occasion of the visit of the British Iron and Steel Institute . . . and also to the various representatives of northern steel works traveling with the party as members of the American Institute of Mining Engineers. Without any exception these critics have pronounced the analyses to be absolutely satisfactory. . . .

The visitors were not content to take the qualities of the steel for granted on the strength of an analysis, however good it might be, . . . a variety of tests of the physical qualities of the steel were made in a most severe and searching manner. A piece of the runner of an ingot which had just been poured, was taken into a blacksmith shop and there drawn out, cooled, bent and twisted, first cool and then hot, welded, cooled again, bent over, smashed open and the members of the party declared themselves satisfied in the highest degree. . . .

The value of all this cannot at present be adequately summed up or perhaps estimated. It was the general belief of the English and German visitors that, great as had been the development of the South during the past ten years in the production of iron, we are destined to see greater still during the next decade, based on the production of steel.

In October 1890 I was invited to join . . . the southern contingent of the Iron and Steel Institute of Great Britain, together with their companions, the Deutsche Eisenhuetteleute Verein of Germany, both societies being the guests of the American Societies of Mining and Mechanical and Civil Engineers. The southern contingent made up three special trains of Pullman cars and I greatly enjoyed the association with them for six days. As the result of our examination of the steel made at Chattanooga and the endorsement of its high quality by these scientific men, I became fully convinced that the proper line of development for TCI was to go into the manufacture of steel. I proposed to Duncan that we should ask the Nashville, Chattanooga, and St. Louis Railway to endorse the bonds of a separate steel company to be located at South Pittsburgh to make steel from South Pittsburgh iron by the

Talbot process, as we had just seen it done in Chattanooga. This suggestion came to naught, but from that day forward as will be seen I never dropped the prosecution of the thought.

In January 1893 a TCI management committee would report on an internal investigation of the possibilities for steel production.

In this country there are four recognized processes for the manufacture of steel—to wit, the acid Bessemer, the basic Bessemer, acid open-hearth and basic open-hearth.

In the manufacture of acid Bessemer, the materials to be employed must be selected to suit the process. The iron used must be of a certain chemical analysis, which restricts the injurious metalloids to very narrow limits, the most essential one being phosphorous, which must not exceed one-tenth of one per cent. The same rule applies to the acid open-hearth.

In the basic Bessemer process the material used must also be made to conform to the process. . . . the difference being in the lining of the converter, which must be basic [acid absorbent] instead of acid. In the basic Bessemer practice it is necessary to have a very much larger percentage of phosphorus for the purpose of keeping up the heat in what is known as the "after blow." . . .

The basic open-hearth process contemplates a much wider range as regards the character of materials that can be used. It is a process that can be adapted to the materials to be used, the only restrictions that are absolutely necessary, being low silicon and low sulphur.

In the consideration of these questions, your committee is unanimously of the opinion that the Tennessee Coal, Iron and Railroad Company can only afford to make steel out of their own raw materials and products, and at a point where they can obtain the largest amount of liquid metal at the lowest cost. We do not deem it advisable to submit a report that would contemplate the manufacture of an iron other than is now made at our present plants at the lowest cost of production. This necessarily eliminates the acid Bessemer and acid open-hearth process on account of the large percentage of phosphorus in our ores, and while it would be possible to manufacture a basic Bessemer pig carrying as much as two per cent of phosphorus, it would necessitate the abandonment of what are known as Red Mountain ores [the Birmingham ores] and the substitution of the brown ores of Georgia and Alabama. This would materially increase the cost of pig iron, to what extent it is impossible to say, as the mining and bringing together of 1,000 tons of brown ore daily has never been attempted in the South.

For the above reasons the consideration of the process to be employed was reduced to the basic open-hearth. This process can deal with a pig iron carrying any reasonable percentage of phosphorus; the less the better, however. Low sulphur is essential, but the question of sulphur is not a serious one with southern irons. . . . All the higher grades of southern coke irons are comparatively free from sulphur.

This leaves silicon as the only substance to be dealt with. The present method of working the basic open-hearth furnace contemplates the use of pig iron low in silicon, and also the use of a large percentage of scrap, usually from twenty-five to fifty per cent. The necessity for scrap is to reduce the silicon and carbon in the charge. The difficulty of obtaining scrap in large quantities in the South is so great that your committee could not recommend the adoption of this process unless some means could be employed which would avoid the necessity of using scrap. The reasons why scrap cannot be obtained in the South are that there are so few manufacturing establishments, and the only scrap obtainable is agricultural and railroad scrap. The greatest source should be from old rails, but the introduction of steel rails in the South is of such a recent date that a very small percentage has been worn sufficiently to be sold as scrap. . . .

Gray forge pig is the grade upon which our furnaces can be run most successfully and at the lowest cost. . . . To use this iron without scrap the silicon must be practically eliminated before it goes into the open-hearth furnace. The only process by which this can be done cheaply and effectually, of which your committee has knowledge, is the Talbot process. . . .

The theory of the process is as follows: The slag used is known as a basic slag, being low in silicon and high in oxide of iron and lime. When the molten metal comes in contact with this molten basic slag, the silicon in the metal is transferred to the slag, and a large percentage of the metallic iron in the slag is transferred to the iron. This process is almost instantaneous and produces a metal practically desiliconized and with the phosphorus and carbon partially reduced. The metal is then ready for treatment in an ordinary basic open-hearth furnace in the ordinary manner.

There has always been more money in selling pig iron than in making it. Stockholders in New York would want the agency for their particular friends. Banks who lent us money in Cincinnati would want it for their friends. Mr. Hillman, our vice-president, wanted us to do without agents and have his relative Mr. Gray act as our general sales agent and sell direct to the customers. There was a shuffling of these arrangements every few months, and accusations by one that another was selling in his territory and depriving him of commissions. As all this business was nominally in my care it threw a great deal of needless annoyance and vexation into my life.

Naylor and Company having expressed their willingness to surrender the general agency for selling our pig iron, which had been given to them by Bond, Mr. Baxter and I agreed with Rogers Brown and Company to handle the business on the basis of 1¾ percent commission, instead of 2½ percent which we were paying to Naylor. [Naylor then] repudiated the supposed understanding with Baxter and made claim for damages, demanding six months notice of termination of contract. To avoid litigation with Naylors, they were reinstated as general pig iron agents, thus reducing their rate of interest on advances and their rate of commission to match Rogers Brown and Company, and also taking 15,000 tons of iron and paying cash for it to relieve our very urgent necessities. Rogers Brown and Company demanded fulfillment of contract for our sales agency. We were always in hot water on that subject.

On June 9, 1891, we settled amicably the claims of Rogers Brown and Company, who became satisfied that we had acted in good faith. On July 13 Archer Brown [of] Cincinnati offered me the position as president of the furnace to be built at Toledo. It would have been a very profitable thing for me if I had accepted it, but I was too loyal to TCI and its future to consider any other proposal.

In June 1888 Colonel Ensley said he did not want any salary as chairman of the executive committee, and only agreed to take it to cover payments . . . that he had made and that were not desirable to put on the books, or for me to know of. I learned that this had to do with classification of convicts by state officials. The salary check for Colonel Ensley [was] to be . . . paid to another person, a prominent politician. As there was nothing on the books to authorize [the payoff] I flatly refused and was ordered to do so by President Baxter, who said he would take all the responsibility. This sort of thing

confirms me in the opinion that [the convicts] should never pass out of the
hands of the state, but the work done by them should be sold for the account
of the state.

*Bowron's diary of July 14, 1888, reveals that the payoff of $1,200 was to the
Alabama congressman John Hollis Bankhead, formerly the warden of the state
prisons. Bankhead had been suspected by state officials of manipulating the
lease system to his personal advantage, though no formal charges were ever
made. A prominent Democratic politician had written privately in 1883 that
"Bankhead is a thief of thieves, in my opinion, but it won't do to say so without
proof." Bankhead had left the prison system but apparently remained influential with his successors, especially the current warden, Reginald H. Dawson.*

*The payment from TCI was probably for Bankhead's services in connection
with recent lease negotiations. The previous January, Nat Baxter had secured
for TCI a ten-year lease on all of Alabama's state convicts. Other bidders for
the lease, primarily competing coal operators, complained bitterly that TCI
had inside information from state officials about what amount to bid. Henry
DeBardeleben, reputed to be in fact the high bidder, later said, "Some bidders
seemed to know more about the basis than others." The convicts were divided
into classes, presumably according to their capabilities, and the state was paid
on a sliding scale from "first-class" convicts down to "dead-heads." The process of "classification" provided much room for manipulating the lease contract
to get "first-class" convicts placed in a lower, or cheaper, category. The common
allegation made against Bankhead was that he and other prison administrators had fixed classifications to TCI's advantage, a view supported by Bowron's
information.[11]*

*The convict-lease system exploded as a political issue in Alabama in 1888.
Probably the most popular basis of complaint was that the state was failing to
get all the money it should from the lease because of the cozy relationship
between TCI and the prison administrators. "The issue of prison management
is agitating the state from end to end," the Montgomery* Advertiser *reported
in July. The Knights of Labor reached their zenith in Alabama in 1888,
having earlier assumed the organizational responsibility of the Anti-Convict
League, and separate conventions of miners were held in Birmingham. The
labor groups offered very public opposition to the convict-lease system. On the
other hand, coal operators defended the system as generally a good thing, if
currently mismanaged in Alabama. DeBardeleben explained frankly that
"convict labor competing with free labor is advantageous to the mine owner. If*

all were free miners, they could combine and strike and thereby put up the price of coal." John T. Milner, a coal operator with long experience using convicts, was elected in 1888 to the state senate partly on the pledge to clean up the management of the convict lease. Milner later held legislative hearings that exposed some of the manipulations of Bankhead, TCI, and the current prison management.[12]

But, as Bowron's diary suggested, TCI and Bankhead were formidable opponents. Criticism of Milner's own treatment of convicts quickly surfaced; evidence showed that the death rate of convicts at his mines was shameful. Conservative opinion-makers came to TCI's defense. In January 1888 TCI's exclusive contract was portrayed as a triumph of reform by the conservative Democratic newspaper, the Montgomery Daily Advertiser*:*

Governor Seay,[13] as is well known, was committed by his whole course in the Senate and all his public utterances to humaner methods in the treatment of convicts. When the question was one of humanity against the dollar, he sided with humanity always. It will be gratifying to those people in Alabama who agree with the Governor on this matter, to know that the award made yesterday gives promise of securing for the State a more enlightened administration of its penal system. . . .

The company that got the convicts under the award of yesterday have worked, for several years past, a large number of State convicts and their record has been, so far as we know, good. Their proposition was the best financially that was made and in addition they agree to erect a new prison complete with all modern appliances, to build schoolrooms and homes for teachers, and to pay the teachers also. This is a long step forward and in the right direction.

The departure in the new plan is the congregation of the entire body of State convicts in one place, and in the requirement that one of the inspectors shall always be present at the prison. In this there is a guarantee against many of the worst abuses of the system under which the convicts were dispersed here and there over the State.

In Tennessee the company would prove to be less successful in protecting the lease. A major confrontation over the convict lease suddenly broke into the open in July 1891 at Briceville, in Anderson County in the eastern part of the state near Knoxville. The Briceville conflict originated in a dispute between free miners and a Tennessee coal company which had denied the miners a contract the previous April, then locked them out when they struck, and replaced them with convicts hired from TCI. On two occasions in mid-July 1891, large assemblages of miners—one of them estimated to have 1,500 men—forcibly removed the convicts from the Briceville mines and shipped them to Knoxville. After the first incident, Governor John P. Buchanan, a Democrat of the Populist wing of the party, led three companies of the state militia in returning the convicts to Briceville, only to have a second liberation occur. The miners looked to the Populist governor and the state legislature for relief, expecting them to repeal the lease. When the governor promised to call a special legislative session to decide the fate of the lease, the miners ended their siege.

But the state of Tennessee depended on the convict lease for revenue, and the end of it would mean the state had to take on the expense of a penitentiary. Powerful industrial interests at TCI and elsewhere wanted to keep their convict-labor supply. The legislature refused to abolish the lease and passed a law making it a felony to interfere with convicts. In the aftermath of the legislature's failure to provide relief, the Anderson County coal miners freed the convicts again in October and November 1891. A bitter struggle then ensued between TCI and the state government, which blamed the company for failure to keep the convicts imprisoned.[14]

The following August miners at TCI's Tracy City operation, angry at being reduced to half time while convicts worked long days, removed the convicts from the TCI mines and burned a prison stockade. They shipped the convicts to Nashville. The Tracy City revolt sparked another clash in Anderson County in which miners attacked militiamen guarding the convicts, killing several troops. The 1892 conflicts challenged the convict-lease system in virtually all industrial sites where convicts worked in Tennessee. Only a great show of militia strength in late August 1892 brought the struggle to a close. By the end of the 1892 troubles, most Tennesseans realized that the system was probably more expensive to defend and maintain than a state-run penitentiary would be. The state of Tennessee ended its convict-lease system when TCI's contract expired in early 1896.[15]

In July 1891 troubles developed of the most serious character imaginable, a veritable "Pandora's box" for our company, connected with the convicts. To go back a little way, the main penitentiary in Nashville had burned down. We, the TCI Company, were the lessees of all the convicts, [though we] subleased a large proportion of them to Cherry, O'Connor and Company, which firm was practically represented by Dr. William Morrow, the other

Leased convicts, Birmingham, c. 1907 (courtesy of Birmingham Public Library Archives)

partners having died or sold out. It seems that [Morrow] carried all his fire insurance with what are called "wild cat" companies, and he could not collect the money. The fire destroyed not only the buildings belonging to the state, but also the machinery, iron-working and woodworking, great stores of seasoned lumber, paint, finished wagons. The loss was extremely heavy, and it ruined Dr. Morrow, and the convicts employed there were thrown back on our hands. We paid a lump sum to the state, and the lease became extremely oppressive, having these men to feed, and clothe, and guard, and getting no work from them. We leased some of them to the coal operation at Briceville in the Coal Creek region. I learned afterwards that the roof [there] was bad and the coal soft and dirty, the royalty high, and the mine unprofitable.

On July 20 the miners and a mob captured both the convicts and the guards at Briceville and Coal Creek and shipped them bodily to Knoxville. The governor called out the entire state militia. The state demanded that we should withdraw convicts from Briceville, as the easiest way of relieving it from its duty of maintaining order and peace and guaranteeing us the use of the labor for which we were paying. On August 26 we obtained an injunction restraining the convict inspectors from removing the Briceville convicts, and a special session of the legislature was called to deal with the convict situation.

In October the Supreme Court . . . decided in our favor that the subleases of convicts were legal. Incensed at the decision of the Supreme Court, the miners burned the stockades at Coal Creek and Briceville and turned loose 320 convicts to go where they pleased. On November 2 they released convicts and burned the prison at Oliver Springs. The governor offered $5,000 reward for the leader and $250 each for his associates. I proposed that we should notify the governor that we considered the lease broken, but Baxter objected to any policy antagonizing the state. The result of this was that the governor laid all responsibility for the release of the convicts on us for not providing sufficient guards to keep the prisoners safe from the mobs. The governor refused to send convicts who had been rearrested back to East Tennessee on the ground that the attorney general declared subleases invalid, even in the face of the Supreme Court decision.

On March 28, 1892, under instructions from the president I gave the company's note for $2,500 as a margin on 500 shares of stock bought for the benefit of a Nashville newspaper proprietor[20] for the benefit of his influence through the public press on the legislature. I objected and only did it under positive orders. On April 14 the state comptroller approached one of our officials agreeing that he would recommend the legislature to settle our convict disputes amicably if we would give him pointers as to buying stock. No wonder honorable men wish to keep out of politics as a rule!

On July 6, 1892, the state of Tennessee filed a bill to collect from us the lease money without making any deduction whatever for the value of the services of the men who were turned loose by the mobs, and on the contrary included in its bill claim against us for all the expenses of putting down the public insurrection, and alleged that the trouble all grew out of our making subleases which were illegal. This seemed to be remarkable when the Supreme Court had approved them.

On August 8 our men at Tracy City . . . threatened to release the convicts. On August 13 the miners burned the Tracy City stockade and shipped the convicts to Nashville. The warden called on us to ask about supplies to feed them, and I told him that the governor had already been notified we would not receive them there. On August 15 the convicts at the Inman ore mines were turned out and sent back to Nashville by the miners. On August 16 the mob attacked the stockade at Oliver Springs but was repulsed. The governor called out two companies of militia and to our amazement suggested our collusion with the mob, to which Baxter made a very vigorous reply. On August 17 the warden at Oliver Springs, although reinforced, surrendered without resistance, and the convicts were sent back to Nashville. The government inspectors decided they would cancel the lease. On August 18 the miners besieged Coal Creek, and the entire state militia converged there. The inspectors served notice of cancellation of the lease in twenty days unless certain things were done. General Carnes sent relief from Fort Anderson, and thus dominated the Coal Creek situation. The board of convict inspectors reversed their policy, and instead of notifying us of cancellation they ordered us to take the men away from Nashville.

There [were] innumerable negotiations with different lawyers trying to reach some basis of compromise. The state legislature had been called into special session and had failed to accomplish anything, and the state now attempted to coerce us into meeting its arbitrary demands by making huge tax assessments against us, which would have cost us, we estimated, $250,000 per annum and would have shut us down. On December 14, 1893, we agreed on a settlement with the state of Tennessee after more than a year of most violent and intricate negotiations and situations, the truth being that the state officials, machine politicians, were afraid of each other, each wanting the honor and glory of fixing things.

5

Depression

In response to the hard times in the iron industry, TCI in 1892 spearheaded a consolidation movement among major producers. As a result, two large companies, De-Bardeleben Coal and Iron and the Cahaba Coal Company, merged with TCI. The combination more than doubled both TCI's iron capacity and its mineral land holdings and, like the one in 1886, brought new promise but also more problems. TCI now carried $9 million in bonded debt which would have to be funded through the hard years ahead, a burden that would keep Bowron and other managers constantly fearful of bankruptcy. The huge debt would delay much needed capital expenditure, especially for developing a steel-making capacity. It made the company even more dependent on the Wall Street financiers who could help to keep the company afloat but who were more interested in profiting from their own trading in TCI stock than in improving the company's stability. Indeed, "insider" trading was the rule, not the exception, among TCI executives, Bowron included, though the practice was hardly illegal at the time. After the merger John Inman remained the dominant board member, but two new men showed large influence: James T. Woodward, chairman of the Hanover Bank, and Walter S. Gurnee, a midwestern railroad developer turned New York investment banker.[1]

The merger also brought into the TCI management many new personalities who inevitably clashed with the men already in place. Truman H. Aldrich, a mining engineer descended from the prominent New England family, came in from Cahaba Coal, a company he founded after several successful years in business with Henry DeBardeleben. DeBardeleben, of course, was the most formidable of the new managers. Born in Prattville, Alabama, in 1841, he was certainly the most flamboyant and probably the most talented entrepreneur in nineteenth-century Alabama. Bowron said of him, "I never knew any man in Alabama so gifted in finding valuable deposits of minerals and so absolutely impractical in their development." DeBardeleben was responsible for putting together the properties that formed the Pratt Coal and Iron Company, which TCI took over in 1886, and the DeBardeleben Coal and Iron Company, which would merge with TCI in 1892. He had owned or controlled at one time or other what ultimately would be the vast majority of TCI's Alabama holdings. He was without peer as a promoter and locater of capital in faraway places. "It's many a man," said a Charleston, South Carolina, lawyer who invested heavily in DeBardeleben's Bessemer enterprises, "[who] has been lured upon the rocks of Alabama by that siren tongue of DeBardeleben." [2]

The TCI management, however, found DeBardeleben difficult to work with. He frequently made promises he could not keep, and he had a strong impulse to dominate any enterprise with which he was connected. He gloried in the role of Birmingham's leading capitalist, enjoying such designations as the one given by the *Wall Street Journal*, the "Christopher Columbus of Birmingham." But he could be his own worst enemy too, as he showed in 1893 when he attempted to "bull" the TCI stock on a declining market in an effort to gain full control for himself and his friends. Having promised to "squeeze the shorts"—that is, hurt speculators who had bet that TCI stock would go down—he himself got squeezed absolutely dry in his "long" position during the 1893 panic. He lost what was for the time, certainly in the South, a great fortune—perhaps $4 million in TCI stock. "Life is one big game of poker," DeBardeleben later said, knowing how it felt to lose big. He stayed on through the 1894 coal strike, during which his tough antiunion tactics would serve to help defeat the miners, and then left TCI to try to recoup his fortune. [3]

The 1893 panic and depression put strong downward pressure on wages and precipitated what would be TCI's greatest conflict to date with organized labor. Alabama coal miners had organized with some success under the Knights of Labor in the mid-1880s. The formation of the United Mine Workers of Alabama in 1890 brought new energy and enthusiasm, and the first districtwide strike occurred that year. It ended in defeat for the miners, partly because black coal miners failed to support the strike. The biggest showdown between capital and labor came when TCI determined in early 1894 to slash its rate paid for mining each ton of coal to thirty-five cents, a measure the company deemed necessary to cope with the depression. It followed earlier cuts and brought Alabama miners' support for a nationwide coal strike in April 1894.[4]

James Bowron began in the early 1890s to comment extensively on American politics, for which he had a natural curiosity and about which he would develop very firm opinions. The economic issues of the day—tariffs and currency—preoccupied him, as they did many Americans during the hard times. An inflated currency made credit all too hard to find for an undercapitalized industrialist, and free trade undermined the southern iron-makers' advantage against English iron in the northern markets. He became an outspoken hard-money protectionist—in many ways a conventional Republican businessman.

When I came to America the English public understood that Samuel J. Tilden had run for the presidency as a reformer, and I think my sympathy was distinctly with him as against Rutherford B. Hayes. My instincts have always been those of a reformer, and as the Democratic party posed as the party of progress my sympathies were with it when I landed. It was not long however before they were completely alienated, and I turned to the Republican party as the saviors of the country when in 1878 the Democrats largely accepted the currency proposition equal to the "South Sea Bubble," that people could make themselves rich by running printing presses, and that a quarter cent's worth of green paper with the government's name stamped on it was equal to a gold dollar in value.

Of course this was no worse in principle than the subsequent heresy of the Democratic party in agreeing on the say-so of William Jennings Bryan that fifty cents worth of silver with the government's name stamped on it was equal to a gold dollar. These fallacies have long since been exploded, and no one could be found today willing to endorse the Greenback party. My instincts as a businessman and financier went out to men like James A. Garfield, afterwards president, and John Sherman, as the pillars of sound finance.

On November 8, 1892, the government of this country was turned over to the Democrats, and I was deeply discouraged. I ought to have had sense enough to sell every share of stock that I possessed and take the losses instead of waiting to take them the next year. There was a triumphant Democratic procession through Nashville which I looked at with deep disgust. The only thing that pleased me was the lantern carried on the float of the ice man with the words: "It's a cold day when we get left." I thought that a piece of true humor. The Democratic party has always been a party of experiment instead of conservatism.

Bowron to the Chattanooga *Tradesman*, late 1892:
I believe the year 1892 will pass into history as a memorable one in the annals of the iron trade as having witnessed the culmination of over-production of pig iron in the South. It has been no surprise to thoughtful men that the prices of Southern pig iron this year should have gone not only below all previous records of American iron, but also considerably below the contemporary quotations on the cheapest iron produced in England. It has for five years been foreseen that a time of reckoning was coming for the owners of capital who would persist in investing it in the construction of additional blast furnaces in the South, where 80 per cent of their product would have to seek an outside or distant market. . . .

The general expectation that this year would witness a large increase in the purchases of iron and steel by the railroads has not been verified; nor has the consumption of iron by the producers of cast iron pipe been equal to that of recent years. The natural dullness in the iron market produced by these two most important factors has been enhanced by the steady and ceaseless encroachments made by soft steel, which has been taking the place of wrought iron in many directions. . . .

The effect of the changed fiscal policy to which the incoming administration is pledged, presents an element of difficulty in the way of forming an estimate of the outlook for the coming year. The abolition or large reduction of the duty on pig iron would prevent the sale of Southern pig iron in the East; for although pig metal is now selling at Birmingham at [about] Middlesbrough prices, and has sold this summer as much as $1.75 below them, the freight to Eastern cities ranges from $4.01 to $4.61, whilst English iron may be, and frequently is, brought across as ballast at from $.60 to $2 per ton in steamers which rely upon the grain or cotton freight for the payment of the expenses of the round trip. . . .

These considerations strongly increase the probability of Southern iron producers making for themselves and converting a large part of their product into steel. The experience gained at Chattanooga and Birmingham, is sufficient to show that this can be done with the very best mechanical and chemical results.

In January 1894 Bowron expressed his concern about the impending Wilson-Gorman tariff, which lowered tariff rates on many articles, in a letter to a Nashville newspaper:

I beg to state that the effect of the proposed Wilson tariff bill upon the iron trade, including subsidiary and allied industries, . . . will be distinctly bad and adverse. This country already enjoys the blessings of free trade from the Atlantic to the Pacific oceans and from Canada to the Gulf of Mexico. It enjoys free and unrestricted competition, which gives the inhabitants of this country in every part of its wide area, the advantages both of accumulated skill and capital and of the mineral deposits which have been thus far exploited under the influence of this competition. This country, however, is so large that the consumptive markets are found chiefly in the older parts of the country which are more densely settled and which have accumulated the bulk of the manufacturing capital. Statistics show that about 82 per cent of the pig iron produced in the South, i.e., in the states of Alabama and Tennessee, is exported beyond the limits of those states to find a market. The railroad companies act with marked liberality in the encouragement of traffic and the development of the manufacturing and mining industries along their lines. The large amounts of railroad mileage now in the hands of receivers show too plainly that as a rule the traffic of the country is conducted at rates which are not profitable to the roads, and it is not possible that the adverse effects of the proposed Wilson bill can be compensated for by any material reduction in the cost of getting to market. . . . The proposed ad valorem duty of 22 and ½ per cent computed upon the . . . Middlesbrough price of $8.50 would be $1.81, which, with the addition of the $1 freight, would make the price of

Middlesbrough iron $11.31. . . . This on the face . . . would appear to give Alabama iron an equal chance in the eastern markets, but it should be remembered that the present [Alabama] selling price is admittedly (and notoriously in many cases) below the cost of production and cannot be . . . sufficient to pay depreciation and wear and tear of plant, much less to leave any profit for the use of the capital invested in the business.

As it is absolutely certain that those who remain in the business do not desire to follow in the long procession of manufacturing industries that have passed into the hands of their creditors during the past year, there will, therefore, be only one course left open for them to pursue in the event of the passage of the Wilson bill with its present proposed tariff upon pig iron, viz.: to reduce wages in every direction. There has been no reduction in the standard rate of wages paid for mining coal in the Birmingham district within the past four years, and a general readjustment of wages throughout the coal mines, coke ovens, iron ore mines and upon the lines of transportation, would, in the aggregate, perhaps enable the producers of iron to continue to fight for the markets of the eastern coast which are so directly threatened by the proposed legislation.

It seems needless to ask what effect the proposed bill would have upon the purchasing power of the people, for if their wages are to be reduced 25 per cent their purchasing power in many cases will be reduced still more. The necessaries of life which are produced at home in the shape of flour, corn meal, beef and pork will not be cheapened by the Wilson bill, neither will the rent of their houses be reduced by it nor the cost of purchasing the cotton clothing, which is chiefly worn in the South. After the workman has paid present prices for articles of food, for his rent and for such clothing as is suitable for the climate in which he works, he will not be apt to find much money left over for investment in the imported woolen goods, carpets, Cuban cigars, and the champagne which Mr. Wilson kindly offers to him at a cheaper rate.

Bowron's views on political economy and international trade now reflected an intense American nationalism, which he communicated in August 1894 to an old English friend who had recently warned him against the evils of protectionism:

You cannot, of course, expect me to sympathize with the [English] standpoint ... on the tariff question. [It] may appear to be as true as the Holy Gospel to Englishmen, and appear the veriest nonsense and puerility to me.... Free trade is right for England. It would be the most superlative act of unselfish philanthropy if we were to adopt it here. It would build up other nations at the expense of ours.... In what way would free trade in this country cheapen the production of our coals or our pig iron? We have got a protective system which very properly, as you admit, enables us to pay higher wages to our workmen than English rates, and yet what? Why, we are making pig iron at less than 24 shillings [$6.00] per ton, including everything except coupon interest on our bonds, and we are mining immense quantities of coal at prices ranging, according to condition and thickness of same and mode of access, from two shillings per ton to 3 shillings [$.75], fob at colliery. We are selling black furnace coke today as low as 5s. 3d [$1.40]. Now with all your boasted advantages of free trade in England, how near can you come to touching this? ... The simple fact is that the greater ingenuity of this people puts it ahead of the English nation, wedded to old methods and possessed with a profound measure of conservatism, and this ingenuity and progressiveness is very largely the result of the higher wages paid and better conditions existing in this country. We have better natural resources; we have more practical ways of developing them and of applying ourselves to reap the full benefit of our conditions, and we do a thing while England is talking about it! There is no hope on the round globe for England ever to compete with this country in anything at all that this country sets itself to achieve. If we wanted to build a bigger navy than you have got, we would do it, for we make better steel, better armor, better guns, and better engines, and can build swifter ships and build them in one fourth the time; and if we wanted to tax ourselves we would have double your revenues. How much more, therefore, can we take away trade from you in such a small thing as making pig iron and mining coal.

On October 17, 1894, I made my first political speech in Alabama, being in the interest of the candidacy of ... Truman H. Aldrich for Congress. He lost the election on its face, but was counted in by the Republican majority [in Congress] on the ground of [vote fraud by supporters of Aldrich's Democratic opponent]. I remember bringing down the house by a quotation from the gospel of Matthew in support of protection versus free trade. It seemed to me as though the Republicans present surely did not read their Bibles; they seemed so surprised.

On November 6 there was a tremendous Republican landslide, the whole country resenting the new tariff. On the strength of this victory our iron sales were very heavy and I had hard work to keep up with them.

On January 25, 1892, Baxter proposed that we should commence paying dividends on the stock so as to put it up on the market and then sell out and both quit. I told him that the nervous strain was telling on me as well as himself and I felt that I would have to quit myself at the end of my then present term. The same day [my brother] Joe came to borrow money to move his family to New York. In the midst of all these troubles and perhaps partly because of them I was bothered at this time with an attack of the grippe.

On February 18 Baxter and Shook left for New York with [a] memorandum which I had drawn up as to the necessity of the company making steel so as to take care of its surplus of pig iron, but they came back from New York without having accomplished anything. On February 26, being in New York myself with Baxter, I brought up the steel proposal very earnestly, and discussing it with Naylor and Company, they said we could make money more easily by combining the southern furnace companies and putting up the price of pig iron, something that could be done in those days but could not be considered now under present laws.

BOWRON DIARY, February 26, 1892:
Lehman[5] suggests that we buy out the DeBardeleben [and] Sloss Companies. Baxter wires Seddon[6] and Duncan wires DeBardeleben to come on for conference.

February 29, 1892:
Jere Baxter[7] arrives to assist in the "bull" campaign. . . . [Nat] Baxter tells Woodward[8] his plans for consolidation and both Woodward and C. C. Baldwin[9] buy stock.

March 1, 1892:
Seddon arrived and had conference with Baxter and seems anxious for a trade. . . . Baxter repeats to me gist of conversation with Seddon and asks me to draft some scheme as a basis for negotiations.

March 2, 1892:
Drafted scheme for consolidation based on capitalization of net earnings (less fixed charges) plus so much per acre for unimproved property.

March 4, 1892:
Seddon asks stock for stock, and to assume his bonds claims. [His] net earnings last year [were] 356 thousand but last six month 216 thousand.... From 4 P.M. til 1 A.M. at work with Seddon and DeBardeleben. DeBardeleben willing to trade on proposed terms, but Seddon kicking and demanding everything in sight.

March 7, 1892:
Negotiations til 1 A.M. Sloss people very stubborn. Apparent break off of everything.

March 8, 1892:
Stock to 44 and ½ on apparent failure of negotiations. Took Turkish bath and bought underwear.

March 9, 1892:
In session til 2 A.M. and finally agreed with Seddon and Johnston[10] on behalf of Sloss. Sold three hundred shares at forty six to "hedge" during the day, thinking all was going off, but found DeBardeleben was going to buy stock quietly.

March 10, 1892:
Bought five hundred shares at 47 and ½. Stock rose to 50 and ¼ on news of agreement when from Christian[11] [came a] telegram refusing to endorse or concur in it. Sloss people go back on the whole thing and demand the formation of a new or fourth company to absorb all the other three. Stock fell back to 49. Over 23,000 shares sold this day.

March 11, 1892:
Sold out all my 1200 at 49 on apparent break up of everything. Sloss people all squabbling amongst themselves. Christian against our charter, our name, and everything else.

March 12, 1892:
I recommend [to] Duncan, Baxter, Shook to go on and agree with DeBardeleben and leave Sloss out and later to take in [the] Cahaba and Woodward [companies]. In afternoon Baldwin urges the same and we sign up memorandum with DeBardeleben accordingly.

March 14, 1892:
Sent out general Associated Press dispatches announcing consolidation with DeBardeleben. Bought 1500 shares at 49. . . . Sloss people bear the stock and try to spread distrust and dissatisfaction. Knock stock down to 48.

March 15, 1892:
Waiting for DeBardeleben's people to come on: little to do meantime. Sloss people issue scurrilous reports through Dow Jones and Wall Street Journal and sell the stock short. Arrival of A. T. Smythe, [Moses] Lopez and [David] Roberts and [J. D.] Adger.[12]

March 16, 1892:
DeBardeleben stockholders decline to ratify DeBardeleben's trade and ask more. Everything looks blue.

March 17, 1892:
From 9 A.M. to 2 A.M. engaged in final session. Smythe a strong but courteous fighter. Agreed on all points finally yielding them five and one-half percent on dollars out of treasury stock. They not seeing that two and one-half cents of this came from themselves. Drafted rough agreement and then to bed, having bought at seventy seven cents on the dollar payable in stock a company having a larger surplus earning than our own, and a larger relative treasury surplus. Our surplus earnings being $270,000, theirs $320,000. Our treasury surplus $568,000, theirs $554,000.

March 18, 1892:
The agreement signed by both sides at 9:30 A.M. Ratified by board at 11:00. Smythe elected director and put on executive committee. Letter from Sloss representative trying to reopen negotiations.

DeBardeleben . . . made the statement that the steel plant should never be put at Ensley. This coming from the largest individual [TCI] stockholder seemed pretty conclusive. DeBardeleben said . . . if the Bessemer Land Company would take $750,000 of bonds he would take $250,000 himself toward the proposed steel plant at Bessemer. About this time the Bessemer local newspaper broke into big headlines: "Out of the darkness into the light—The long looked for steel plant at last in sight." But it too was counting chickens, or at least steel plants, before they were hatched.

BOWRON DIARY, May 14, 1892:
Baxter says that as DeBardeleben will be our largest stockholder he [Baxter] will support him as [president] if he wishes the place.

May 16, 1892:
Baxter and Shook worried and annoyed at [DeBardeleben's] reckless [and] extravagant statements[,] seemingly intended to reflect on them.

May 17, 1892:
Baxter incensed at [DeBardeleben's] conduct. I counsel conservative and dignified forbearance.

June 24, 1892:
[DeBardeleben] . . . on the alert to snub McCormack.

February 14, 1893:
Went with Baxter to see DeBardeleben at train. [DeBardeleben] says he has bought TCI [stock] . . . in New York and made $25,000. Has control of 120,000 shares. Will buy out Charleston crowd. . . . Platt tells him to have no Tennesseans in office. . . . That U.S. government will encourage naval construction in the Gulf. That he has laid all the foundations for a big bull pool in the stock and wants us to join him. That he will have a majority Southern men in next board and that I will be on it.

February 18, 1893:
DeBardeleben says has seventy thousand shares. That Cahaba stock will all join him in pool for one year. Wants to tie up stock, encourage short interest and squeeze it. There are 4,000 shares short now. Wants Inman on board. Not fully decided on other New York men.

Poor fellow! The finish of the pool was by no means bullish. On February 24 and 25 TCI stock [was] raided by "bears" and dropped from 31 to 25½. Brokers called me again. The simple fact was that they had learned of DeBardeleben's heavy holdings. He had been wined and dined by brokers and was very talkative, and they knew some things and guessed others as to the amount of stock which he had and which was chiefly margined by other stock of the same kind. Inman offered to take 10,000 shares off his hands to help him, but DeBardeleben declined saying it was unnecessary. I mention this matter because Justice Charles Bricken of the [Alabama Court of Appeals] spoke most unjustly and incorrectly once in my presence to the gen-

eral effect that the TCI crowd had pulled DeBardeleben in and stripped
him of his fortune, which was estimated at nearly $2 million when he went
in. The truth of this will appear as I write. I attempted to correct the justice,
but he very imperiously declined to be informed.

On March 7 my brokers insisted upon my selling more TCI stock in view
of the appearance of the market. I sold 300 shares at 26¼. On March 13
I attended a board meeting in New York at which Mr. Platt tendered his
resignation, . . . after which we were working until midnight with a steel
committee endeavoring to arrange terms for the use of the Talbot process.
A lively scrap ensued between the Tennessee and DeBardeleben crowds as
to the offices for the following year, which finally settled itself with Baxter
chairman of the executive committee; DeBardeleben president; Aldrich,
Roberts, and Shook vice-presidents in the order named; self secretary and
treasurer, office at Nashville, my salary being raised from $5,000 to $6,000
a year. I had asked them to give me a secretary and relieve me from the
clerical labor of writing on account of my thumb, but was disappointed.

On March 23, 1893, the newspapers said that Inman had bought 25,000
shares from DeBardeleben privately. Baxter wired me that DeBardeleben
was relieved from complications, and it was supposed that this would stop
the "bear" raids upon the stock, but evidently he was still carrying a large
amount more than he could support, and the trouble was not yet over. On
April 29 Inman wired us that he bought 12,000 shares from DeBardeleben,
and again we thought that the situation was cleared up. The stock was down
to 18¾, or just about half what it had been on January 31. I tried to buy
more at this low price, but my brokers declined to buy it for me. It was just
as well, for it closed at the end of the year at 15.

On May 4 [there was a] panic in New York. National Cordage Company
stock dropped from 78 to 26. Under these conditions, with two of the Nashville banks closed and the other two limiting their withdrawals to $100 per
head, everything [was] as blue as indigo. On May 24, Inman wired that he
had bought 13,000 shares more from DeBardeleben, which closed him out.
Now what Inman had to do with leading DeBardeleben on into a big bull
pool, which he had told me he had formed, and getting 120,000 shares on
margin, I would like Justice Bricken to explain.

On June 1 the secretary of the [South Pittsburgh] pipe works came to me
for help as he could not get anyone to discount his customers' paper for him.
I tried to get someone in Nashville but could not. The brokers in Chicago
who handled many of our discounts failed [on] June 3, and the situation

Henry F. DeBardeleben, Alabama industrial entrepreneur (courtesy of Whitney DeBardeleben)

became increasingly difficult day by day, as gold was going out of the country and the U.S. Treasury was rapidly coming to a silver basis. I learned of two blast furnaces in Alabama that had not paid their payrolls for three months.

On June 21 the First National Bank of Birmingham called upon us to send cash down to help it make our payroll. [The] Louisville and Nashville Railroad [was] dunning us for payment of freight bills. Merchants' Bank of

Cincinnati and the Bessemer Savings Bank call[ed] us for payment of our loans. On June 22 [there was] a run on the First National Bank of Birmingham. An Associated Press telegram stat[ed] the run was caused by our failure to pay our men the past Saturday. [This] broke our stock to 15. On July 17 ten banks failed in Kansas City, Topeka, and elsewhere. On July 18 thirteen [more] failed. On that date we paid the Fourth National Bank, New York, [15 percent interest] for money on bills receivable. On July 22 [there were] bank failures in Louisville and Knoxville. TCI 6 percent bonds sold at 73. On July 25 six banks failed, and our home bank, the First National in Nashville, refused to renew our note for $6,000, but finally agreed to renew $4,000 of it. On July 26 [more] panic in New York. The Erie Railroad [went] in the hands of a receiver. Louisville and Nashville Railroad [stock fell] to 48, TCI to 10½. On July 27 the First National Bank of Birmingham [was] unable to furnish the currency for our Blocton payroll, and we had to ship it from Cincinnati.

On July 31 the Fourth National Bank, Nashville, refused us a renewal even of a little $15,000 note, but the Louisville and Nashville Railroad discounted our paper . . . to cover [the Birmingham ore mines'] payroll. The Mechanics' Bank, New York, refused us any commercial discounts, and we only covered our payrolls by the kindness of Matthew Addy and Company, Cincinnati, advancing against shipments. Two Birmingham merchants, Adler and Cosby, came to Nashville to get pig iron, bonds, or anything else against our notes, thinking we were going to fail. Birmingham banks refused to pay any checks over $25 and we sold Adler 1,000 tons of pig iron and $17,000 of DeBardeleben bonds [acquired in 1892 merger] in exchange for our notes. This pleased both parties.

On August 2 the First National Bank of Birmingham failed. Birmingham merchants threatened suits for their open accounts, and we ordered another furnace banked. At this point gold began to be shipped from $3 million to $6 million per day from England in payment for stocks purchased for English account at the panic prices. On August 5 President Garth of the Mechanics' National of New York allowed our check to go to protest, refusing bills receivable sent him for discount against which we had drawn checks. The First National Bank of Nashville only [sent] out our payrolls by driblets of about $2,000 per day. [On] August 7 I observed our payroll was being filled by the bank largely with dirty old notes and nickels and dimes that looked like the scraping of the barrel.

On August 9 the First National Bank of Nashville suspended [payment].

On August 10 the American National of Nashville suspended. There was a run all day upon the Fourth National, which refused to make payments to anyone in specie of over $100, but would pay any amount in clearinghouse funds. All banks at this point began refusing to accept checks except for collection. Indeed this seemed necessary. I had drawn a number of TCI checks on the First National Bank of Birmingham, which had suspended, and the checks were refused and returned to me by the holders. I took them up by checks on the First National of Nashville instead, and in due time got them back from the holders for the second time. I then redeemed them by checks on the Fourth National of New York, and they were duly paid.

At this point one of the strangest experiences of my financial life began. Three of the banks in Nashville, the First, American, and Commercial, were in the hands of the federal government bank examiners acting as receivers. The Fourth National was the only bank still in operation, and it was declining to pay out specie for more than $100 on any one account in any one day. We had many thousands of dollars of notes out in circulation given for commercial purposes, and as they would mature they would be sent, or had already been sent, by the holders for collection at maturity. Some of these came to the banks in the hands of the bank examiners, and if we offered checks on New York and Cincinnati they said, "No, we cannot take them. We are government officials under bond, and we have no authority to accept anything but money." We had one note for about $5,000 in the hands of the American National Bank. I said to the examiners, "Please telegraph the Fourth National, New York, and ask if our check for this amount is not good." He did so and got reply that we had much more than that to our credit, but that they did not certify checks by telegraph. It looked as though our note would have to go to protest, but finally my friend, President Keith of the Fourth National, said, "Jim, you give me your New York exchange; if he will take it, and I think he will, [then I will]." So this was done and the note was paid. I always loved Mr. Keith, because he was the only man in America that used to call me "Jimmie" instead of "Mr."

It became necessary for us at the Nashville office to devote our principal efforts to corresponding with the different people to whom we had issued notes. We had to write to every man and say: "Our note to you for so much will mature such a day. We cannot get cash funds in this city with which to pay it." We would then give him a list of ten or fifteen good bills receivable held by us and ask him to take one or more of them in partial payment, with our endorsement added, and give him a check on New York for the balance.

When a man would reply to us that he had paid away the note we then had to push the correspondence along to the party he had paid it to, and this business took up practically two-thirds of our time.

On August 28, the country being broken as the result of four-months' control by the Democrats who had come in on March 1, and the U.S. Treasury being saved from going to protest only by the patriotic action of J. P. Morgan in getting up a gold fund amongst New York banks, President Cleveland, who was bigger than his party, forced the repeal of the free coinage of silver bill, the repeal bill passing the house by 110 majority. The effect of this was magical. Seven national banks resumed the next day. We were so nearly flattened out that for the first time on record, August 31, we were unable to pay our own salaries.

On September 1 Walter S. Gurnee agreed to lend us $100,000 on pig iron collateral at 1 percent a month, which helped us. On September 6 the Fourth National of Nashville removed the $100 limit and resumed ordinary payments. The Louisville and Nashville Railroad agreed to take $100,000 DeBardeleben bonds at 85 as a credit upon our notes, and it seemed as though the crisis was passed. It will hardly be [believed] that during this period of violent strain we had been unable to discount such paper as that of the Carnegie Steel Company, although we had offered it in Pittsburgh at 15 percent per annum. On October 5 Gurnee discounted one of these notes at 12 percent, the Hanover National having asked 20 percent.

On September 12 Truman Aldrich wired from Birmingham: "No meat, no meal, no money." Do what I might, the people who were suffering for these things seemed to feel that I ought to manage somehow to provide the money. Aldrich in particular was so mad about it that he said he would quit if Mr. Gurnee would consent. On October 30 we had a strike at Blocton of the miners because of the delayed payroll. Aldrich said openly that he would not blame them, which was a trying position for us when our general manager would talk that way. On November 20 Aldrich was so mad at the merchandise accounts being in arrears of payment that he wrote me he would make it a personal matter and that one or the other of us must get out of the company. I wrote him an appropriate letter, and November 25 he apologized gracefully.

On October 24, after the pro-silver men had failed to bluff the president into a compromise, they accepted the House repeal bill of the Bland free [silver] coinage act, and this was followed by a boom in stocks, and the next day our New York bank, the Fourth National, resumed regular discounts.

The year 1893 was only the first of several years of trial and trouble such as I always look for under Democratic control. The party seems to be afflicted with some violent demagogues and iconoclasts who glory in upsetting and pulling down everything that exists anywhere.

Bowron assessed the causes of the economic crisis and suggested how to overcome them in a letter to the Chattanooga Tradesman *in November 1893:*

Dear Sirs:

I have waited a little while in replying to your favor of November 3rd so that events might shape themselves somewhat, for we are living in a transition age and it does not do for a man to be too prophetic. You ask several questions, which I will reply to seriatim.

THE CAUSE OF THE PRESENT DEPRESSION IN IRON INTERESTS:

First and chiefly, the over production of pig iron by "boom town" blast furnaces. Secondly, the intense competition between railroads which broke down rates to a point that prevented the necessary expenditures on permanent way and rolling stock from being maintained. Thirdly, the steady substitution of steel for iron, which has maintained in activity and relative prosperity the furnaces and mills based upon the output of steel whilst those based upon iron output declined in activity and prosperity in inverse ratio. Fourthly, the distrust in American securities caused by the insane effort to maintain a constantly growing national pyramid of silver inverted upon an apex of gold. This lead [*sic*] from 1889 to 1892 inclusive to an excess of exports either of merchandise or precious metals over imports of the same, of four hundred and eighty millions of dollars, which represented the return of so much European capital to its owners. The continuance of this movement led in the spring to largely augmented withdrawals of gold and produced the disastrous panic with which we are all familiar. . . .

IS THE MARKET FOR OUR RAW PRODUCT EXPANDING:

Yes; it is expanding largely in the extreme East, on the Atlantic Coast and in the New England States. Southern iron has also replaced English pig iron on the Pacific Coast. There has been no expansion of the Southern demand for pig iron during the past year.

WHY HAS THERE BEEN SO LITTLE PROGRESS MADE IN CONVERTING OUR RAW MATERIAL INTO MERCHANTABLE PRODUCT:

In the fact of the universal substitution of steel for iron and the gradual falling out of the race of one finished ironworks after another, there has been no encouragement for the investment of capital in the direction of any of the forms of manufactured iron in the South. There is little accumulated capital in the South, where (regardless of the opinions of the tax assessor's [sic]) the iron trade has been far from profitable, and the capital that is available is not at all disposed to sacrifice itself in the construction of works that may be and will be superceded as soon as the South commences to produce steel on an important scale. In my opinion the metallurgical position of the South has arrived at a point where no further progress will be made until steel is produced on a large scale and economically. As soon as this is done the whole South and Southwest states will become a home market for the Southern producers of iron, who, instead of paying from $2.50 to $4. per ton to reach a market with their pig iron, will be protected against Northern and Eastern competition on a similar distance and a similar freight.

The depression worked a severe hardship on coal miners, who in 1888 had agreed to a sliding scale for payment based on the market price of pig iron. The scale was pegged at forty-five cents per ton on the 1888 pig iron price of $13 per ton and set to go up two and a half cents for each dollar rise in pig iron. Forty-five cents was meant to be the minimum paid, but by 1890 companies lowered their minimum to forty cents as iron prices fell below $13. During the panic of 1893, the rate for coal went down to thirty-eight cents per ton. For the average miner digging five to ten tons per day, the reduction represented a substantial loss of income, considering that he had to pay for dynamite, tools, and his helper out of his gross pay. The severity of miners' predicament everywhere led to the nationwide coal strike in April 1894.

The TCI management was far better prepared for the conflict than the miners. It had not only greater financial resources but also better access to political authorities, who could help their cause in many ways. TCI's main tactic was to keep up a basic level of production with convict labor and free black miners who were skeptical of the union and then to wait for government intervention to stop the inevitable violence between strikers and the company. The strategy worked perfectly, thanks in large part to Henry DeBardeleben and Governor Thomas Goode Jones, a lawyer who formerly represented the Louisville and Nashville Railroad and thus had close ties to Birmingham industrialists. Within a few weeks of the start of the strike, Jones sent the state militia to Birmingham to quell violence. As violence continued through the summer of 1894, Jones and the militia became more determined to end the strike. Finally, in late August, the miners gave up and accepted a rate of thirty-seven and one-half cents per ton.[13]

On April 11, 1894, our Alabama miners proposed an arbitration on the subject of wages, but the next day backed out from it and ordered a general strike. We proposed to reduce the existing scale . . . for digging to 35 cents [per ton]. Between the Democratic silver panic of the last year and the shadow of impending tariff changes the whole country was at a standstill, and reduction of prices was necessary in every direction.

Alfred M. Shook to George McCormack, March 10, 1894:
It was the sense of the [TCI board of directors] that all labor pertaining to the mines that had not previously been reduced, should be reduced 25%. No time was fixed when this reduction should take place, as it was impossible to get the committee to agree upon a policy. Mr. A[ldrich] earnestly advocated the banking of all the furnaces now, which would enforce the closing of the mines, and let them stand in that condition until the men came to us with a proposition to go to work at a reduction of about 25%. DeB[ardeleben] favored the moving of all the convicts to Blue Creek mines, mining coal enough there for all the furnaces, and closing down the other mines. Baxter favored a compromise position, which was to shut up one mine at a time and let it stand until you could find somebody who would take it by contract at a low price, and push the contract business as rapidly as possible. If this action forced a strike, well and good, and if not, continue to shut up one mine at a time and contract it out until all the mines had been let out on contract, thus consummating the reduction without any stoppage. They finally agreed that enough convicts should be moved from Pratt to the Sumter mine at Blocton, to run the latter mine, and that the men thrown out of work there would be told that they could get work at Pratt at a reduction of about 25%. In this way, if any strike is brought about before the expiration of our contract with the men it will have to be forced by the men themselves.[14]

Henry DeBardeleben's notice to Blue Creek coal miners, April 1894:
A job at Blue Creek is a desirable one. This is a rare chance for all first
class colored miners to have a permanent home. They can have their
own churches, schools and societies, and conduct their social affairs in
a manner to suit themselves, and there need be no conflict between the
races. This can be a colored man's colony.

   Colored miners, come along; let us see whether you can have an
Eden of your own or not. I will see that you will have a fair show. You
can then prove whether there is intelligence enough among colored
people to manage their social and domestic affairs by themselves in
such a way as to command respect of the people at large. It is not likely
that you will have another such chance to demonstrate to the world that
you are capable of governing your social affairs without the aid or interference of the white race.[15]

By May 1894 a general coal miners' strike was in force in fourteen states
of the union, so that our troubles were by no means local. They came from
national causes. On May 19 we blew out the South Pittsburgh furnace, the
Whitwell miners having struck, and we shipped away the goods from the
commissary, and told them they could stay out as long as they wanted to.
The same day the Pratt strikers assassinated one of our labor agents. Five
hundred of them assembled at Pratt slope Number Five intending to blow it
up but were dispersed by the sheriff with forty deputies.

   On June 26, 1894, the local executive committee requested Truman
Aldrich to look after pending coal contracts and to let DeBardeleben handle
the coal miners' strike, as a result of which June 30 Aldrich resigned, feeling
his pride hurt at authority being taken from him and given to DeBardeleben
to put down the strike. A very intelligent man, highly educated, a man of
much energy, it seemed a pity that there should have been such continuous
friction between [Aldrich] and his various colleagues. I admired him personally and was deeply grieved that he was always more or less censorious
of me because of my official failure to pay the local creditors promptly.
Heaven knows I would have paid them if I had had the money!

   [There were] evidences over the country of the miners losing ground.
They could not get high wages when the operators could not get high prices
or in some cases sell their coal at any price. The strike in Iowa collapsed,
and there were evidences of weakening in Ohio and Pennsylvania. At this
time also, in addition to the coal miners' strike in fourteen states of the

Industrial workers, c. 1900 (courtesy of Birmingham Public Library Archives)

union, there was a fearful railroad strike extending from the Atlantic to the Pacific and from Canada to Birmingham. On July 7 the federal troops fired on the rioters in Chicago where miles of loaded freight cars were blazing on the tracks.

On July 16 a murderous attack was made at Pratt mine by the striking miners on the men at Number Three, six being killed. This broke up the strike. The next day there was an indignation meeting in Birmingham, and fifty-four men [were] put in jail. Governor Thomas Goode Jones told the strikers that men who wanted to work should be allowed to work and would be protected in doing so, if he had to lay a dead miner on every cross tie between Birmingham and Pratt mines.

BOWRON DIARY, July 27, 1894:
300 Italians to be put to work at Blocton.

August 11, 1894:
Total poll of district 40[,] majority against settlement. Our men vote for settlement[:] [Pratt Mines] 245–15, Blue Creek 18–29, Blocton 112–160. Sloss men against it. Blocton open vote deters 150 advocates

of settlement. Committee says Blocton strikers holding out because of [Llewellyn] Johns[16] advice[.] He promising to get them 40 [cents per ton]. Baxter instructs DeB[ardeleben] to fire [Johns].

On January 5, 1894, Baxter began, and practically continued from that time forward, negotiations on the side in connection with street railroad matters. In fact, the handling of street railroad matters in Nashville, Chattanooga, Birmingham, or other and more distant cities became his principal occupation, and to attend to these matters in which he hoped to make very large sums of money, he practically ignored his duties as president of our company, and they fell upon me. Mrs. Baxter told me on January 10 that her husband was so nervous that he could not talk to the family five minutes without breaking down, and he told me that it was a constant thing for him to be unable to sleep and to get up and get dressed and go out and walk about the city two or three hours in the middle of the night, and then come back and distract his mind by reading some light French novel. It goes without saying that under these conditions he could not help me in handling the company's affairs, and I had to underwrite many of his duties.

We were leasing a lot of convicts to Jere Baxter, our president's brother, who was using them in building the Tennessee Central Railroad. As a matter of fact he never paid for their hire. We felt that even if he kept them up and supported them we were so much in, but he was not able even to do that, and daily, to my distress, I was ordered by my president to make various payments from time to time to them to help keep up the convicts. I knew we were piling up bad debts, but I was powerless under the direct demand of my president.

There [was] marked friction [in Birmingham] between Aldrich, De-Bardeleben, and David Roberts as to duties and general management of the company.

BOWRON DIARY, July 18, 1894:
DeBardeleben [disapproves of] McCormack's nomination as general manager which he objects to at present as Aldrich has made all district think [McCormack] is the big bee of the whole country.

July 26, 1894:
Talk with DeBardeleben whose amour propre is wounded by Baxter consulting Inman and then Roberts before him. He is impeding

George B. McCormack, Tennessee Coal and Iron executive and Bowron ally
(courtesy of Birmingham Public Library Archives)

Roberts in coming to Birmingham and objecting to McCormack being
general manager for fear they will divide his power and glory in the eyes
of the people.

September 7, 1894:
Shook says DeBardeleben has formed a new company to run at Bessemer. . . . [DeBardeleben] told [Shook] he was ready to leave the TCI
in 20 or 30 days. [Shook] wants his place. Thinks Roberts will go with
[DeBardeleben]. Will support me for third vice-president.

October 13, 1894:
DeBardeleben reported as having charge again of outside company work and snubbing McCormack.

October 18, 1894:
DeBardeleben urges Baxter to sign the contract with him for ore, saying he will turn in his resignation as vice-president immediately. Agreed to on that understanding.

The executive committee sent John C. Haskell[17] down to investigate. His report drew a proposal to abolish the office of the general manager and to move the office of the treasurer to Birmingham. Baxter urged me to see the members of the committee individually and to fight and lectioneer against the removal of the office to Birmingham, which I would not as I could see that finally such a move must come.

On June 6 James T. Woodward, president of the Hanover National Bank, turned up unexpectedly, having been to Birmingham. One of his objects was to find out how the company was being managed and who was attending to its business and doing its work. He said he would not consent to any steel-works being put up by the company out of which anyone else should obtain any collateral advantage in which the company did not participate. This was a blow at the proposal to build a plant at Bessemer where DeBardeleben's land company would reap much benefit.

In July 1894 Baxter [had] received a joint letter from Inman and Woodward complaining of his not visiting the works in Alabama, and saying that unless he went down there twice a month the stockholders would move the company's offices down there. At this time . . . I could only get audience with [Baxter] on business of the company by going to his house at night, as he was absent all day long on other business. In September Inman and Woodward requested the removal of [the corporate] office to Birmingham by the first or fifteenth of October. [Baxter] asked me to go to New York and ask for delay until March, which I did for the simple reason that all our notes were maturing at Nashville and I did not want to move down to Birmingham until I could have time to start a new series, which of course I would make maturing at Birmingham. This was quite promptly agreed to in New York when I presented the subject. They talked to me very frankly about the management and admitted that I was doing the work and was entitled to some better position than secretary and treasurer.

Bowron to Truman Aldrich, November 18, 1894:

In reply to your kind inquiry as to my personal status in all the negotiations for reorganization and promotion . . . I am afraid I can only say
that I have not any. I enjoy confidential relations with every officer in
the South and . . . have striven to lubricate the machine and avert friction, but as David Copperfield went to Agnes to be advised and comforted concerning his suit for Dora, so my colleagues discuss with me
their separate hopes and none seem to think that I have any. It does
seem odd though to any one who knows the inside life of the Company.
In the last twelve years there have been 6 Presidents, 14 Vice Presidents, and 6 General Managers. I alone have been without any break a
General Officer of the Company during that time, yet I remain today
where I was at first, viz. at the foot of the list of twelve officers. . . .
Having in the last few years had three different Presidencies offered me
in the iron trade, I am free to say to you that it does begin to seem
rather anomalous that I should be the only general officer without a
place on the Board, the Executive or the Governing Committee. The
old adage says that "all things come to him who waits," but I have
waited so long that I begin to fear nothing more will ever come my way
if I remain with the TCI Co. . . . My present feeling is to wait patiently
a little longer and then if nothing turns up in my favor, sell my stock
and retire from active business life, and occupy myself with such lines
of study as are congenial, which pressing of brain work has so long
unfitted me for.

On December 5 I found [that] our lawyers, one of whom was Baxter's
son-in-law, were drawing on the company for salary in advance of its maturity. Baxter [was] accepting the drafts without my knowledge, no entry whatever on the company's books. It can hardly be believed that [a] company of
the magnitude and importance of ours could possibly be handled with such
friction and such ignorance and such neglect of duties. I have read that
Providence takes care of blind men and sailors—I think it must also have
taken care of our company.

I received a letter from Walter S. Gurnee saying that he wanted me to be
first vice-president and asked me to suggest plans for organization and salaries. I visited New York in January 1895 and was again assured that I should
be made vice-president at the coming election if Inman consented. On January 25 Inman wrote Baxter that the company could make no promotions and

if I wanted to leave it I ought to give them some notice. [Inman said] that Aldrich had been suggested for president if his, Baxter's, affairs prevented him from giving attention to the company. Mr. Inman certainly ruled the company with a rod of iron. All the others were in favor of my promotion, and one word from him stopped the whole business.

On February 26, 1895, I shipped my desk and papers, and also a safe, to Birmingham, and on February 28 resigned the chairmanship of the state YMCA committee, and on March 3 at 9:00 P.M. left for Birmingham with a sad heart, believing that I was leaving a cultured, beautiful, aristocratic city to go and live in a sort of exaggerated coal mining village, with nothing but workmen and a few superintendents.

Birmingham

The iron industry recovered slowly from the 1890s depression. For a time during 1895 things looked up, only to turn downward late in the year with the threat of war with Great Britain over the Venezuelan boundary dispute. Depressed prices continued through 1896 and 1897, and at times James Bowron still feared that TCI might fail. Partly in response to the hard times, Bowron and other Birmingham industrialists developed a growing internationalist perspective on marketing TCI's iron. In 1894 10,000 tons of cast-iron pipe was shipped from Birmingham to Japan, and pig iron exports grew rapidly throughout the decade, going all over the world and rivaling the great English iron centers in the market. In 1899 and 1900 Bowron would be TCI's primary salesman abroad. This international marketing and stronger domestic sales began to pull the iron economy out of the trough. But when profits appeared in 1899, major TCI shareholders began to clamor for dividends. Bowron knew all too well how heavy the company's obligations were from the long years of depression and the recent efforts to modernize production, and he adamantly opposed paying any dividend. He knew that the company would have to borrow the money. When he was overruled, he moved to sever his long relationship with Tennessee Coal and Iron.

Relationships between TCI's major stockholders and its southern managers remained rocky, even after the departure of Henry DeBardeleben in late 1894. John Inman's influence ended when he suffered financial disaster in the cotton futures market in the summer of 1896 and then died under mysterious circumstances. The announced cause of his death in November 1896 was nervous prostration, but associates would later say he committed suicide. After Inman's death, James Woodward of the Hanover Bank and the financier Walter Gurnee exerted the dominant influence over the TCI board of directors. They generally distrusted the southern managers. Nathaniel Baxter's inattention to duty and his resistance to moving the company office to Birmingham angered the New York directors, especially the hard-boiled Woodward, who knew that Baxter was more interested in his private enterprises than in the company's well-being. The disposition of the Ensley Land Company, which went bankrupt in 1897, created bad feelings when the property ended up in the hands of two TCI managers, George McCormack and Erskine Ramsay. The conflicts between Birmingham and New York would make the late 1890s an uncomfortable period for Bowron, even after economic conditions improved.[1]

The late 1890s also provided some highlights for Bowron and Birmingham. He, Alfred Shook, and other TCI executives finally overcame the obstacles to steel production and put their company on the way to competition in a major American industry. Bowron took immense personal pride in this achievement. Along the way he became a major fixture in the business elite of Birmingham, a city that, as it turned out, he would like better than he ever imagined.

I was very cordially received in Birmingham in all directions and am reminded of the expression of my friend, Bishop Charles Quintard of Tennessee, who said that when he went to England he found that to be a member of the [Church of England] was to be respectable. To be a clergyman of it was to have entrée to the best society. But to be a bishop of it was like carrying the key to the Kingdom of Heaven. I found on coming to Birmingham that to be in the iron trade was to be respectable; to be an officer of an iron-making corporation was to have the entrée to the best society. But to be the chief residential officer of the largest corporation was to carry the key to the Kingdom of Heaven. In Nashville where I had resided for nearly thirteen years I had many friends in the churches, schools . . . but I had never taken any commanding position in the

Birmingham's main street, 1895 (courtesy of Birmingham Public Library Archives)

social life of the city. In Birmingham I found it was not so much a question of what a man's grandfather had been, but the question was and still is, "What does he do?" I had come in other words to a progressive city of earnest industry.

Birmingham, like all other young boomtowns, had suffered seriously in the hard times through which we had passed in the previous two years. Real estate was hardly salable at fifty cents on the dollar of its previous value. The city reminded me of a great big beetle turned over on its back kicking very hard to get on its feet, but really quite uninjured. Some of the people who are today very wealthy consulted me as to whether they should hold on to their real estate or try to sell it. I spoke very cheerfully about the prospects of the place and encouraged everyone to hold on. If I had possessed some money I might have made a large fortune at that time by buying real estate. All thought that the transfer of headquarters of the largest corporation from Nashville to Birmingham meant much to the city, and they could not show me too much attention and kindness.

I got my desks and safe into the office on March 4, 1895, and transacted the usual day's work, interviewed various newspaper men, enrolled as a member of the local YMCA, and attended the meeting of the local musical society, the Mendelssohn Society, which was a good day's work. On

March 13 [I] attended the First Presbyterian Church where I formed a friendship with Dr. A. B. Curry, the pastor, and Mr. Hawkins, the chairman of the state committee, YMCA. After church I went around to the YMCA where they informed me I had been elected a director the previous week. To my surprise I was called on to act as pianist at the First Presbyterian Church prayer meeting, and although quite incompetent, I filled the bill, because I never refuse any religious service that is offered to me, and I never make excuses for the character of my performance, but do the best I can.

On May 1 I had rather a curious experience at the house of a most kindly and genial old soldier who had invited me to spend the evening. On arriving there I found the dining room spread with a supper and the neighboring room with claret and cigars. They informed me it was a vestry meeting of a certain church at which they undertook to raise a subscription to pay off the church debt of about $5,000, and it was largely done amongst those present. I was not a member of that church, and yet to my amazement they elected me as a delegate to their state convention. But I told them that it was absurd and I insisted upon being released from any such unsuitable nomination. It was the oddest mixture of church and society that I had ever seen.

By October 20 I seem to have dropped into full service at the South Highland Presbyterian Church, taking part in the Bible class and choir in the morning, and leading the Christian Endeavor and the church service at night, and have been in very close and active association with the church and its affairs from that time forward. I resumed music lessons, this time from Mrs. Guckenberger, who insisted that my voice was a high baritone and not a bass, and that I should practice high music, and [I] did in fact begin to carry my voice up to "G." She was right. My voice is much fuller in the higher register and is absurdly weak when I try to sing on the bottom of the bass clef.

On May 15, 1895, Adah came down from Nashville again and after twenty minutes inspection we decided to purchase the house between Fourteenth and Fifteenth Avenues South and fronting on Twentieth Street, owned by Dr. Gillespy. I negotiated with him for a day or two, finally closing the transaction on a basis of $13,000, $3,000 down and the balance over one, two, or three years, the cash down to be paid when the house was delivered to me October 1, as he was then living in it, and notes to bear interest from that date. Five hundred dollars on account thereof [was] to be paid on the signature of the contract to bind it. At this time I only had $300 available in bank and borrowed $200 until the end of the month from George B. McCormack so as to make my first purchase and bind the transaction. I had no money but I had plenty of nerve at that time, and this was an excellent purchase for the place is reasonably worth $50,000 today [1916].

In the spring of 1895 the condition of business began to improve. We had gone through a year and three-quarters of most distressing conditions since the Democratic success in the autumn of 1892 with the infliction of their free silver and free trade policies upon the country. But the natural energies of at that time 70 million American people could not be held down indefinitely, and the pot began to boil again.

I have heard of a Jewish rabbi whose congregation in Germany wanted to give him a housewarming, and it was agreed that each member should go to the house with a bottle of wine and empty it into the rabbi's wine cask. After they had finished a pitcherful was drawn and they began to serve it around so that they might sample the composite wine. One after another tasted, looked a little oddly, and passed it on to the next. By degrees looks broadened into smiles and smiles into a hearty guffaw of laughter. Each one of the economical and thoughtful Jews had decided that if he put a bottle of water in it would not be noticed but would blend with the wine. So that they got about 200 or 300 bottles of water, and the consequence was a failure. So with the iron trade. As soon as business began to improve each owner of a blast furnace thought he could put it to work and it would never be noticed among all the others. So before the country had time to recover from its panic, it was broken, so far as pig iron was concerned, under the weight of production.

I had the idea that I could make money that year, that things were going up, and I started in by trying to buy some TCI stock, but after the experience of the last two years my brokers refused to buy me any except on actual cash margins, so I bought 500 shares through the Hanover National Bank on the security of my South Pittsburgh pipe works stock, paying an average price of 29¼. I was so confident prices were going up that I recommended my associates in the pipe works to buy heavily of pig iron, which they did and made good money on it.

We began now to have a little easier sledding. With the advancing prices of pig iron the banks began to offer us 6 percent money instead of 8 or 12 percent. In other words they were no longer afraid of our immediate failure. On June 7 we advanced prices another twenty-five cents and sold 12,500 tons at the advanced price. DeBardeleben told me he had proposed to the executive committee that he would build a steelworks at Bessemer and sell it to us at cost and 10 percent profit, taking our bonds in payment. This certainly looked as though we would get a steelworks at Bessemer, and I felt greatly encouraged and bought 500 more shares of TCI.

On July 15, 1895, the New York *Herald* developed a savage two-column "bear" attack on TCI stock, which dropped 3½ points.

New York *Herald*:

If the Stock Exchange authorities do not desire that the public should "keep out of Wall Street," they should make going into Wall Street as safe as possible by stopping all blind pool gambling and striking from its lists the securities of every concern that refuses to make intelligible and businesslike statements of its finances. Even when such statements are made there is risk enough and to spare; for they can be skillfully adjusted so as to create a false impression upon those who look at them superficially. A great many foolish and reckless people who go into Wall Street to speculate would not take the trouble to examine such statements if they were made. They are gamblers, pure and simple, and nothing can be done—nothing should be done—to protect them. A striking illustration of the extent to which this class can be influenced by mere market manipulation and by the circulation of street rumors and will fail to search for information that is at hand, may be seen in the recent course of an industrial company that publishes a fairly full annual report in pamphlet form, albeit not very widely distributed— namely, the Tennessee Coal, Iron and Railroad Company.

About the first of February Tennessee Coal [and Iron] . . . was selling under $14 a share. Since then, aided by the improvement in the iron industry, its manipulators have marked it up to nearly three times that figure—it left off on Saturday round $37. The advance in its market valuation is about $4,500,000, a sum equal to the entire earnings of the company for a period of seven or eight years. Early in the rise reports were circulated that the company had contracted for the sale of its output of months ahead. Then, as the price of pig iron advanced from time to time, enormous prospective profits for Tennessee Coal were figured out, and it was rumored that dividends on the preferred stock, which were suspended two years ago, would be resumed, and now there is talk about a dividend being earned on the common stock "if" pig iron only advances to a high enough price. . . .

In the spring of [1886] the shares of the company were introduced on the Stock Exchange, starting about 38, and the first big deal was made. The share capital was then $3,000,000 and the bonded debt less than $1,000,000. In the fall it was announced the company had bought the Pratt properties in Alabama. The Tennessee Coal stock was then concentrated in the hands of the insiders, and in connection with this purchase they made a magnificent market for it. The capital stock was trebled and $1,000,000 of bonds issued, and shareholders of record on December 22 were given "rights" to subscribe for the bonds at par and get a bonus of $3,000,000 in new shares—a stock dividend of 100 per cent. The public bit. The stock in December sold at 118 and then, in the same month, at 37 and ½, "ex rights." Flushed with success, the insiders created some more "rights"—namely, to subscribe to shares of the Ensley Land Company. . . .

Then came a master stroke, which gave some color to these glowing estimates—a dividend of $1 a share on the stock was declared and paid—the first and last in its history. The stockholders had scarcely got this dollar into their pockets when it was juggled out again, and by the same old expedient—more paper and more "rights." An issue of $1,000,000 of preferred stock was made, and stockholders were given the right to subscribe and take it on surrendering $840,000 of their common stock and $657,000 cash. By giving back his $1 and about $6 more in cash, the stockholder got a new piece of paper on his own property.

The next big deal was made in 1892, when the properties of the DeBardeleben Coal and Iron Company and of the Cahaba Coal Company were purchased. In connection with this, the company increased its common stock from $9,000,000 to $20,000,000, paying the $11,000,000 of the new stock for the properties in question, besides assuming $4,100,000 of their bonds. By this the Tennessee company got a lot more lands, of which it had already an ample supply, and seven more or less antiquated blast furnaces. . . .

To make a long story short, it may be noted that the earnings of the whole property last year were less than a third of the "official statement's" estimate for 1888, although the bonded debt meanwhile had been doubled and the capital stock more than doubled. The dividends on the preferred stock are cumulative at eight per cent, and although it takes but $80,000 a year for this, it is now two years in arrears. In fact, if proper charges were made it would appear that the company has never earned the interest on its present bonded debt. The official report for the year ended January 31, 1895—they did not sell $800,000 of Treasury bonds that year—admits a deficit of $68,000 on interest requirements, and this after charging $107,000 to capital account and $182,057 to a "surplus account" which has run up to $386,553.

The report also shows a net floating debt of about $1,000,000. In his report for 1893 Mr. Bowron, the secretary and treasurer, remarks that the bookkeeping "surplus," carried along from year to year, was not in divisible shape, but represented improvements to property and formally asked permission to "write off all or a large part of this sum in lieu of depreciation or reduction of capital valuation," and adds, "Nothing has been done in this way for the past three years." He has also been permitted to charge off a little, but by no means a large part, of it. It is this property, with a lot of antiquated furnaces and depreciated plant, which will require enormous expenditure to put [it] in efficient order.

Bowron, Baxter, and Shook responded to the story with a categorical denial that TCI watered its stock, falsified its reports, or operated "antiquated" furnaces. However much truth there was in the Herald *story, it appears to have had little effect on TCI policy.*

Believing that a man never gets poorer by taking a profit, I decided to sell the 1,000 shares I had bought through the Hanover Bank, which had cost me an average of about 29½, and I sold them from 44 to 46, making a profit of about $14,290 on the transaction, which enabled me to pay for the house which I had bought six months previously. I think I was justified in this transaction, buying stock when it was down at the bottom and after two years of serious depression. This of course placed my affairs in a much more satisfactory condition.

Having sold the stock under my own control I . . . wrote Mr. Baxter urging and insisting that he should either sell my 900 shares for my account or send the actual stock to me.[2] I got a letter from him in reply intimating that he would make a claim on me for the share of profits he might have made if he had not carried stock for me with his own credit or collateral. As a matter of fact, he did not. I gave him my notes at the beginning secured by pipe works stock and paid 10 percent interest to Mr. Inman for discounting them and paid the notes in full, and was now entitled to my stock. This placed me in the distressing position of having strained relations with my president. In

September 1895 I had a long and friendly conversation with Baxter in which he offered to sell the stock as soon as he paid for his, and I was to allow him one-fourth of the profit for his having taken care of the matter. As a matter of fact if he had let me manage it myself I would have made twice as much money, and I may as well say that he did not sell it, and after repeated urging and demands on my part I found months afterwards that he had not got it. It had been mixed with his own affairs and lost sight of.

On December 20, 1895, came [President Cleveland's] Venezuelan war panic. TCI [went] down to 24, Louisville and Nashville [Railroad] to 40. Inman had been proposing to buy 150,000 tons of iron and Gurnee had been proposing to lend us $100,000 on pig iron as collateral. Both of them now withdrew these proposals. We decided to blow out two furnaces and reduce the miners' wages five cents per ton. These were the first effects of the war panic. On January 2, 1896, I was informed that before Cleveland's belligerent attack against England Mr. Gurnee was willing to have put $1 million into a steelworks for us.

Instead of lending us money, Mr. Gurnee wrote that he would want all his loans paid off that month. Mr. Inman wrote that his firm and the Bank of America would want all their money that month. These loans aggregated between them about three-quarters of a million dollars. I had about as much chance to pay them off as I had to jump over the house. On January 15 Mr. Inman, who controlled all our affairs with his little finger, put up his rate to 9 percent on his firm's loans, seeing that we could not pay them. Baxter [was] not coming near the office on account [of] negotiating street railroad matters. Our two vice-presidents [were] away. No one [was] present to sign payroll checks. My troubles were numerous. At the same time the president of the Sloss Company broke loose cutting prices heavily. This induced buyers to retire from the market. At the same time the Ohio Falls Iron Works of New Albany, Indiana, failed owing us $6,000. Failures were increasing and several of the smaller furnaces began to blow out.

On January 22 the executive committee in New York wrote suggesting that the publication of our earnings [be] held back to allow speculation by those having advance information. [A] resolution was also passed asking on how many days President Baxter had been in the office recently. [They asked] also for particulars of the debt to us by his brother for the use of convicts in building the Tennessee Central Railroad. It really seems impossible to understand how he managed to hold onto his position, but he did manage, and as I had his work to do it made my position very much harder.

[While] preparing for our annual meeting I found to my distress that the working capital of the company had been reduced one-quarter of a million dollars during the year by the incessant expenditures upon the property. I told President Baxter that the company was in a perilous condition financially. On February 24, whilst paying 10 percent to Mr. Inman, the chairman of our executive committee, who should have helped our credit, I succeeded in borrowing more than $80,000 in other directions at 8 percent. I told [Baxter] that I could not bear the nervous strain of running the finances without any working capital. I was lying awake at night many nights after 2:00 A.M., and I must have relief or quit. He said he would stop the capital expenditure and keep it stopped or he would quit. Unfortunately he made many such promises but never kept any of them.

I found that Baxter was still making drafts against the company in respect of unearned salary and having Colonel Shook to accept them in the name of the company, of which transactions there was no record on the company's books nor any authority for them. I wrote John Inman . . . and requested him to have it stopped. On May 6 James T. Woodward arrived here and I showed him the drafts, having received a telegram from Inman to do so, and Woodward said Baxter's resignation was the only course open to him. [He said] that it was an open scandal that Mr. Baxter should stay away from here and neglect our business. Inman [wrote] that Baxter was insolvent and that he recommended me to take legal proceedings against him if I thought it would be of any use. He also ask[ed] for my opinion as to the suitability of George McCormack to succeed him. As I had been doing all of Baxter's work for the past two or three years, I was naturally disappointed that Mr. Inman thought nothing of me, but I cordially recommended McCormack for the position. On May 14 [when] President Baxter [made] a draft on the company for salary, although he was already paid in advance to the middle of June, I wired the executive committee for instructions and received a reply forbidding the payment.

As this seemed to bring matters to a head, I felt compelled to write Baxter demanding delivery of my stock or payment for it, and threatening legal proceedings. Of course this was a very painful position for me to assume with my immediate superior officer. On May 27 Mr. Baxter arrived, and I had a long personal conversation with him, and he explained where and how he had lost nearly $400,000 in the past four years and threw himself upon the "mercy of the court." So I relinquished all my claim for the profit that would have come to me if he had sold the stock as he might have done at my request. This stock cost me about 19 in 1893, and I sold my own in 1895 at 46, so if he had sold it at that time as I asked him to do I would have made about $24,000 on the transaction. I, however, told him that we had worked together for many years and I was not a man to trample down one of my associates when he was in trouble. I would agree to cancel the entire transaction and simply let it stand as though I had lent him the money to be repaid with 6 percent interest, and he could just make me his note for the amount to be paid as and when he was able. He was very grateful.

On June 4 Baxter returned [from New York] saying the executive committee would do nothing to help the company and that we must "scuffle through" if we could. Instead of helping us, Inman wrote demanding more margin on his loans secured by pig iron, and I could only write him that we had not got it. At this time the Louisville and Nashville Railroad, which was always exercising a benevolent and paternal control over the district, helped us by renewing $30,000 of our notes given in payment for freights. On June 29, after great and strenuous efforts with our customers, I succeeded in getting notes from enough of them in advance of due periods of settlement to meet our July 1 interest, and so we bumped over that rock without foundering, which had seemed impossible.

The Democrats, who never learn anything, finished their national convention in Chicago and, heedless of the fearful panic of 1893 on the free silver proposition, they again at the invitation of the silver-tongued orator from Nebraska, William Jennings Bryan, adopted a free silver platform, refusing to endorse President Cleveland's administration. This was immediately reflected by the renewal of the free silver panic of 1893. The very same day the Mechanics' Bank in New York refused us any further discounts. The Populists followed two or three days later endorsing the free silver ticket. TCI stock which had been 26 in June, only six weeks before, dropped to 15. Our Chicago note brokers turned down sale of paper and things tightened weekly. On July 20 large amounts of gold [were] drawn and stocks fell heavily, TCI to 13. Gurnee wir[ed] for iron to cover his $50,000 loan, and we had [no iron]. My millionaire boss, Mr. Inman, wired me to try to cover the August 1 interest as it would be a "card" for me. We tried to place a note of the Carnegie Steel Company for $17,891 in Pittsburgh and offered 15 percent to discount it and could not sell it.

With the greatest possible difficulty I covered the August 1 interest, the Hanover Bank refusing the commercial paper we had sent there for discount, but Inman protected [it]. The situation becoming still more strained, the Chicago Stock Exchange was closed. [There was] additional panic in New York, and banks [failed] in other directions, including New Orleans. On August 6 our strongest Birmingham bank requested that we reduce our loans secured by pig iron from $25,000, and I responded by threatening to put out four or five blast furnaces and corresponding coal and ore mines and to throw 5,000 men out of work, on which they withdrew the request. We were again helped by the Louisville and Nashville Railroad as we could not meet our note to them for $30,000 in cash. It accepted commercial paper in lieu.

On August 14 we made our record low water sale. We had not made the Pratt Mines payroll for July, which should have been made on or about July 20, and it is marvelous that our men continued to work. There was no earthly chance of our getting $30,000 for it in any other way, and we sold . . . 5,000 tons of Number Two foundry at $6.20 per ton spot cash, the iron to be piled separately on a piece of ground to be leased to the buyer. We followed this by the sale of a cargo . . . Number Four foundry [iron], to Japan at $5.75 per ton at the works. I think these were the lowest.

On September 5 politicians began to predict the defeat of Bryan and the free silver ticket, and we began to place some commercial paper again with our banks. But we made our payrolls for August on that date [only] by McCormack advancing $7,000 out of his personal savings and I $2,000, at 6 percent and without security. September 7 seemed to mark a turn in the tide, and we sold over 20,000 tons of iron and advanced prices fifteen to twenty cents and placed a $15,000 Carnegie note in Pittsburgh at 8 percent. On September 16 our August earnings showed a deficiency of $10,169, less than our interest, on account of the low-priced sales of pig iron. On the following day, after the publication of the worst earnings we had ever had, stock rose to 20½, which shows the folly of supposing that stock prices on the exchange are governed primarily by the intrinsic merits and values of the concerns.

I [had] word that Mr. Inman was sick at Saratoga. As a matter of fact he died there [on November 3] and never returned to business. He was on the younger side of middle age, tall, well built, a strong man of splendid brain power, and should have made a great figure in this country. He had everything apparently in his favor, but I think he burnt himself out with overwork and too great ambition. Such things seem pitiful. I do not know why he never seemed to take any interest in me and blocked the efforts of other directors to advance my position several times. I was sorry that this was his attitude.

Walter Gurnee wrote that he wished his advances reduced. The Louisville and Nashville Railroad was carrying us at this time on our notes for about $120,000, and its chairman, August Belmont, wrote to Baxter to come to New York to . . . give him assurances of the payment of said notes. I went at

Baxter's request to New York and saw Belmont, who said the traffic department was too eager for business and could not be trusted to watch credits.
They had taken control in New York, and credits were to be cut off, and we
were to make cash settlements in future, and were to pay the notes as they
fell due. As a matter of fact I did pay the notes as they fell due, but I did not
pay the open accounts, as I took the credit without asking him for it.

James Woodward was furious and said we ought to shut down both furnaces and mines and break the Louisville and Nashville Railroad. [He said]
that their railroad was hard up, and they had asked him to discount our
notes. His vice-president [at the Hanover Bank inferred] . . . that he could
get our paper for nothing if he needed it. I offered to bet him $25,000 that
TCI had never made a bogus note to anybody. They took it all back and
came as near to apologizing as it was possible for them. It was the worst
bulldozing crowd in that bank that I ever encountered in my life.

Believing that with the impending Republican victory and the defeat of
free silver there would be a large advance in stocks, I again committed the
imprudence of making a large purchase on borrowed money, buying 1,000
shares each through the Hanover National Bank and Moore and Schley.
These purchases rang[ed] from 29¾ to 32, and within two years, carrying it
all that time paying never less than 6 percent interest upon it, I had the
satisfaction of seeing it quoted at 19.

On November 3 [we] witnessed an overwhelmingly Republican victory, a
general landslide. Banks [took] all the commercial paper that we had. Gold
pour[ed] into the treasury. Cables and telegrams in all directions ask[ed] for
iron at low prices. Another bank in New York restored usual discount
arrangements, and the bank in Cincinnati revoked its request for payment
of its loans and wrote us that it would willingly increase them.

On account of Inman's death, [we] received formal notice from Inman
Swann and Company to pay off all loans as they matured. At this time we
owed his firm more than $600,000. On November 16, my birthday, I [was]
in New York borrowing money in different directions and commencing to
pay off the Inman loans. On December 14 I originated what I had never
heard of before, and what is now constantly done in every direction, namely,
the practice of borrowing on open accounts receivable. By assigning both
the pig iron and coal accounts receivable I borrowed about $350,000, partly
from the Hanover Bank and partly from Walter Gurnee, with which to pay
off the Inman loans.

Everything looked as though we were going to get on our feet again, and
right there came another stumbling block in another stock panic in New

York on December 18, on account of the Senate committee reporting a resolution to acknowledge Cuban independence. Of course anyone who knew anything about Spain knew that it was a third-class power and not to be feared, but this country had been so long out of war that the very thought of such a thing sent cold shivers down the backs of capitalists. Banks began to fail in Chicago and St. Paul. Mr. Gurnee began to be scared about his loans the previous week.

My stock that I had just bought at an average of 31 was down to 24, so there was $14,000 apparent loss in a month. To cheer myself up I sang in the *Messiah* at St. Mary's Church, the first performance I believe in Birmingham, with an audience of 485 people. We were a small but ambitious crowd. We had six sopranos, five altos, four tenors, and six bassos. I am counted as one of the latter, although my voice is nearer tenor than bass.

I had bought a billiard table ten feet by five feet with pool pockets from the Brunswick Balke Company for $240, and set this up in the house, and for several years thereafter I derived immense pleasure from it, and so do my children to this day. I . . . have the satisfaction of having made the highest record score on it at English billiards that has ever been made on it since it was put up. It is a game that I strongly recommend as a game of skill with some element of chance. It is a sociable game where almost any number may join and they may be chatting. Conversation does not interfere with the game.

On December 25, 1896, between tennis on the court in the morning with six sons participating at once, all players, music in the house, and billiards in the evening, we had a very happy Christmas day.

On April 19, 1897, [came] the outbreak of the Turco-Greek War. It should have had nothing to do with our affairs, but it knocked our stock to 19½. I had been carrying stock since the autumn of 1896, having got it then at an average of 31. Here was an apparent loss of about $25,000 in seven months besides the money which I had paid out in interest for carrying it. Oh! How foolish. I realized that if we had the money and the working capital we could pull through, and that sooner or later these times would change. But the question was whether the company could stand it, and whether I could stand it.

On April 23 the railroads notified us that they would help by a reduction in freight rates of two and one-half cents per ton on red ore and coke, and ten cents on limestone. In a conference . . . of furnace men and railroad men, President Smith of the Louisville and Nashville Railroad told us that low freight rates alone would not save this district from bankruptcy. [He said that] we must have steelworks here, and also have cheaper coal. [We should] reduce the mining rate and stand a strike if necessary. He then decided to reduce pig iron rates . . . fifty cents to help the situation somewhat further. We asked the miners to make a concession to prevent the mines closing down. Our Pratt miners voted in favor of it, Blue Creek and Blocton against it.

At this point, James T. Woodward encouraged us by saying that we could have plenty of capital to run the business . . . whenever we established confidence [in our management]. I wrote him back that if I had not established confidence in the twenty years I had been in this country, and practically [as long in TCI's] service, I would rather pull out and quit and establish [confidence] somewhere else.

Bowron to Woodward, April 28, 1897:

In the 15 years that I have been in this Company's service, there has never been a period of two months that I have been free from the gravest anxiety and care. I have had to contend with successive Boards of Directors and administrations whose anxiety has been to create new securities, water the stock, water the bonds, and provide enormous charges to be met, and to order continuous expansion in the way of new construction or acquisition of property by purchase with floating debts upon the same, and there has never on one occasion in the 15 years been any provision made for the floating debt of any property so purchased by us and taken over. I have done as much as any one living man can do working by day and lying awake at night studying and planning and sweating blood from my heart's core in this Company's service; and if it is now necessary for the gentlemen who are absent to "be convinced that the spirit referred to was abroad"; namely, the spirit of economy and conscientious service on my part, then I want to step down and out. . . .

It is not any spirit of indifference on the part of the Company's officers . . . that makes our business to-day unsatisfactory or our condition one of embarrassment from day to day. It is the simple fact that . . . the Company's bonded debt has been at times unduly expanded and a load of interest has been left for us to meet which it taxes all our ability and ingenuity to meet in these times of unprecedented difficulty and scanti-

ness of margins much as the industrial world has had to face for the
past four years.

Mr. Woodward with two other of our important directors came down from
New York to look over the situation on the spot, and expressed their desire
and intention to help us. Woodward said to me, "The company will pull
through," and deprecated my talking finances to the others. Of course this
was encouraging, [except that] I had already closed out my stock. In late May
I had sold within the next few days half of my TCI stock from 21½ to 22,
thus at least stopping interest [payments], and on May 3 sold the remainder
at 19½.

As if I had not enough trouble and anxiety I was called into consultation
by my physician . . . who told me that I was on the very verge of an alarming
illness caused by mental strain and worry. I was threatened with diabetes.
He prescribed mental rest, sea bathing, and exercise. How was I possibly
to get them? If I had left for a week the company would have gone to protest.
I was cut off from bread and all starchy foods and limited to fish, eggs,
cheese, salads, and green vegetables. There I was: worry driving me into
illness, and the prospect of possibly a dangerous illness and early death leaving my affairs involved and my large and young family inadequately provided
for. [This] increas[ed] my care apart from the seemingly hopeless condition
of the company.

On June 10, having sold 6,000 tons of pig iron with orders for about
16,000 tons in front of us and offers of loans in New York and Cincinnati at
6 percent, and my doctor telling me that analysis showed my condition distinctly improving, I took heart and bought 1,000 shares of our stock at 22½,
which . . . I had sense enough to sell at varying prices over the next ensuing
ninety days ranging from 28¾ to 35, so that I recovered in that ninety days
about $10,000 of the loss previously made, and this helped things very much.
It is an old adage and a good one that a man never gets poorer by taking a
profit. If you see a reasonable profit take it. Don't outstay your market.

In 1895, on the belief of George McCormack that he could make basic
iron, we had commenced experiments in the Alice furnace. It had always
been supposed that our Alabama pig was too silicious for use in the basic
furnace and that we could not get the silicon down in the blast furnace
without carrying so large a burden of lime as to make the furnace cold and
the cinder pasty. [That would result in] a lime-set and [we would have to]
have the furnace scaffolded. The discovery however of large bodies of mag-
nesian or dolomitic stone in East Birmingham . . . seemed to solve the ques-

tion, as its use in the furnace would give a more liquid cinder and allow the carrying of a burden heavy enough to hold down the silicon without the furnace sticking. On August 22, 1895, we made our first sale of 500 tons of basic iron at $9.25. On August 30 we sold to the Carnegie Steel Company 25,000 tons subject to trial of the first 1,000. On September 4 we sold 20,000 tons of basic iron to the Illinois Steel Company.

In December 1897 Milton H. Smith came down and . . . had a long heart-to-heart conversation with Mr. Baxter. He said that the Birmingham district was practically "broke," and that it could not go on any longer selling half its pig iron at the bare cost of manufacture with no allowance for depreciation, wearing out of plants, and exhaustion of minerals. [He said] that the Louisville and Nashville Railroad had $15 million invested in the Birmingham district and that if the district collapsed with all its very heavy traffic, it would be ruinous to the Louisville and Nashville. He said it was the duty of TCI, as the largest local enterprise, to lead the way into the manufacture of steel, and that he had come to say to us that if we would not do so the Louisville and Nashville Railroad, which was already a stockholder in the Birmingham Rolling Mill, would put enough additional money into that concern to enable it to go ahead.

He and I and McCormack had a long conversation on the subject. McCormack proposed that he [McCormack] and I and [Erskine] Ramsay, Shook, and Baxter should each subscribe $10,000. With this $50,000 signed we would then go to the people of Birmingham and ask them to subscribe another $50,000. Then with $100,000 so subscribed we would go to the Louisville and Nashville Railroad and Southern Railroad and ask them to subscribe a similar amount. With that money we would put a small plant up, small as to the number of its units, but modern as in their size and capacity, where we could deliver molten pig iron very cheaply, and with the profits earned expand the plant unit by unit.

Colonel Shook had come back from New York with the answer of the executive committee that the company would not go into the manufacture of steel. It had no money for the purpose. But . . . the officers were authorized to subscribe to the capital stock of the Birmingham Rolling Mill Company $100,000 . . . to assist that company in enlarging its steel equipment. I . . . wrote a careful and thoughtful letter to James T. Woodward . . . pointing out the impossibility of securing now or at any time in the future sufficient orders for pig iron to keep all our furnaces in operation. Our plants were running down, and we had no money or prospects of any with which to rebuild them. If we had to sell pig iron and nothing else . . . we would drag along at the tail end of the procession instead of being at the head as our size and property ownership would suggest. I wound up the letter with the thinly veiled sarcasm that "knowing our directors to be busy men we wished to say that if they would turn the officers loose we would build a steel plant ourselves and find the money with which to do it."

The executive committee . . . answered [that they were] willing to "turn the officers loose" and would welcome very hospitably any plan for the construction of the steelworks which we could suggest, bearing in mind that the company had no money available for that purpose. We held a conference of officers and decided to proceed on the basis of a plant to handle 400 tons of furnace metal per day at a cost of $500,000 for construction and $200,000 for working capital. M. H. Smith gave general assent to our proposal . . . for the Louisville and Nashville Railroad to subscribe $200,000. He required a preliminary report from Wellman Seaver and Company[3] on which he would go to Mr. Belmont. Wellman [estimated] $609,000 as the probable cost, including a rail mill, or $419,000 if confined to a billet plant. The only trouble about this estimate was that we [ultimately] spent $1,800,000 on the billet plant, and I do not know how much the rail mill cost. Wellman said in his report that he knew no place in the world where steel could be made so cheaply as at Ensley. This was encouraging to the Louisville and Nashville Railroad. We had an extended interview with President Samuel Spencer of the Southern Railroad. Mr. Spencer was a competent engineer himself, and he very quickly saw through everything we laid before him, and agreed to recommend [to] J. P. Morgan and Company to subscribe as much toward the enterprise for the Southern Railroad as August Belmont would subscribe for the Louisville and Nashville.

Belmont agreed to the Louisville and Nashville subscribing $100,000, but we [said] that was not adequate and that we could not build a plant on the necessary scale on that basis. Baxter . . . said Belmont's enthusiasm was a little chilled by the alleged fact that the Birmingham Rolling Mill was not making money on its steel, and I was asked to go to New York and generally warm up and encourage things. On April 4 I met our [board], and Walter S. Gurnee . . . said they "would do nothing." I protested and said if the directors would let us alone we would build a smaller plant, say $350,000, without help from them. He was mollified and said he would help. The venerable old man was very feeble, being approximately ninety years of age. Gurnee . . . made his huge fortune in the inception of the Chicago, Milwaukee, and St. Paul Railroad, of which he had some $2,500,000 underlying 7 percent bonds as a nest egg. He probably also profited from the growth of real estate in Chicago, of which he was mayor somewhere around 1850. At this age and in the condition of his health he was subject to the influence of his family and of his attorney. None of them liked us very much. The sinking fund for the Cahaba bonds [for which TCI had gained responsibility in the 1892 takeover of Cahaba Coal] was heavily overdue, and his attorney was insisting that he should have $100,000 paid on that before he subscribed to the steelworks.

On April 27 our executive committee adopted the report of the special steel committee and authorized the construction of a steelworks at Ensley on the basis of $1,100,000 capitalization. The Louisville and Nashville Railroad [held] us up wanting to impose conditions before it would sign for its $200,000 subscription. Rogers Brown and Company [was] willing to sign for $50,000 [only] if we would give them our foreign agency. On April 30 they wired from New York that the $1,100,000 could not be completed unless we got $150,000 subscriptions here in Birmingham, which McCormack and I worked up within the following two days, I myself making the largest subscription on it, $25,000, which was something entirely beyond my means. I was only able to do it by selling other things.

On June 27 Baxter left for New York to see if it was possible to straighten out the Gurnee demand that was holding back the completion of the steelworks syndicate. We owned some Cahaba bonds which would have been available for the sinking fund, but we naturally had money borrowed on them. The bank agreed to take pig iron as collateral in lieu, thus freeing the bonds. On June 30, this having been carried out satisfactorily, and [our] depositing certain pig iron warrants with Gurnee worth $10,000 as security to carry out our promise, Gurnee signed the syndicate agreement. I officially announced the completion of the deal and the intention to build the steelworks. On July 14 ground was broken at Ensley for the steelworks. All of my work in connection with committing TCI and the entire Birmingham district to the production of steel was then and there, after six years of unremitting effort, successfully accomplished. On Thanksgiving Day 1899 we poured the first heat of steel at Ensley, about twenty-three tons. This was an eventful day for Alabama.

I attended the [1897] meeting of the South Pittsburgh Pipe Works and . . . all officers [were] reelected, including myself as president. We declared a dividend making up 20 percent for the past year, and our quick assets showed five times the amount of our liabilities. As a matter of business the success of this small compact company under my own guidance was a great comfort to me at this time. I had $30,000 invested in it, which had been increased to $60,000 by the declaration of stock dividend, and it was on this latter amount that we were paying 20 percent. What a contrast this was: small capitalization and compact management [against] a large concern [TCI] with watered capital and various factions in the management.

In April 1898 a committee from the Chattanooga and Bessemer pipe works brought in for approval a consolidation scheme for the four southern pipe works, Bessemer, Chattanooga, Anniston, and South Pittsburgh, and we all signed it subject to ratification by our respective boards. In disposing of that matter for all time and reviewing my connection with the pipe trade, first under George Downing's management and later under my own, my books show that I made a profit of about $25,800 on the final liquidation of this investment over and above the cash that I had previously invested. This . . . [paid] no attention to the dividends, which at that time had for some years averaged 14 or 15 percent on an investment that had been issued by stock dividend, so this was equivalent to 25 or 30 percent on the original investment. It was one of the most satisfactory business transactions I ever had or was connected with—small in capitalization, free from bonds, with economical management. Unfortunately, my success in this enterprise led me into a much larger investment under different management and with disastrous results, as will appear hereafter.

In February 1898 the representatives of seven furnace companies gathered together to form a combination for maintaining equal prices, and after two days session we agreed, but when our papers were drawn our counsel, Walker Percy, declared the arrangement was contrary to the [Sherman] Anti-Trust Act and must be dropped. The United States is the only civilized country that maintains this attitude and insists that unrestricted competition is best for the nation. The consequence is, so far as the iron trade is concerned in the South, that the country resembles a wreck chart, and the map is dotted all over with records of tragedies. I am safe in saying that two blast furnaces and rolling mill projects out of three since the Civil War have failed financially. Enormous loss has been suffered in the holding back of enterprise. If these concerns had been allowed to maintain living prices instead of cutting each other's throats and going into bankruptcy, they would have made money. [They also] would have developed districts, built towns, extended railroads, enlarged bank deposits, employed workmen, branched out into subsidiary enterprises, advertised their sections, provided markets for the country producers and small-town merchants, and thus the states would have been greatly enriched. This is the policy which made Germany before the cataclysmal war [World War I] the close competitor of Great Britain in manufacturing and shipping.

In May 1899, on the strong recommendation of my warm friend Archer Brown, of Rogers Brown and Company, in whom I had the utmost confidence, I agreed to take $25,000 with him in the Empire Steel and Iron Company, which he was busy organizing. This was based on an unsound principle, namely, the tying together of scatter[ed] plants . . . , some of them hundreds of miles apart, all of them old, requiring new machinery and equipment. That was a highly speculative time when the idea was to recapitalize things, sell, and get out at a profit. I did finally do so. I put in all $35,000 into his syndicate and over the course of the next eight years I finally sold out all of it at a profit of $4,834. I would have made more money if I had lent the money on mortgage at straight 6 percent interest. It does not pay to tie up a lot of old properties together.

On June 14 Baxter and Shook arrived, and after discussion with McCormack and myself we accepted the offer of the Sheffield Iron Company $850,000 spot cash for the purchase of all its property. This gave us nineteen blast furnaces. Viewed in the light of calm, sober afterthought, it was a mistake, because there was not sufficient trade or demand for foundry iron in the entire country for us to run nineteen furnaces steadily year in and year out.

In June 1898 I attended . . . a meeting of the American Foundry Association and spoke to an audience of 300 foundrymen for one hour extemporaneously, as is my custom, on southern pig iron, its production, quality, and uses, and in some measure on its history. I suppose for that single hour's effort of simply drawing on my knowledge and my memory I obtained more notoriety than for any other one thing I ever did in my life.

Bowron to the American Foundry Association:
How little did I suppose when I came to this country twenty-one years ago and went down in the South . . . that I was coming into the heart of a region which in two decades should supply [iron to] the very country from which I had come. . . . How strange it seems to realize that Birmingham . . . is today the third largest point of export of pig iron in the world—Middlesbrough, England, being the first, Glasgow,

Scotland, the second. . . . Within the eighteen months ending first of January last, there were exported from Birmingham two hundred and ninety-seven thousand tons of pig iron to foreign countries. This iron went to England, Scotland, Wales, Ireland, France, Belgium, Germany, Russia, Denmark, Sweden, Spain, Italy, India, Japan, China and Australia. . . .

Why is it? . . . When you consider the mileage which is involved in the assemblage of materials for the production of iron in other parts of the world . . . you will see the differences. . . . Standing on the top of the water tower, with one of the rifles with which we are making the Spaniards cringe today, you can put a bullet from the top of the blast furnace into the ore mines; you can take a revolver and fire a bullet on to the coke ovens or to the quarries from which the lime is drawn. . . .

A singular delusion swept over this country some years ago which caused a great many people, apparently sane, sober and in [their] right mind, to believe that by the construction of a blast furnace they could turn a cabbage garden or some vacant pine land into an important boulevard of a city, the lots of which were worth at least $1,000 per front foot. So it has transpired that there has been in this country a plethora of blast furnaces, and in the last ten years many of you have derived an advantage at the expense of the creditors of the blast furnaces which have supplied you with pig iron below the cost of production. . . .

The popular delusion about the construction of blast furnaces, necessarily involving a fortune, is responsible for a good many idle furnaces. But the switching off of so large a part of the world's consumption from iron into steel is responsible for a great deal more, and that is a permanent change, and one not only permanent, but increasing. . . . Within the next 30 days, undoubtedly, the papers will be signed which will divert within a year probably one-half of the iron which is now being supplied [to] the Birmingham district [foundries] . . . into the steel works which will be there constructed and there will be a large diminution in the supply of cheap pig iron which is being offered to you from Birmingham district. . . .

I want to draw your attention to this. . . . Suppose you are making stoves or iron pipe, or radiators or sugar machinery, or any other kind of material which can be exported to foreign countries. . . . The distance from Birmingham to the sea coast is only 268 miles. The railroads are liberal . . . I do not know any place in this particular line where a plant can put itself in immediate physical juxtaposition to coal or coke, limestone, pig iron, with a half dozen railroads, with nominal rates of freight to the sea coast for export. . . .

I believe the consensus of opinion of this country is going to lead to a control of the Philippine Islands now that we have them. . . . I believe when we take Puerto Rico we shall keep it. I believe that . . . the insurgents in Cuba, what few of the poor miserable fellows are left after the cruel oppression they have suffered, . . . may find it necessary, for the preservation of order and wealth, and preservation against Spaniards, who remain, to turn it back to us or have an American protectorate. . . . I am confident that the American nation will never again . . . [risk] sending an Atlantic fleet [on] a voyage 13,000 or 14,000 miles . . . [even] if that means the construction of a canal through the isthmus. . . .

I cannot close my eyes to the incident results which will give the Alabama coal fields the control of the Pacific coal trade from San Francisco to Valparaiso, putting steam coal on board at Mobile or Pensacola. . . . There can be no other country which can occupy the Pacific coast as we can, and it will double the value of the Alabama coal fields.

On December 20, 1898, I closed out my last speculative TCI stock which I was carrying, and was out of speculative transactions for the first time in ten years. I sold out sadly too soon, but I was in a condition of such nervous exhaustion and depression from long continued strain that I was compelled to have relief. The highest price at which I sold out was 36. Within the following year the stock rose to 119. I had 3,000 shares in 1897–98, and if I had had nervous strength to carry on another year this stock which I had supported so faithfully for so many years would have brought me a profit of one-quarter of a million dollars. On December 30 I received back from New York the last security of mine that had been held up there as collateral, and closed the year broken down in health, weary and depressed in mind, but comforting myself with the knowledge that I was out of debt. I showed on my books a profit of $23,709 made in that year, and apparently had a credit of $138,939 as the net worth of my estate, but I was not studying so much on the subject of profits. I had borne so long a strain that I was almost at the jumping off point.

I borrowed $100,000 from the Hanover Bank on open accounts receivable, being the only available asset, and James T. Woodward told Colonel Shook that I was a pessimist and a croaker. I wonder what he would have been if he had filled my job. He never had anything to do with me except to lend money on adequate collateral, which money was always repaid with good interest. He made big money by buying the stock when it was low and selling some of it when it was high, and never had a kind word for those who did the work and kept the company out of the hands of receivers.

On December 5, 1899, Mr. Woodward told me that two of our largest stockholders [Walter Gurnee and Cord Meyer] had sold out their TCI stock on the big boom price and wanted to see the stock go down again so that they might buy it in. Meyer . . . told me that he had sold his Tennessee stock at around 120 and that he would buy it again on the fall. He said then there would be [a] crash inside thirty days. He was certainly a splendid prophet. On December 11 TCI stock was 83, on December 18 [it was] down to 61. There was a stock panic in New York owing principally to the trouble in London arising from the successes of the Boers against the English in the South African war.

I looked into the question of our [making] rails . . . and found the Louisville and Nashville Railroad was willing to take all their rails from us for five years at the parity of Pittsburgh or Chicago prices. The Nashville, Chattanooga, and St. Louis and the Central of Georgia were willing to do the same, and the Southern Railway to give half their business to us. This seemed to give us a very fine outlook if we would push our rail mill to completion instead of trying to sell our steel as ingots for which there was no market at all, or as four-inch billets [steel bars] for which there was only a limited market. We authorized the contracts for the rail mill engine and boilers. Our people in New York had been talking to Julian Kennedy[4] of Pittsburgh, who said we ought to spend $800,000 on the mill, and our directors were scared and worried. He was right about it. We never had enough money to work with, either in building or operating. We ought to have raised more and spent more, and then we would have made more.

[On a marketing trip to Europe in April 1900] I had done this: Instead of having one European correspondent, J. Watson and Company at Glasgow . . . I had opened up relations with firms in Berlin, Milan, Paris, and Antwerp for sale of pig iron, steel billets, and steel bare for our account on commission, thus bringing us and our name before the actual consumers. Naturally I could not sell much on any such flying trip where the customers wanted samples. In some cases small sample orders were given, but I had at least roughed out an organization with which to make a start. . . . On June 2

[the] New York directors wired Baxter recommending that I should go back again to Europe for three months, this time to sell our goods.

On my [second] trip of two and a half months I had sold in all 36,500 tons of pig iron on a total expense account, railroad, steamers, hotels, and sundries, [of] $1,152.77, a little more than three cents per ton on the pig iron I had sold as compared with twenty-five cents, the usual agent's commission. So I felt very well satisfied with my journey from a commercial standpoint.

On September 13 I arrived in New York [and] was met by one of our directors, Fred H. Benedict, who was a heavy stockholder and who complained that he could get no information about the company from Mr. Baxter, who did not answer his letters. He and Mr. Boardman, our general counsel, . . . practically took up all of my time, and I told them frankly that the company would never do any good until it was run for its own sake and not run as Mr. Baxter was running it, to please Wall Street!

I attempted to report to President Baxter on my journey, but he took up all my time with his own personal troubles and lawsuits and never asked a single question about my journey. He asked me to take charge of all steel sales as well as pig iron.

BOWRON DIARY, September 19, 1900:
I found finances had been allowed to run into the ground; over 1,000,000 tons of iron and steel on hand, but no money. Not a dollar towards the Pratt payroll day after tomorrow. Deficiency of $200,000 in sight for the month.

I found that the freight accounts were unpaid for two months and all sorts of vouchers in arrears, whereas I had left comfortable working balances in the bank when I went away. I was appalled at the situation and said to my assistant, most trustworthy and resourceful as he was, whilst beads of perspiration stood out on my brow: "Good Heavens! John, how could things have been allowed to run into this condition without attention?" To which he replied: "I told Mr. Baxter thus and so, but he said Mr. Bowron will be home on such a date; leave it to him and he will fix it." I immediately applied to the Hanover Bank for $250,000 loan on securities of the Sheffield Company which we owned. I arranged with the Birmingham Trust Company to renew an arrangement for the issue of storage warrants by them, based on the stock of iron on hand.

In the meantime, owing to the steelworks' losses, Mr. Baxter urged

McCormack and myself to carry them forward as deferred charges, and not show them in the current month's figures. This we declined to do, and on publishing our true figures the TCI stock slumped from 63 to 55. Baxter agreed that we might put out one Oxmoor furnace but would not consent to our putting one out at South Pittsburgh. Neither would he agree to our engaging a traffic man, although I told him my stenographer, good as she was, who had been handling it, was overworked and that a cargo of iron was now on its way to Antwerp without order owing to her being overworked and using the wrong code. I felt greatly discouraged about the situation and the control of the company being in the hands of a man who was so lax and ignorant of its affairs and thoroughly incompetent to fill the position.

I had been gone two and a half months, and had sold 36,500 tons of iron, and had arranged agencies to cover England, France, Belgium, Germany, Sweden, Austria, and Italy for the sale of pig iron, steel, and possibly coal tar and pitch from the by-product plant. During that time [Baxter] had allowed the company to run from a cash basis to one of most serious financial stringency, and yet in the twelve days that I had been at home he never found one hour to discuss with me the affairs of the company! What wonder that I should be grieved and disheartened to the point of despair in working under such conditions! The next day he received some letter from James T. Woodward which nettled him, and he told me that he ought to quit, and that he was working on a street railway deal where he expected to make from $300,000 to $400,000.

I had gotten a letter from Woodward two or three days before this commenting on my having borrowed $250,000 for the company, and saying now that I had so much money to work with he supposed we would run along very comfortably and with large balances. This gave me a text, and I wrote him a straightforward, heart-to-heart letter. I point[ed] out the perfect impossibility of carrying on the company on the existing basis of paying 8 percent dividends on watered stock, whilst practically every dollar of the company's earnings was needed either to pay interest on bonds or to finish the steelworks . . . and the development of the new mines. Either we ought to shut down all construction work, which would be fatal, or the directors should recognize that the completion and development of the steelworks was vital, and stop paying these dividends until we had surplus money with which to pay them. He never acknowledged receipt of the letter.

Woodward wrote that the executive committee would remove the sales department to New York and appoint a new chairman of the executive committee to take charge of it. Benedict wrote me to ask if I would go there and take the appointment and make New York headquarters. I declined on the ground that I was too old and had moved too often. On October 3 one of our directors who never took any active part in our affairs, William Barbour, wrote for me to attend a meeting in New York regarding the employment of an accountant as auditor. I do not know whether they suspected the accuracy of our accounts, but they had good reason to do so, for there was nothing being taken off by way of depreciation, and profits were counted every month on material on assumed selling prices and before it was shipped.

On October 4, after a four-hour session in which TCI stock vibrated up and down six points, the executive committee declared another 2 percent dividend. I only learned of this by rumor from the street. They never had the courtesy to reply to my letter on the subject of finance ... or to ask whether we had the funds available with which to pay such a dividend. I therefore told Baxter, Shook, and McCormack on October 5 that I would resign as treasurer of the company and later dictated a letter stating my inability to run the company's finances without any working capital.

Bowron to Baxter, October 3, 1900:
I presume [the dividend] will be payable November 1, and will require nearly $460,000 in cash to pay it. I do not know how this money is to be provided. The working capital in the business is today not adequate for our requirements, as is shown by the fact that within the past ten days I have been compelled to borrow $375,000, partly from our bankers, and partly from our agents.

I have had the Assistant Treasurer compile an estimate of the receipts for the remainder of the month of October and the necessary routine disbursements. His estimate shows ordinary disbursements on bills payable, interest, workmen's pay rolls, and railroad freights $654,000, with estimated collections from coal, pig iron, bar iron, agents advances, export sterling, and cash on hand $510,000, leaving a deficit to be provided by borrowing of $154,000 [$144,000].

In addition to our routine disbursements within the next 30 to 60 days, we must contemplate payment of Cahaba Sinking Fund $25,000, repayment to agents of advances made in anticipation of collections $75,000; arrears of freight accounts $30,000; total $284,000. To this add the dividend, say $455,000, and it requires the early provision of $739,000. We have already pledged our Sheffield securities with the

Hanover National Bank and our Cahaba bonds with the Birmingham Trust and Savings Company, and we have nothing on hand that would be considered good collateral except our stock of pig iron and steel, and perhaps the stock of the Bessemer Rolling Mill. . . .

I do not know where to obtain these large sums of money. No part of it could be obtained from our banks locally as their loans are already full, and they are trying to reduce them. So far as I see the money could only be obtained in New York, and I do not know any one who would lend it there in advance of the delivery of the collateral. . . . Even this however will not represent the position of the Company, because the improvements that are going on, according to an estimate I have obtained from the General Manager including the completion of the rail mill, soaking pits, coke ovens, coal and ore mines, gas producers, etc. will require $471,000, and this amount which will be required over the next six or seven months is more than the present apparent surplus earnings of the Company after payment of its fixed charges. . . .

I have handled the finances of the Company for 18 years and have always in some way or another seen my way through. But in the present condition of affairs, with an empty treasury at the present moment, an amount of collateral that is not quickly available, and a large amount of expenditures that are necessary to complete work that is already in hand, I cannot see the way to provide the amount of this dividend, or if provided, then I cannot see the way to handle the finances of the Company during the next ensuing months without working capital, without incurring some default and some discredit.

I believe therefore that it would be better for some one else to undertake the solution of this problem, and for that purpose I hereby tender you my resignation of the office of Treasurer of this Company to take effect on the election by the Directors of my successor, or at an earlier date if you should think fit to anticipate their meeting.

On October 8 I received a telegram from Woodward asking me to withdraw my letter for the present, and I authorized it to be withheld for two days. On October 12, in response to Mr. Woodward's request, I went to his country home between Washington and Baltimore and spent the day with him. I denounced the malversation of accounts and padding of earnings to make things look pleasant. I asked him what he would do if the Hanover Bank kept accounts that way, and he said "he would drop dead." He said the directors were my friends and had treated me kindly personally, which I admitted. It would hurt them by the depreciation of their stock if I were to resign at the present time, having been so many years with the company. It would attract attention and cause comment. He requested me to withdraw my resignation and let the thing rock along until the spring meeting and election of new directors and officers, at which time people were always ready for changes. I could drop out on the ground of ill health, and it would attract no attention.

I agreed to this, and he agreed in return that no more dividends should be declared and that he would borrow for us $300,000 in New York to assist in straightening out the situation. He asked me to get up a scheme for financing the company, and I outlined a plan which he approved and which was afterwards actually carried out for the issue of a new fifty-year, 5 percent refunding bond issue for $15 million with all existing physical properties and securities behind it. I told him Baxter was a good trader and that he should move him to New York in charge of sales there, and make McCormack president. He asked what I would do, and I told him that I had enough to live on and had been working then for forty-two years without a stop and was willing to quit and rest.

Bowron to Albert Boardman [TCI director and corporate counsel], November 20, 1900:

Since I have taken over the finances of the Company as a whole in 1882 (which consisted of an overdraft), there has never been a time down to the present, except during two boom periods for intervals of a few months, when the administration of the Treasury has been free from a great nervous strain. I am only known in the South by the creditors of the Company as a man who does not pay their accounts promptly. I have had to stand the personal odium, the reproaches, and the occasional insults of angry creditors who have waited for their money anywhere from four to eight months after it was due. I have had to give my personal endorsements and have been under liabilities for the Company for as much as $1,000,000 at a time when the Company seemed to be in imminent danger of receivership, and when Colonel Shook and myself were the only solvent bondsmen on the bonds. This sort of thing carried on year after year and decade after decade wears on a man's nerves, and I have suffered from nervous indigestion and nervous insomnia; the latter is now entirely cured, and the former very greatly abated, so that I have but little to complain of. I am, however, nervous; I have lost somewhat of the aggressive force and determination that I have had previously, and am more easily discouraged. I realize under these conditions that if I were again to face conditions of strain and panic and difficulty I could not accomplish for the company what I have been able to do in the past; and the effort to do it would undoubtedly bring about in a more aggravated form the nervous disorders previously mentioned and would lead to a break down in health. I am not willing, therefore, to face such a condition. I entirely agree with what you say about it being manly to stay by a concern in time of difficulty, and I have done it. I am the only single official of the company that has re-mained in its service without break for a period of 18 or 25 years, according to the starting point reckoned from. Every other officer has been in and out and in again either once or twice.

On January 9, 1901, we received new bylaws from New York for TCI which abolished the second vice-president's office, thus legislating my friend and associate Alfred Shook out of office altogether without having paid him the courtesy of any previous letter of notification. They also superseded the authority of the president by providing for a chairman of the board. On January 21 Don H. Bacon, ex-president of the Minnesota Iron Company, was elected chairman of the board of TCI. Mr. Bacon had never been con-nected either with coal mining or the production of coke or pig iron, or steel. His entire experience was that of mining ore, and it seemed a somewhat singular selection on the part of the directors.

Bacon ordered that all inventories should [count] . . . iron and steel at cost, and statements of monthly earnings should be based upon the pig iron actually shipped out, instead of assuming profits on material in stock at nominal market prices as Mr. Baxter had insisted upon lo these many years, to my intense disapproval. Bacon suggested our putting into our costs and accounts a provision for depreciation, and I nearly dropped dead when Mr. Baxter said that he had never favored the present system of earnings!! Bacon told me that when he was asked to come into the company and be-come its head he was told that the company had no floating debt. I made a statement for him of what we had, and went over the values of land, fur-naces, and plant with him. Bacon . . . said that he had never been placed in a position in his life where he had to raise any money and he did not know how to go about it. He asked me to take the necessary steps and submit them to a subcommittee which had been appointed. I then prepared the necessary draft prospectus for a general blanket bond of $15 million.

On April 30, 1901, I delivered the keys and papers [at] 5:00 P.M. to J. R. Vail, auditor, and left the office just as a matter of routine without any firing of cannon or ringing of bells, and that evening attended the May festival and sang in the chorus of Elijah.

Retirement

Bowron's exit from TCI had been part of an overall movement of the original local executives out of the company. Nathaniel Baxter, Alfred Shook, George McCormack, and Erskine Ramsay all left at about the same time. Their severance generally had been no more pleasant than Bowron's. Shook was summarily fired in early 1901 for his alleged mismanagement of the TCI steelworks, an action deeply resented by Bowron and the others long involved in the local management who appreciated Shook's determined efforts to get steel production started. Bowron reported that George McCormack quit after Don Bacon had "specially and needlessly assured [McCormack] of his stability" and then had slandered him. According to Bowron, McCormack confronted Bacon with the "perfidy and untruth and told him that he [McCormack] would shoot him if he circulated any more calumnious reports."

The old TCI managers would find plenty to keep them busy. Virtually all would become directors and officers of local banks. Shook and his sons would begin new coal ventures, and McCormack and Erskine Ramsay, the former chief mining engineer at TCI, would start a new and highly successful coal company, Pratt Consolidated. McCormack, Ramsay, and Bowron would also take over management of some of the leading local land companies, most of which had gone bankrupt in the 1890s. Ramsay and McCormack acquired the Ensley Land Company property; McCormack and Bowron would lead in the recovery of DeBardeleben's old Bessemer Coal, Iron and Land Company. Bowron for a time sat on the board of the Elyton Land Company, Birmingham's original development enterprise. Their pasts with TCI were not immediately put behind, however; a lawsuit charging malfeasance against the old executives over the Ensley Land Company would raise the ire of all of them, most especially Bowron.

James Bowron's business investments during his retirement years would prove not to be very successful. He put much time and money in a new iron company that failed, the result of bad advice from usually reliable sources. Having made a very good return on his money in the South Pittsburgh pipe works, he invested heavily in a Birmingham plant plagued with bad management. His only successful investment was the Bessemer Coal, Iron and Land Company, and it would not always pay dividends. Within a few years of retiring, he was distressed about his financial condition.

Bowron's retirement and his disappointment in the YMCA's "modernist" turn led him to greater activism in the Republican party, the prohibition movement, and the Masonic order. In his view, the work of each complemented the other—and his literal understanding of the Bible. He would consider both running for office as a Republican and accepting appointive office but in the end did neither, partly because he disapproved of Theodore Roosevelt's failure to embrace a "lily-white" party. Prohibition appealed strongly to the reformist instinct in Bowron, and he embraced the movement as strongly as he ever had any civic or religious concern. Here was a cause tailor-made for him: a clear solution, based on moral imperative and requiring personal discipline, to a social evil of abundant and far-reaching destruction. Bowron had joined the Masonic order in England but during the hectic years with TCI he had had little time for it. In retirement he would become quite active, and in 1911 he would be raised to the thirty-third degree, the order's pinnacle, in a ceremony at Washington's Masonic temple. He was then one of only seven thirty-third-degree Masons in Alabama.

Bowron had always enjoyed travel, provided that he could take family members with him. His retirement made long pleasure trips possible, and during the remainder of his life he made a conscious effort to visit the various continents of the world he had not so far seen. His trip to the Middle East in 1903 took him to places of deep personal meaning.

Throughout the often turbulent and exhausting 1890s, Bowron had devoted much time and energy to a family that continued to grow. He and the second Adah had a "second" family of children. A daughter, Edith, had been born in 1889, his ninth child. After her came Richard in 1891, Edgar in 1893, Harold in 1895, Robert in 1899, and Paul, the fourteenth and final child, in 1905. At the same time, his "first" family, composed of four surviving sons—Charlie, Jack, Tom, and Fred—and the one daughter, Ada, was maturing and beginning to embark on careers and marriage. James Bowron devoted remarkable attention to guiding the older ones through adolescence and early adulthood and, at the same time, to nursing the younger ones through illness and childhood pratfalls. During TCI's difficult financial times in the 1890s, he often stood watch over the young children at night when measles and mumps swept through his house. In his partial retirement beginning in 1901, Bowron became more attentive, even taking the time to teach the youngest, Paul, to read.

He had already helped the older sons get started in careers. Charlie was an engineer at TCI; Jack, a manager in the pipe industry; and Fred and Tom, bankers. In the coming years, Bowron would make numerous investments partly with an eye toward "placing" his numerous sons in careers. In some cases his efforts proved financially unfortunate, as Bowron would ruefully point out.

On May 1, 1901, I sat on my own front porch, it being a fine morning, and smoked a cigar and watched the people going downtown on the street cars and reflecting how funny it was that I had nothing to do. It was the first day in my whole life since I started work on November 1, 1858, that I had been my own master with no one to tell me where to go and what to do. It had been a pretty long grind, and if at that point I had expressed my satisfaction and had decided nevermore to go into a business transaction it [might] have been better for me. It is impossible to tell. I am quite willing to believe that the events of my subsequent life have worked out on the whole to my advantage.

Although I was now out of TCI, [the company] lent me the private car, and the railroads had got so accustomed to hauling me around as an old dead beat that they did not hesitate to do it again, so that we left with the whole family, nine children and nurse . . . for St. Simons Island [in Georgia]. We went to Brunswick and took a boat to St. Simons Island, and, to our dismay, Richard developed fever that morning, casting a damper on our holiday. We had a pretty good time, the rest of us, bathing every day, walking along the beach, the little children learning to swim in water three inches deep and all of us resting up pretty well. After the brine we washed off by taking a shower at the artesian well, which spouts sulfur water about twenty-five feet high.

On July 16 Harold fell off the porch on his head but was more frightened than hurt, and we told him not to do it again. Being a good obedient child he did not, but fell off next time on his foot instead and sprained his ankle so that he could not walk. By this time Dick's fever had apparently about broken up, and we would have felt much better, but Edgar began to show some disturbance. From July 19 to 23 Edgar showed fever every day, and we called in a visiting doctor who gave him medicine and advised that he could take the journey [home] safely. We . . . arrived on July 25 [in Birmingham] where we could get Edgar safely to bed and under the care of our good family physician. On July 27 Edgar's fever was declared to be typhoid, and we nursed him at home, I naturally giving him a good deal of my time by day. His fever reached its height on July 31 at 104.8 degrees, and then gradually subsided. On August 1 all hands went to bed, being the first night in weeks without any of us having to be up with invalids.

[Also] on August 1 I was informed that Don Bacon had requested Charlie's resignation. He tendered his resignation to take effect September 1. On August 12 Charlie was offered the position as assistant to the president of the Alabama Consolidated Coal and Iron Company . . . and accepted it. In June 1903 the Echols-Smith Hardware Company, in which I had subscribed some $5,000 stock for the benefit of Fred and to get him a position, had reached a point where it wanted . . . either to raise additional capital or to merge with some other concern. As the principal stockholders did not seem to be entirely in agreement with each other, I was appointed a committee of one to negotiate the whole proposition. On July 2 the Echols-Smith Hardware Company agreed to accept the proposition of Milner and Kettig to buy out the business and absorb it. On July 13 Fred started in with Milner and Kettig in their city sales department.

Dick started with the TCI at Ensley [in 1911], the beginning of a highly successful career. It may not have appeared so when they put him on the hottest, dirtiest, and hardest work they had. But C. J. Barr[1] told John Fletcher,[2] who had recommended Dick, that he "had tried at least thirty rich mens' sons out there and had never found one yet that had grit enough to stick." But John told him that Dick would stick, and he has done.

In May 1902 I went . . . to Philadelphia where I attended a meeting of the American Institute of Mining Engineers, and entertained my future son-in-law, Dr. J. S. McLester . . . desiring to have the opportunity of sizing him up. On May 18 [he] asked and obtained our consent to marry my splendid daughter Ada, a match which has always been from that day to this a source of extreme gratification to me.

Arriving home [from a business trip on] July 4, 1902, I found that Edith was in the Davis Infirmary with a severe case of typhoid fever. Later in the month I spent a couple of days [in Chicago] . . . and was called home on urgent telegram as to Edith's condition. It is perhaps hardly necessary to say that during that journey from Chicago I was consciously and constantly talking to the Lord about her condition and urging him to grant her recovery, and she changed for the better during those hours, the crisis passed, and she commenced to recover. This seemed to be the second time in her life that the Lord had called for her and had been persuaded to relinquish his call. It is not surprising therefore that on the third call he should have insisted on taking her sweet spirit to himself. On August 13 Edith had her first solid food, the fifty-second day of her illness. On August 19 she had so far recovered as to be able to stand, and the nurse left.

On February 3, 1903, we landed in Alexandria [Egypt] and were very much amused at the meeting of the East and West: an electric light in the bedroom and a little one-cent wick floating in an oil lamp as big as a postage stamp in the bathroom. A touch on the electric bell brought a trim French chambermaid, but to step to the door and clap one's hands brought a tall, dignified, swarthy, turbaned Moor, so you had your choice to speak either French or Arabic. One lady of [our] party . . . declined to learn even six words of Arabic and was dependent upon me at every meal to order what she wanted. I found no difficulty whatever in the next six weeks in acquiring about 600 words of Arabic and to read and write a few of the simplest little words, but like everything else, one forgets it for lack of practice.

From Cairo we started up the Nile, not on the big tourist steamers, but on the smaller trading steamers which stop at every river town. They carry the Europeans on the upper deck and natives on the lower. The opportunities of observing native habits are very much better in this way. On our first day up the Nile I was interested to see fifteen persons carrying corn stalks to fire one brick kiln, and at a sugar factory over fifty men stoking with cane trash, instead of using any kind of automatic conveyor.

We visited the splendid temple of Denderah and then stopped at Luxor for about four days, visiting with profound interest the mighty ruins of Karnak and the "tombs of the kings" across the river. I cannot, however tempting the opportunity, undertake to write a lecture on Egypt and Palestine in my brief biography. I have often given them to American audiences. I will only remark that the inscriptions and the paintings in the tombs of Egypt, the pyramids and others, are convincing evidence that, 2,000 years before Moses wrote the first books of the Bible, the Egyptians recognized the immortality of the soul, resurrection of the body, future rewards and punishment, based on a trial in the great Assize Court. As these records go back within 1,600 years of the Flood, which geology establishes being in post-glacial days, and as that period could have been bridged by the overlapping lives of five of the early patriarchs, it is my belief that the original knowledge of resurrection and immortality given by God in the Garden of Eden, in what we now call Mesopotamia, was transmitted orally through a few patriarchs to the tribes which afterwards became the Assyrians and left their records in Nineveh and Babylon whence the same knowledge was carried into Egypt.

[In] Jerusalem [we] visit[ed] of course the so-called Church of the Holy Sepulchre and ... Golgotha and the "Garden tomb" on which so large a proportion of Protestant scholarship has agreed. I need not say there more than that the so-called holy sites revered by the Catholic church were selected by the Empress Helena in the third century, she claiming that they were miraculously revealed to her. I am satisfied that the Lord was not crucified or buried within the present wall of Jerusalem. But I could not but respect the emotion of the Russian pilgrims who visited the so-called holy places. I watched one poor fellow weep until he had thoroughly wetted a big stone and then wiped it dry with a large colored handkerchief and went off and repeated the same performance at another site.

You may ... omit the purchase of rosaries that have been blessed by the priest and laid upon the so-called sepulchre or the alleged stations of the cross on the via dolorosa, knowing that the lapse of centuries has covered the streets which the Savior trod with many feet of accumulated debris and rubbish. But after you have seen all that I have mentioned and more, and reflected that it is the same landscape, sea, and sky on which the Lord looked, and that the paths and roads are those on which He walked, and that the miserable dirty, whining beggars, blind or lepers, craving your assistance, look like those who blocked His path, it is easy to appreciate much of what one has read and learned, and to realize with deep emotion and reverent joy and interest the privilege of walking where He has walked and "in His steps." I think one finds in this world a measure of what one looks for. If the Christian seeks to be reminded of the life of the Master, he will find what he seeks.

On January 27, 1902, I had a stiff argument with the YMCA people who were urging that I should serve as a trustee. I positively refused to do so unless the trustees should be a self-perpetuating body, holding property under a deed of trust for the express purposes to which it had been originally dedicated. There was at that time becoming apparent in the YMCA what has since then become much more so amongst the churches, a spirit of skeptics and latitudinarianism. I have always taken the old original views, commonly known as the "old time religion." I have never had any sympathy whatever with the Gnostics or the Pelagians. I think the Bible means just exactly what it says: that the Lord Jesus was the Son of God and of the virgin Mary, and was made man and lived amongst us, and suffered death for us, taking upon himself the sins of the world. In this faith I have lived and in it I shall die.

I have no sympathy with the modern skeptics that prate about Jesus as a great prophet, a wonderful teacher, and a splendid example for us to imitate, nor have I any sympathy with or tolerance for those who . . . scoff at the fall of man, the story of Adam and Eve and of Jonah, and find many other mares' nests. I have spent fifty years in studying and teaching the Bible and know it to be true from cover to cover. It is proved by its own character, by the agreement of numerous writers of all classes of society, writing over 1,500 years in different countries, in different languages. It is confirmed by the impossibility of human writers originating its thoughts; also by geological and astronomical evidence, by contemporary history, and by modern archae-ology. Holding these views, I was not willing to give money or to accept money for the new YMCA building with any chance that some board of directors at some time, tinged or tainted with heresy, might turn it into a club or institute, or in some other way deviate from its original purpose.

On August 25, 1902, a deputation embracing the district attorney, post-master, internal revenue collector, and the clerk of the U.S. court came to ask me to head the Republican ticket for the legislature. I was willing to have done so but my family objected on the ground that I had had for so many years nervous strain and worry that it would not be wise. I presided over the Republican county convention and note with gratitude the statement of the Birmingham *News* that my address was an eloquent one. The first para-graph as reported read: "When I first came to Birmingham seven years ago I started to plant some magnolias in my yard and was informed by Mr. [Braxton B.] Comer[3] across the street that I would never live to see them grow; but as he was a free silver Bryan Democrat, he was wrong, as such men usually are; as the trees have grown and flourished and now one can sit in the shade of them and rest. So now I believe the time has come to plant a white Republican party in Alabama, and in a few years it will grow big enough to shelter many of our misguided Democratic brethren."

I presided as temporary chairman over the Republican state convention, speaking for one hour to 600 white delegates. At that time if we had been let alone the state and the "solid South" would have been split. When 600 white delegates could gather together in Birmingham at one convention it showed that people were getting tired of the errors of the Democrats, who were only held together like the staves of a barrel by the hoop of maintaining racial supremacy. I said that the hoop had been knocked off, that the white men had the numbers, wealth, and intelligence, the votes and the prestige, and that for anyone to prate about Negro supremacy was to show that . . . one was living like the man of old with an evil spirit amongst the tombs. I said when this hoop was knocked off the staves would fall in every direction, and that the young men who approved the Republican doctrines of uniformity of law from ocean to ocean, protection for American labor, sound money . . . should line up with the Republican party, and that there would be far too many of us to be afraid of political or social ostracism.

At this time many people were expressing themselves in that way, and I can name a dozen of the most prominent men in Birmingham who were in sympathy with the movement. President Roosevelt, strong and vigorous as he was . . . made a mistake. He should have encouraged the movement, which would have split asunder the solid South, but instead of that he looked apparently only at the influence of the Negro vote in Indiana and one or two other northern states which were close, and pronounced against a southern white Republican party, and showed his displeasure by displacing from office the district attorney and the internal revenue collector, on the alleged ground of "pernicious political activity." This discouraged the movement and put the South back again into the old rut in which it is still rolling. I may say in leaving this matter that although I sat seven hours in the chair without leaving it and received the report of the committee on credentials, not one word of protest was made as to any unfair treatment having been accorded to the colored delegates or candidates of the convention.

In 1906 I was told both ranks of the Republican party had agreed on me as a compromise candidate [for governor] and that I would be compelled to run by moral pressure. Following this came a deputation of sixteen to insist that I could harmonize the party and must run. I positively declined to do so however on several grounds, including the hostility of President Roosevelt to a white Republican party in the South, which I insisted was necessary to split the "solid Democratic South," as white Democrats would not go to a Negro party.

On November 26, 1909, [I] ... had an interview with the postmaster general [Frank Hitchcock], who said that President Taft had spoken to him as to my nomination for postmaster for Birmingham. [He said] he had no endorsements on file, and he could not act without some, and was anxious to know what would be the attitude of the newspapers. I told him that I was quite sure they would be satisfied with the nomination, and he asked me if I could get letters from them to that effect. I said that no doubt I could, but I would not. Hitchcock looked surprised at this, and I said to him that I had never asked any man living for a job, a position, an office, or a vote, and I never would do as long as I lived. I had filled a good many offices of responsibility either with or without remuneration, some of honor and hard work, but they had always been conferred upon me without my seeking. [I said] that I believed the office should always seek the man. He appeared annoyed and told me that I must certainly understand that the United States of America did not find it necessary to go around and thrust offices upon people as a favor.

I said in reply that was not my attitude. I had come to this country as a foreigner. I was a believer in the fiscal views of the Republican party—sound money, protection. I had always lived either in Tennessee or Alabama, which were Democratic states, and ... although I had taken active part in England in local affairs I could not as a Republican in the South be elected the guardian of the city pound, and therefore I would like a federal office simply as some kind of recognition. If he thought fit to confer the office upon me I would feel honored by it, and would work as diligently to make it a success as I would to make a blast furnace a success. So we parted. I was told afterwards that P. D. Barker of Mobile, the national Republican committeeman, said that he would be d___d if Bowron or Erskine Ramsay or any of those kid-gloved Republicans should have the office. It must go to someone who would hustle up votes. He did not speak that way to me about it, however, and I learned that the newspapers in Birmingham gave much prominence to my apparent nomination, this being followed by swarms of letters and telegrams being sent to the postmaster general endorsing my name.

Bowron did not get the appointment. His primary support for it among party activists came from Joseph O. Thompson, a white from Tuskegee who, because of close connections to Theodore Roosevelt, was ineffectual with William

Howard Taft's patronage dispensers. Some Bowron supporters accused Frank Hitchcock of trying to curry the favor of black Republicans, but in fact the contest for the Birmingham postmastership appears to have been an affair between two "lily-white" factions.[4]

In 1907 I gave thirty-seven Bible class lectures of about fifty minutes each, being absent abroad about three months out of the year. I attended thirteen sessions of the committee appointed by the city council, about four hours each, investigating alleged graft, and delivered the following addresses, thirty-two in number.

Jan. 4	Cadmean Circle	110 minutes	Religions of Palestine
Jan. 6	Salvation Army	15	Mrs. Orchard's funeral
Jan. 23	South Highlands Presbyterian Church	30	Evangelists' Service
Mch. 5	Foreign Mission So.	60	Mexico
Mch. 14	Jefferson Theatre	10	Kindergarten work
Apr. 18	Majestic Theatre	10	Treble Clef Club
Apr. 17	S. H. Presbyterian	30	Evangelists' Service
Apr. 20	Athletic Club	20	Athletics
Apr. 20	Masonic Temple	10	Ethics, 18th degree
Apr. 24	Masonic Temple	30	World's development in 50 yrs. 32nd degree
May 1	Masonic Temple	25	History of Babylon
May 14	YMCA	10	Athletic Christianity
May 31	Woodlawn Church	43	High School Commencement on "Hurry"
June 11	S. H. Presbyterian	10	Brotherhood meeting, Cooperation
June 12	S. H. Presbyterian	30	Evangelists' service
June 22	Oskar II	35	Religious sympathy
June 29	Oskar II	30	Fulfillment of Prophecy
Sep. 30	High School	30	Commercial value of education
Oct. 13	Jefferson Theatre	55	Prohibition
Oct. 18	S. H. Presbyterian	90	Norway

Oct. 24	Ensley, open air	15	Press Club, Commercialism
Nov. 5	First Baptist Church	10	Law & Order League, Objective
Nov. 7	Paul Hayne School	20	Opening new playground
Nov. 20	Masonic Temple	15	Faith, 18th degree
Nov. 21	Masonic Temple	20	Duties of citizenship, 32nd degree
Nov. 23	Hillman Hotel	30	Ground for Optimism
Dec. 8	S. H. Presbyterian	10	Church finances
Dec. 12	Medical College	60	Norway
Dec. 18	Masonic Temple	60	Explanation of rituals, 18th degree
Dec. 22	YMCA	30	Panics, causes and remedies
Dec. 25	Masonic Temple	15	Christmas thoughts for Knights Templar
Dec. 29	YMCA	60	Religious life in Norway and Russia

In 1907 Jefferson County voted 5,523 for prohibition and 3,848 against it, which was very satisfactory to me as I had been rather active in promoting this temperance movement. I will here say that the Bessemer [Coal, Iron and Land] Company of which I was an official had been selling building lots and building materials to Negro miners for two or three years, payable by monthly installments. Prior to the panic every man had the fullest possible employment. After the panic half the mines on Red Mountain were shut down. Many men got work alternate weeks, but with half time and prohibition we found our collections were better than with full time and whiskey. I heard real estate men say that they had never been able to collect their weekly rentals from miners as well as they were doing. It is the old story: fill up the hole where the money drains out of the workman's pocket into the beer barrel, and he has money with which to buy food and clothing and furniture, and then some left over to make himself and his family happy; whereas the money spent for drink brings nothing but disease of the nervous system, and liver and heart troubles, paralysis, insanity, crime, vice, shame, and poverty. It is I believe the one most potent influence in all the world used by the devil.

Bowron giving a public address, c. 1900 (courtesy of James French)

"James Bowron . . . on Prohibition," a pamphlet appearing in about
 1912:
If the . . . existing sky-scrapers in Birmingham . . . could be carefully
burned down without hurting anybody or injuring adjacent property,
the loss would be much less to Jefferson County than is now produced
by the consumption of a corresponding value of money invested in the
purchase of liquor which is burned up in the bodies of the consumers,
leaving in its train distinct injury to liver, brain, nervous system, stomach and arteries. . . .

As an employer of labor I have the deepest sympathy in these days of
high cost of food for the laboring man, who works long and hard and
has very little money left. I most earnestly desire that his little surplus
should go every month into the purchase of a home, furniture, food and
clothing for himself and family, instead of going into liquor which leaves
him nothing to show for it at the end of the year but a debilitated
constitution. . . .

The whole question to my mind is so one-sided that it hardly admits

Woman's Christian Temperance Union march in Birmingham, November 1909
(courtesy of Birmingham Public Library Archives)

of any discussion. The legal axiom is "Salus populis suprema lex"
("The public health the highest law"). In the interest of public health
we take precautions against the spread of smallpox, cholera and typhoid
and yellow fever; we order suitable sanitary precautions to be taken;
food stores to be screened; marshy places to be drained; foul places to
be disinfected; we order holes to be fenced around to prevent the un-
wary from falling into them; we have laws to suppress anything in the
nature of a public nuisance—and what can be a greater public nuisance
than the sale of a narcotic poison which stupefies the brain, temporarily
and destructively energizes the blood, destroys the will-power, infuri-
ates passion, injures the body, wastes the time and squanders the
money.

Throughout the South the white man is placed next to the colored
man, and the moral burden is upon the white man of being his brother's
keeper. Too many of the colored men, alas, have not the self-control to
govern their passions, and hence to put whiskey into the hands of a
negro is as great a crime against society as to turn him out with knife
and pistol.

On February 3, 1913, after I had gone to bed, I [would be] called up by someone to be informed that a near relative of mine[5] was at the hotel Hillman on the verge of delirium tremens and threatening suicide. I simply would not have known how to act in such a case, and my son Jack most kindly and considerately took hold of matters and handled them for me. No wonder that I am such a strong prohibitionist when I have had such object lessons very near to me amongst my relatives. I called to see the poor fellow the next day and found him full of remorse and sorrow, and apparently deeply touched by being kindly treated instead of scolded. It is a disease beyond question, and we cannot scold people for diseases.

In April 1905 at the Masonic Temple of Mobile I participated for the first time in America in Masonic work. I felt that my memory was perfect, but I was almost thrown down at the first sentence, because my worthy friend and brother Ben M. Jacobs answered me before my question was half finished. He had not suspected my deliberate and dignified manner of interrogation.

There is nothing whatever in Freemasonry demanding secrecy. I have been admitted to all of the degrees that are recognized as standard in England or in the United States. I have not only been admitted to them but have assisted in performing practically all of the ceremonies, or have been at the head in turn of each one of the various bodies conferring such degrees. I may therefore speak admittedly with authority. There is nothing within the compass of Freemasonry that might not with perfect propriety be printed on the front page of every newspaper. The allegations made by its enemies, especially the Roman Catholics, as to its alleged infidelity and its blasphemous or profane character, are absolutely unfounded and mere scurrility unworthy of notice. To the question, why then should there be any secrecy concerning it, I answer that those things, matters, and principles which are public property and common knowledge excite no interest. If only a limited number knew that grass was green, the sky blue, and gold a reddish yellow, the interest in such knowledge would be more or less acute. Freemasonry therefore builds upon the common factor of curiosity as a means of promoting interest in its rituals and principles. If it be asked why it is restricted to men, I would answer that it typifies character building, and typifies this through the medium of temple building, which in Solomon's Temple was confined entirely to men.

My complaint against Masonry is that the lodges devote too much time to foolish repetition in the ritual to the same question or answer, wasting much time that might be applied to commonsense description of the purposes of the ceremonies. There is too much verbal load on the ear and too little instruction load inside of it! Hence, many people never get beyond the external forms or become truly versed in the philosophy of the order. On the other hand some who give themselves earnestly to Freemasonry allow it to take the place of their religion, and that is not right. Masonry undertakes to promote the true fraternity of men and to inculcate liberty of thought, speech, action, and worship. It permits a Christian, Jew, or Moslem to meet on one common footing, the belief in the fatherhood of God and the brotherhood of man. It does not, however, require that any man should cease to hold his own religious principles less dear because he gives to the other man the perfect right to differ from him, and the very first Masonic pledge that is required assures the novice that nothing will be required of him which shall interfere with his duty to his God, his neighbor, or himself. A true Mason therefore should be a better citizen, a better neighbor, and a better man in his relations to his family, his business, society in general, and to his church.

I first decided to join the order definitely after sitting up discussing the matter until nearly daylight with my noble friend and leader, Thomas Whitwell, and I took my first degree in the old room of the Tees Lodge #508, Stockton-on-Tees, my native town, at the hands of Ralph Graham, a dentist of that city, who was the worshipful master in that year. Having taken the second degree in due course I was raised to the sublime degree of a master Mason on the first of June, 1869, and at the same place duly received my certificate from the Grand Lodge of England, which was then presided over by the earl of Zetland, whose mansion was not many miles away from my subsequent residence at Redcar. In these two parent organizations I made due progress, filling the various subsidiary offices in the lodge of inner guard, junior deacon, senior deacon, junior warden, and senior warden. In the meantime, however, I had moved as recorded previously down to Redcar prior to my marriage in 1870, and very soon became a member of the Marwood Lodge #1244 and was rapidly promoted in it through the intervening steps until I became the worshipful master, into which office I was inducted July 7, 1874.

During my year of office the Romish church got in its work on the marquis of Ripon, who was also one of my not distant neighbors living in the county of Yorkshire, and who had succeeded the earl of Zetland at his death. I think the old gentleman had been the grand master for twenty-six years. The marquis of Ripon had not long held the office before he became a pervert to Romanism, the system which will not permit any individual opinion, and requires its members to forsake any secret order as they may not carry any secret in their own souls that is not to be given to the priest in the confessional. The Roman Catholic church rejoiced greatly therefore when the marquis of Ripon resigned his office as grand master of England and renounced his membership in the order. Their joy, however, was short lived, for the Grand Lodge asked and obtained the consent of the Prince of Wales to become its grand master, and he was with great dignity and éclat inducted into the office in the Royal Albert Hall, London, April 28, 1875. We were required to appear in evening dress, white gloves, and full Masonic regalia, no jewels or emblems, however, being permitted except those recognized by the Blue Lodge and the Royal Arch. It is my impression that there were nearly 5,000 present. I am speaking now of the Prince of Wales who at the death of Queen Victoria became King Edward the VII.

Having been by the kind feelings of my brethren elected and pushed forward to office in the Alabama Consistory, I became in the Rose Croix Chapter master of ceremonies, and later in the Alabama Consistory prior, preceptor, and master of Kadosh. I worked hard and faithfully, and having some fair degree of ability due to voice and manner, my brethren were pleased always to accord me a high degree of commendation for my performance of ritualistic work. My memory is so good that I have always been entirely independent of books or notes, and have been able to perform the ceremonies without the constraint which follows reference to notes. I have had infinite pleasure from my association with the Masonic order. I have made a great many friends in it, and sincerely hope that by my numerous addresses and teachings I have done some good and reached some people with inculcations of high morality and ethics whom I might never have reached in any other way.

Bowron would later give his explanation of the meaning of his Masonic devotion in an article entitled "Responsibility":

In the great light of Masonry it is said every one of us must give an account of himself before God, and again that no man can answer for his brother or give himself a ransom for his brother. . . . All the scriptural teaching to us Masons is that of the individual discharge of duty.

The whole world depends on the performance of duty. We sleep soundly at night in our homes because of our faith in the performance of duty by policemen and firemen, or in the sleeping car because of our faith in the locomotive engineer watching his signals and his steam, and the conductor receiving and properly interpreting his orders. . . .

Our duties are twofold—to God and to man. . . . Do we maintain the sanctity of God's day or use it for our own purposes? We are charged by the Book which we honor "not to forsake the assembling of ourselves together as the manner of some is." Do we assemble ourselves together habitually and constantly, with fidelity, to praise and honor the Great Architect of the Universe or do the allurements of the office to look over our mail, the golf course, a baseball game, a trades union meeting or an automobile ride in the country keep us from the performance of this duty? . . .

Every Mason should take part in the public affairs of his country—national, state and local. In this I claim and submit to my brethren that he is required . . . to use his own judgement and not to give his vote and influence to the control of any one else. No party caucus can bind me. I have never voted in a primary, because I will not consent that any one else shall tell me for whom I shall vote. My conception of duty is that each man must vote in every election and not ignore it because of the trouble and time involved in going to the polls. . . . I submit that the true Mason would rather be right than successful. He should be willing to be in the minority, to see his candidate defeated but have his conscience clear rather than to vote for a successful candidate and feel that he had voted against the conviction of what is right. . . .

I submit that the duty of the Mason is to investigate and form his own opinion, looking at both sides, and that he should seek information not to support and bolster up an opinion already formed or received from some one else, but to enable him to form his own independent opinion upon which he can stand. . . . It has been said and has become an adage—"vox populi, vox Dei"—but this is not necessarily true unless the public voice is the outcome of thoughtful investigation. One need only refer in our own country to the wave forty years ago of unsound financial opinion which would have made half a cent's worth of paper into a dollar by imprinting upon it the bank note without maintaining metallic reserves for its redemption at par. The folly of this has been adequately demonstrated by the issues of fiat money in Germany during the war and in Russia since the revolution, and yet in 1878 the theory was taken seriously by nearly half the people of the United

States. I point to this to show that no true Mason can afford to take the voice of the majority, as the voice of God, to define for him his duty in life.

In February 1902 George McCormack requested me to proceed with the preliminary organization of the Valley Iron Company, to make pig iron at the place now known as Battelle [in northeastern Alabama]. This was the beginning of all kinds of trouble and disastrous loss to me. The proposition consisted of a body of mountain land . . . [with] a vein of coal about three feet thick in the top and one of [iron] ore four and one-half feet thick in the bottom. The ore was light in iron but high in lime. The coal was dirty and needed washing. These were the objections. On the other hand, the property was right on the main line of the Alabama Great Southern Railroad, and was watered by a creek. The coal could be brought down an inclined plane from the top of the mountain, the loaded cars carrying the empty ones up. There was no railroad freight to pay either on the ore or the fuel and no limestone required. We drew our plans for every saving of labor and fuel. The wasted heat from the coke ovens was carried to the boilers to raise steam for the powerhouse. Steam-operated compressors [were] to send air up the mountain for coal cutting machines in the mine, and the steam also operated a generator to furnish electric current to the ore mine at the other side of the railway for the electric drills and the hoist. All this scheme looked perfect on paper.

I do not think I erred in the precautions I took before going into this enterprise, and yet I was thrown down very hard. Before I decided to put any money into it, I was favorably advised by McCormack [and] Erskine Ramsay. I also had the property examined and was advised favorably by James L. Gaines, former general manager of TCI Company, . . . and my own son Charles, on whose sound engineering judgment and conservatism I relied considerably. During its development it was visited twice by Frank H. Crockard, later vice-president and general manager of the TCI Company, . . . and on each visit he increased his stock subscription. I insisted upon a drill hole being put down in the valley to test the ore and gave the core from it to McCormack to be analyzed at the Woodward Laboratory. The analysis showed 28 percent iron, but in operating the blast furnace we never got more than 22 percent yield. We shipped a carload of coal . . . down to the Woodward Iron Company to be made into coke, and McCormack told me that when it was drawn it could not be distinguished from the coke on the yard made from the Pratt seam. There was evidently something wrong about this because the Battelle coke is . . . thick and chunky, without the slightest resemblance to the Pratt coke.

In late February 1902 I spent several days in the East interviewing different friends, largely those with whom I had been associated in TCI, bringing before them the proposed Valley Iron Company scheme. But they were all very busy men and their means largely occupied, and I did not get much encouragement from them. [Later,] after taking several subscriptions [in Pittsburgh] I went on to Columbus, Ohio, where my friends John G. Battelle[6] and Henry A. Marting[7] signed for $50,000 each, which with the $25,000 or $30,000 subscribed in Pittsburgh gave the subscription list quite a boost. Ramsay and McCormack signed for $50,000, and so did I for a similar amount. This was too much considering my means. To carry out my subscription . . . I sold my preferred stock in the Alabama Steel and Ship-building Company[8] at 82. This was a mistake. It [soon would be] worth over par, but I was afraid of the future of TCI under Mr. Bacon's management.

After I had raised the money . . . and was gone for some months [on the Middle Eastern trip], I returned to find that the plans had been changed in my absence, more money spent, and that there was insufficient capital. To avoid financial difficulty the furnace was most unwisely started before the ore mine was sufficiently developed. The ore contractor took advantage of our position and shipped out large quantities of draw slate along with the ore, all stained red together, which was highly refractory and took half a ton more of coke to the ton of pig iron than it should have taken. This in a nut shell was the cause of the failure of the company [in 1906]. It was a disastrous enterprise for me. I have drawn the salient facts together here to show . . . that so far as I can see I was not morally chargeable with negligence in going into this enterprise on a large scale.

In 1905 George B. McCormack said he thought he would make me a proposition to exchange some of his Pratt Coal Company bonds for some of my [Valley Iron Company] stock. He and Erskine Ramsay amplified this statement by agreeing to deliver me $25,000 of Pratt Coal bonds for $25,000 of my Valley Iron stock. I think this was done partly out of remorse and partly out of sympathy. The last time we had been up at Battelle together . . . I was seized with violent indigestion from which I was [then] suffering so constantly, . . . and I think McCormack became alarmed at my condition. These fits of indigestion were due to hyperacidity of the stomach, the predisposing cause of which is mental anxiety and worry. I had put $60,000 into this business and had been pushed over the brink by McCormack. I was not satisfied with the coal, which was too thin, and he argued me out of my dissatisfaction. I was not satisfied with the ore and wanted further analysis of it. Before I could get it he told me he had accepted the option on the property and that we were committed to take it. This grieved me very much as I thought it entirely premature. He, being also at this time the general manager of the Woodward Iron Company, had the control of making the coke from the samples of coal that we sent down and also the samples of ore, and someone undoubtedly committed fraud on him and us, for the analyses were distinctly better than the ore proved to be. He told me himself that the [Valley Iron] coke . . . could not be distinguished from the Woodward coke on the yard, whilst it is really absolutely and utterly different.

He must have realized that he had let his foot slip in some of these matters and in consequence allowed me to be involved to a ruinous extent. At the same time he was under no legal obligation whatever to do any such thing, and I have always given credit to himself and Ramsay for their action as being governed by warmhearted sympathy and personal friendship. I do not know what the bonds cost them, and it does not matter. I know what they were worth to me, and it was a godsend to have such a promise made.

The celebrated (as it afterwards became) Ensley Land Company suit was filed [in 1902]. It disclosed the most wonderful flight of imagination possible, claiming that for years Baxter, Shook, Warner, Bowron, McCormack, Ramsay, and possibly some others had been planning and plotting to acquire the property of the Ensley Land Company.

The Ensley Land Company was a boom land company. The original capital was $10 million, and TCI sold to it for $5 million in stock about 4,000 acres of land in and immediately around Ensley. There was nothing at Ensley at the time except the blast furnaces and the company's office and laboratory. The balance of Ensley was nothing but bare ground or corn patches. The other half of the stock . . . was sold to the TCI stockholders at ten cents on the dollar as a privilege.

Under the management of Judge H. G. Bond . . . money was spent freely in cutting trees, making streets and sidewalks, building a better-class hotel, and a few houses of different kinds. I do not know what they did with their money. William Duncan and Bond would never allow any small industry to start there as they were always going to have some big thing, telling me that the Pullman Car Company was going to move down there, or at least make a southern branch, or things of that sort. This had taken place in 1887, ten years before, and salaries and taxes had been going on until the company had been compelled to issue mortgage notes at 8 percent, and finally [in 1897] it fell into the hands of its creditors. Percy Warner of Nashville[9] bought the entire property to protect the judgment owned by his father's estate of less than $20,000. He bid the amount of the debt, and any subsequent creditor had the right to come in and redeem it if he had thought the property was worth more. But no other creditor seemed willing to do so.

I had never at any time had anything whatever to do with the management of the Ensley Land Company. I had not even been a stockholder in it since November 1888. I never had but a few hundred dollars invested in it, and my books show that I sold my stock and closed out my interest in it in 1888 at a profit of $39. At one time I was elected on the board of directors to make up a quorum; I do not now remember even what year it was. My attitude towards the Ensley Land Company was one of hostility and vexation of spirit, because I had all the financial trouble of our company and more than I could take care of, and I resented bitterly being coerced by my president and general manager to advance money for the Ensley Land Company which we needed desperately for our own obligations, and which I knew and told them we had no legal right to pay.

As, however, the property had been sold by the sheriff and bid in by [Percy Warner], and there were several other judgments pending against it, it did not seem that [TCI's] majority interest was worth a postage stamp. How could one dream that at this time I was planning and plotting with Baxter, Shook, McCormack, Ramsay, and Warner to acquire this property and beat TCI out of its interest?

In 1897 Napoleon Hill of Memphis[10] had brought suit against TCI as a stockholder in the Ensley Land Company, of which he was a judgment creditor, claiming . . . that we had only paid ten cents on the dollar for our stock, and . . . we were liable for the other ninety cents. Our general counsel, Walker Percy, advised me that we were liable and that the situation was a very serious one. [Percy said] that we must earnestly endeavor to push into operation some scheme of arrangement with the creditors for the reorganization of the Ensley Land Company to save ourselves. This was simple enough. We should get someone to act as trustee for the creditors and redeem the property out of the hands of the judgment creditor. [We should] then endeavor to develop the property by encouraging the locating of small industries . . . to give, if possible, value to the stock. Nobody could be hurt by such a movement.

The suit further alleged that my sale as trustee for the creditors of certain plots of land to Ramsay and McCormack . . . had been made with the full knowledge on their part and on my part that the steelworks would be located there. [It alleged further] that I was really selling what I knew would be extremely valuable real estate for a mere pittance of what it would have been worth if the facts had been known, and that we were all in the scheme together to divide profits. The transactions were absolutely fair and straightforward. No human being had one cent of graft or secret profit or commission so far as I know; certainly I had none. I have been in much litigation in my life, but this suit was the only one which ever reflected on my moral character and charged me with being a fraudulent trustee.

My own conscience being perfectly clear, I applied to President Bacon of TCI to assign Mr. Percy ... to defend me. It was leveled against me in respect of acts done wholly as the servant of TCI. He refused, and I afterwards found [he] was giving every possible information and help to the other side. Bacon was a very suspicious man, and I think his mind had been poisoned before he came down here, but a stronger character would have made some investigation to see whether he was deceived or not.

On March 4, 1907, the Supreme Court of the United States denied the application for appeal in the Ensley Land [Company] suit, and so this finally and permanently ended the outrageous charges and litigation against my friends and myself, which through the personal malice and mean suspicious minds of two or three narrow-minded lawyers had been pending against us for six years. Think of all the expense for time, witnesses, stenographers, not to speak of the heavy fees to the counsel. Just think that [we] would not get this back from the other side, let alone get any damages. In England the unsuccessful litigants would have been taxed with all of our costs as well as their own.

August 9, 1899, was a bad day for me. I went to Anniston, Alabama, and spent the day with J. K. Dimmick, who was the general manager then of the American Pipe and Foundry Company, and I agreed to go in with him in starting a pipe works in Birmingham. It was a very unfortunate decision. I ought to have recognized that I had my hands pretty full and should have been putting away money then in bonds or real estate instead of going into fresh industrial enterprises. D. R. P. Dimmick [J. K.'s brother] came over, and we signed up the subscription list for the new pipe works in which I started off with $20,000. This would have been all right if I had stayed there, but I was foolish enough over the course of some years to increase it to $90,000.

There [was] a great disaster at the Dimmick Pipe Works in the spring of 1900. The roof . . . fell down during the process of construction, three men being killed and twelve injured. It would not be in operation before August, and . . . orders for 10,000 tons of pipe had been cancelled on us because of the delay. This accident was due . . . entirely to carelessness by failing to prop the trusses as they were set up, so that when one fell they all fell, like a pack of cards going down together.

In 1902 Mr. Dimmick put his son Fred in as president, [though he was] only twenty-six years old. This was a mistake. Fred Dimmick was . . . an exceedingly nice fellow, but had not the executive ability required for the position, or the courage resolutely to hold down expenditures. I was provoked at [J. K. Dimmick's] methods of business and the way in which, having controlling interest in the stock, he was writing up his own salary. This feeling gradually increased as [my son] Jack was my representative in the business and did not receive what either he or I thought fair consideration. I pointed out that it was a difficult position for Fred Dimmick to be buying iron from the Williamson Iron Company, in which he was one of the three partners. I had been promised a salary as vice-president and ought to have had the purchases of iron put into my hands as I had more experience in such matters than anyone else in Alabama.

I had got to the point of drafting a bill . . . to file against J. K. Dimmick for abusing his power as the controlling stockholder for selfish purposes. We had some very straight up and down conversation, however, and Mr. Dimmick stated that much of the commissions appearing on the books to have been paid to himself, which I had denounced as illegal, were paid out again by him as secret commissions or bribes to other people to give us their business.

At this point Miss Charlotte Blair, the secretary of the company, chipped in and for some reason unknown to me manifested a violent dislike, not to me, but to Jack, insulting him and vilifying him in a way that could not be borne. Mr. Dimmick was evidently afraid of her, and instead of accepting her resignation, he to our great surprise asked Jack if he would move to Philadelphia and take a position . . . in his general brokerage business. In pursuance of this Jack resigned as treasurer of the pipe works, and Mr. Dimmick told me that he would give $1,000 for Miss Blair's resignation. It seemed strange to me that he did not ask for it or call a meeting of the board

of directors to relieve her from her position. It was a pitiful position for a
president of a company to occupy—afraid of his secretary!

In 1904 Dimmick asked for the resignation of Miss Blair. The understanding was that Jack was to take the position either of secretary and treasurer or manager. Miss Blair left in a rage, and devoted herself thence-
forward to raising the money to start the American Cast Iron Pipe Works in
opposition to the Dimmick Pipe Company, and with the express purpose of
breaking the latter. Did not Shakespeare say, "Hell hath no fury like a
woman scorned?" She got in her work all right.

*Charlotte Blair, the forty-three-year-old daughter of a Camden, South Caro-
lina, Confederate major, had learned the cast-iron pipe business as the stenographer for a Virginia manufacturer in the 1890s. She participated in the
establishment of the Dimmick works and sat on its board of directors, by some
reports the only woman in Alabama occupying a corporate board seat at the
time. After her break with Dimmick, Blair acquired the backing of the Atlanta
businessman John J. Eagan and founded a new company, American Cast Iron
Pipe Company (ACIPCO). It would become one of the most successful iron
pipe manufacturers in the United States, with its headquarters in Birmingham, though Blair would not live to enjoy its triumph.*

At the [1909] annual meeting of the pipe works . . . I offered several resolutions which were adopted as to monthly meetings of the board . . . and
other actions to put the business on a businesslike footing, instead of meetings being held whenever J. K. Dimmick wanted them. In fact for the first
time the concern was on a fair business basis of management, but it was too
late. The excessive and continued expenditures on plant and equipment and
so-called improvements had tied up the company's working capital, and it
was not able to pull through the storm. If it had been free from bonds it
could have shut down and waited for better times.

On March 18 we virtually agreed in conference with President John J.
Eagan [of ACIPCO] and J. R. McWane [11] to sell our pipe works . . . for
$526,000 [in] 6 percent cumulative preferred stock in that company. If
this arrangement had been carried out it would have given me practically
$100,000 of that 6 percent preferred stock. I thought at that time that my
financial troubles were about all over. There was no reason under Heaven
why it should not have been carried out. [Then] a very unfortunate thing
happened: a casting crane . . . at the pipe works fell. This caused [Eagan

Charlotte Blair, secretary of Dimmick Pipe Company and founder of American
Cast Iron Pipe Company (from *History of the American Cast Iron Pipe Company*
[Birmingham: n.p., n.d.])

and McWane] to suspect our roof was in bad condition, and they insisted upon it being specially examined by an engineer on their behalf before they went any further. The engineer reported that the roof needed quite a good deal of money expended upon it to put it in proper condition. They insisted on abating the original purchase [price] proposed by quite a considerable sum to cover the estimated expense of the new roof. J. K. Dimmick undertook to repudiate the whole transaction on the ground that we would make lots of money ourselves and did not need to go into any such consolidation. His son Fred and I tried to hold him down.

The pipe works, being top-heavy and tottering towards its fall, J. K. Dimmick . . . now proposed to take away his son [Fred] East and put in a practical man from another pipe shop as manager. In other words, he had squeezed all the juice out of the fruit and was willing to throw away the rind. On February 6, 1911, I was informed by a director of the First National Bank that they would apply for a receiver the next day for the pipe works unless J. K. Dimmick returned $10,000 which he had repaid to himself the past week out of the funds of the company. This caused a meeting of creditors of the pipe works the following day . . . and a two-months' breathing spell was agreed to by the local creditors, all the small ones to be paid off at once. In June 1911 the offer of the U.S. Pipe Company was accepted for the pipe works. [There was] only enough money to pay the debts of the concern, nothing to be left for the stockholders. Thus went my $90,000 of stock, which in 1907 had a book value of $144,000!

Renaissance

Bowron's retirement ended abruptly—and happily—in 1910 when he was given an opportunity to save a failing concern, the Southern Iron and Steel Company. As with so many southern iron enterprises, the history of this company was a story of outside control, heavy debt, and poor decision making. Bowron would be brought in because of his financial expertise, but in fact he would have the opportunity to function as the chief executive officer for more than a decade. He enjoyed the role and in time had considerable success, partly because he had more managerial authority than he ever had at TCI. The board of directors of this company was weaker and less intrusive generally, owing largely to the fact that bankruptcy courts had governed the company for extended periods. Although he initially had to contend with a supercilious English aristocrat as board chairman, Bowron eventually would deal primarily with two major northern stockholders, both more informed about the company and respectful of Bowron's judgment: James Platten, a banker, and William Coverdale, a design engineer. By the time the company had stabilized in 1914 and been reorganized under the name Gulf States Steel, Bowron was on his way to the pinnacle of his business career.

Despite the new business responsibilities, Bowron kept up his civic and religious commitments. He joined a new cause, the women's suffrage movement, that he believed would inject more morality into politics. In 1915 he engaged in conflict with the ministerial and lay leadership of the South Highland Presbyterian Church over how closely Biblical authority would be enforced in the pulpit. The church earlier had experienced rifts between fundamentalists and modernists; in 1910 the elders had examined their young minister, the Reverend Sterling Foster, about his suspect interpretation of the Bible, and when Foster would not say that he believed that Jonah had literally lived in the belly of a whale for three days, he was forced to resign. James Bowron had nothing to say in his autobiography about Foster's departure, but Foster's daughter, Virginia Foster Durr, would blame Bowron years later for contributing to the firing.[1]

He was clearly at the center of the controversy surrounding Henry Edmonds, a young modernist who came to the South Highland pulpit in 1913. Bowron's account leaves the distinct impression that he was Edmonds's primary antagonist in a controversy over Biblical interpretation, but Edmonds would suggest otherwise in his own autobiography. Without calling the name of the person, Edmonds identified as his chief opponent an unnamed fundamentalist fanatic whom he labeled an extreme premillennialist. This man opposed reform movements because he believed that the more rapid the advancement of human degradation the sooner the second coming of Christ would take place. That did not represent the attitude of the reform-minded Bowron. But Bowron's hostility to Edmonds, and particularly to the religious values he represented, should not be underestimated. A man of firm religious convictions already, Bowron had become increasingly determined to uphold strict Calvinism and Biblical literalism in his later years.

Spaniards have a proverb which says, "When one door shuts another opens." This is used by them in rather an unfeeling way: someone dies and they quote the proverb meaning that someone else is born to take the place. I have so often noted the goodness of God in so directing my life and affairs that, when I should find myself blocked in one direction, another way should open to me. I have had so many lessons of providential care and protection that I would be indeed ungrateful and stupid if I should fail to recognize this. After the crisis in my affairs owing to Joe's failure in Spain, when I was swamped with difficulty in England, I was offered a salary threefold greater than I was then receiving, to go to America, and I took it. When the English directors, rich and lazy, desired to

William P. G. Harding, Birmingham banker and director of the Federal Reserve Bank (courtesy of Birmingham Public Library Archives)

save trouble by selling out our American company to the Tennessee Coal, Iron and Railroad Company, leaving me stranded without a job in a strange country, I immediately had one offered me by that company as secretary and treasurer. When the pipe works paid its last dividend in 1907, falling into trouble because of the panic, the Bessemer Coal, Iron and Land Company started up and paid up to 1910.

Now, when the Bessemer Company was on the point of stopping its dividends, and the pipe works getting ready to go over the precipice into bankruptcy, and I had about one-third of my necessary expenses in sight by way of income and was sixty-six years old, an age when not one man in a thousand can get a new job, the dear Lord who had always helped me when I needed it before helped me again. That is His way of doing. The waters of Jordan were cleft in twain for the Israelites to march through into the promised land, but they did not clear apart until the soles of the feet of the priest in the front of the procession touched the brink of the water. It was about like that with me.

In July 1910 Erskine Ramsay . . . suggested to me that the Southern Iron and Steel Company was in more or less financial difficulty, which I already knew, and that they wanted someone to take the position of vice-president and treasurer and pull them out of the hole. The parties interested had asked the First National Bank to suggest someone, and he personally had suggested me to W. P. G. Harding, the president of the bank, as the right man—in view of my record in so successfully handling the finances of the Tennessee Coal, Iron and Railroad Company. He thought the salary would be perhaps as much as $9,000 per annum.

On August 3 Mr. Harding . . . said that if I would take charge of the finances of the Southern Iron and Steel Company, he would use all the power of the bank to back me financially and make my administration successful. Later in the morning I [met] Cecil A. Grenfell of London, who told me that he was a member of Parliament from a borough in Cornwall, and that he was the brother-in-law of the duke of Marlborough, having married the duke's sister; that the stock of the Southern Iron and Steel Company was controlled by Englishmen who had put a great deal of money into it, and that they had been told that I was an Englishman of large financial experience and thoroughly familiar with coal, iron, and steel of this district. [He said] they wanted the benefit of my services. He said that they were earning their interest but were embarrassed for want of ready money. The president, W. H. Hassinger, was discouraged, and they did not know just what to do.

I learned . . . that the payrolls were being delayed, and no payments at all made to ordinary creditors. President Hassinger declined to see creditors, who, I was told, piled up in the corridor and waited and could get no satisfaction or money either. That was the local situation, and some people were then talking about presenting a petition in bankruptcy. I knew very little about the status of the company or about its affairs at that time. Of course, I had known all about it originally.

It was originally the Alabama Steel and Wire Company [which] built in 1898 a rod and wire mill at Ensley closely abutting on our TCI blooming mill. In fact, that plant was built on land that we gave them, and we furnished them with red hot billets going over the fence on a conveyor. After that company broke amicable relations with the Tennessee Company, being accustomed to use Bessemer billets and not open-hearth [steel], it bought billets in the North and paid freight on them, which was an expensive proposition. [It] then decided to make its own. They played fast and loose with Bessemer [Coal, Iron and Land] Company as to locating in Bessemer, [but] instead they had located near Gadsden. The citizens of Gadsden [promised American Steel and Wire] $150,000 in donations, of which only about three-fourths was ever paid. There they built a blast furnace, open-hearth steelworks, and blooming mill, as cheaply as they could be built.

They bought ore lands . . . at Porterville and Gaylesville. The former ore was unworkable at a reasonable cost, having about a foot of ore on the top, another foot on the bottom, and a foot of rock in between the two. The latter was only a twenty-inch bed of ore anyway. Neither one could be mined economically. They had some brown ore over on the Georgia line dreadfully mixed with chert, which was found unprofitable to work. They had a coal mine at Labuco, on which they had spent some $60,000 and abandoned as unworkable; another coal mine at Graves in North Birmingham, where Captain Graves owned the surface above the coal mine for the extraction of shale for a brick plant. His operations had so shattered the top that it was a mere collecting point for water to run down into the coal mine below. Out of the eight boilers at that mine, seven were used to pump water! One, only, was used to hoist coal.

[The company] did, however, buy the Virginia mines from Truman H. Aldrich, six miles west of Bessemer, and in doing this, whether they knew it or not, made a "ten-strike." For that coal is not equalled in the state, being the cleanest and best coking coal, producing a coke of not exceeding 9 percent ash from unwashed coal.

There was a blast furnace at Trussville which had an excellent supply of water and of sand for the casting bed and nothing else of any practical value.

The furnace was too small and needed a new bustle pipe and hot blast main. The stock house was ready to blow down and did blow down a few years later. The engine house was partly held up apparently by the engines. The washing plant and conveyor were so cumbrous and ill adapted as to be absolutely unworkable. It is hard to see what advantage this agglomeration of troubles was to the Alabama Steel and Wire Company.

The company began to ship ore from Porterville . . . to the furnace at [Gadsden] to make iron, and there to be converted into steel in the open-hearth plant, rolled into billets, those billets shipped to the rod mill at Ensley and there to be rolled into rods, drawn into wire, and made into nails or barbed wire. Thus there was quite an amount of cross hauling and extra payment of railroad freights.

[Failure was] not surprising . . . with such a staggering load of trouble. Too many things to look after, all scattered. It would have been a miracle if it had done other than fail, as it did in the panic of 1907, and as Mr. A. R. Forsyth, who was secretary and treasurer of the company, [told] me, when they were adjudged bankrupt he exclaimed "Thank God," and went home and slept for a week.

[In the 1907 reorganization effort] they had gathered together quite a number of people of high rank and financial standing. Amongst these was the firm of Bourke-Schiff and Company of London, being of the same family as Mortimer L. Schiff of Kuhn-Loeb and Company, the great German banking house in New York. Mr. Cornelius Vanderbilt, Jr., a relative of the duke of Marlborough, was also a director of the new company. Mr. Grenfell stated that the great house of Rothschild was also interested. These people amongst them put up [about] $3 million of new money, and it was not enough for what they wanted to do.

Mr. Grenfell always complained that they had grossly overestimated the mineral resources and the values of the property which they were describing. This is very likely. My experience teaches that enthusiasm is the dynamic power which is needed to accomplish things. The enthusiastic promoter makes light of difficulties and always looks on the bright side of everything. Otherwise, he would never succeed in promoting.

They made Mr. Hassinger president, and he, although an able man and a very successful one, for whose judgment I had high regard, made what appeared to me to be two colossal mistakes, either one or the other of which was sufficient to wreck the company. One was that instead of locating at Bessemer . . . where he would have been close to the Virginia Mines, and where he might have purchased at that time the Raimund ore mines which were afterwards acquired by the Republic Iron and Steel Company, he selected Gadsden as the strategic center of the company's operations. If he had spent that money in removing ... to Bessemer ... the history of the company might have been radically different.

The other great mistake was [the money] that he spent upon the brown ore mines of Georgia ... [including] the payment of existing second mortgages and receivers' certificates and ... the construction of a central power plant with electrical equipment and connections with washers, reservoirs, pipe lines, standard- and narrow-gauge railroad tracks, approximately $1 million. That sum would have purchased the Raimund ore mines at Bessemer and [would] have gone a long way towards the building of a blast furnace at that point. It seems somewhat difficult to believe, but all this expenditure was made apparently on faith of the old workings and open cuts, and the surface indications at other points, and not a single drill hole was put down in the virgin ground to find what ore was there available. As it finally turned out, the company had all the facilities it needed for a large and profitable production of ore except the ore itself, and practically every dollar of the money that was invested in [the Georgia] enterprise was lost. The ore produced therefrom cost more money to put it on the railroad tracks than ore of a similar quality might have been bought for in the open market without one dollar investment of capital!

On the other hand, ... they did construct at [Gadsden] a rod and wire mill on a large scale, of the most solid construction and efficient character. That plant stands today unsurpassed in the entire country. There is nothing better of its class and character. In that construction they spent some $1,400,000.

Their money had given out, [and] they had no one in charge of finances— that is, of raising them. Construction was not finished. Market conditions were very unsatisfactory. Margins were small. Costs were high. The tonnage of brown ore produced was inadequate. To cap the climax they were capitalized at $17 million stock and $10 million of bonds. There were also debentures, and at the time spoken of a large amount of floating debt. Some of the parties who had furnished machinery, or even the steel which had gone into the buildings, held mechanics' liens and were threatening to enforce them, and others were threatening to file petitions in bankruptcy.

The office came to me as every other one has come to me, unsolicited. I felt however that I ought not to be too modest, but put my best foot foremost, and so I inquired how much they were paying Mr. Hassinger, and they told me $25,000 per annum. "Well," I said, "if I accept this position, it means giving up the life of a country gentleman, with nothing to do but study in the library, make speeches at political conventions, Masonic lodges, and take a little general part in public life and affairs. It means getting back and sweating blood in dealing with creditors, lying awake nights studying how to meet the bills and payrolls, but you cannot afford to pay me as much as you are paying Mr. Hassinger. You are paying more than the company's finances justify, and I would not consent to your paying more than $15,000 for the position." After nine years of being my own master I became again the humble slave of a company, to keep office hours and to be bossed around by everybody from the directors at one end to the stenographer at the other!

I got a telegram from the executive committee in New York to be very cautious in giving people notes unless receiving large concessions. This both annoyed and amused me. It showed the committee knew nothing of financing industrial operations. If an account is open and overdue, you may be sued upon it now. If you make a note for the account you have put off the evil day of payment so far, and your creditor is satisfied because he has something he can use in bank. It was in this way that I succeeded in carrying TCI through its many years of financial difficulty.

I had found to my horror when the July statements were submitted to me that we were losing on operating account $1,000 per day, totally exclusive of the bond and debenture interest accounts, which with interest on floating debt aggregated nearly $2,000 per day. I realized that a company in such condition could not go along very far, and my efforts were therefore directed to "sparring" for time, postponing payments, realizing on liquid assets, and studying the situation to enable us to make positive and sound recommendations for the future of the company. On September 16 our steel plant manager . . . gave me a memo that it would require $164,000 to bring on the steel plant to a capacity of finishing 300 tons per day. It is hard to describe the difficulties of carrying on business with people who were producing some of our most necessary supplies, such as sulfuric acid, aluminum, and tool steel, not to speak of merchandise for the commissaries, declining to sell us except with sight draft attached to bill of lading.

On January 2, 1911, I went to Gadsden and that night addressed the Gadsden Business Men's Club for an hour and a quarter. The newspaper said speaking of me in advance that I was a man of "wide and accurate information." I am disposed to believe that they thought otherwise when I had finished talking to them that night. I sat for several hours after dinner listening to one speaker after another singing of Gadsden's advantages, and all agreeing that they were greater than those of [the] Birmingham district, and that iron could be made in Gadsden more cheaply than in Birmingham. When I arose at half past eleven to reply, [I] told them that Gadsden was handicapped by freight rates and thin seams of ore [by] at least $1.50 [per ton] in the making of iron as compared with Birmingham. The gloom and silence could have been cut with a knife. I proceeded to explain to them how it was necessary to carry the material produced into higher forms of finished goods instead of attempting to sell semifinished material. But from then on I was man of very doubtful popularity to say the least.

I . . . learned that the [company's executive] committee had set a salary of $25,000 per annum, and traveling expenses, for Mr. Grenfell as chairman of the board, and apparently he was going to travel . . . between England and America at his pleasure at the company's expense. I was not willing to do all the work and have someone else take so large a salary and the honor of accomplishing a successful reorganization. [Grenfell] wrote me that he hoped he could rely on my support of "his" administration. I was thunderstruck at such a letter, for it was a gross breach of faith. I had come into the company five months before at his request upon the express assurance that I was to be the head of it. To save expenses I had cut the president's salary from $25,000 to $12,000 cash, and cut down our offices and our staff, and instituted every possible economy. At a stroke comes another who had openly admitted that he was "not a business man" to draw $25,000 per annum without any stated duties, to rank over me, so that if anything were accomplished to put the company on its feet, I would get no credit for it! To say that I was indignant would be to say too little. I could not afford to throw up my situation, besides which I was gradually liquidating the large indebtedness of the company and thus helping the district, so I swallowed my wounded pride and went on.

Grenfell wrote urging me to engage an additional sales manager for wire products, and I replied that our sales department was already selling more stuff than we could produce, and I was unwilling to pile up needless salaries. Grenfell . . . [sold] 10,000 tons of axle billets. I wired him to withdraw the quotation as we had no facilities for producing axle billets; no testing machine, no equipment for chipping, or anything. He estimated our present net earnings would run $500,000 per annum. I estimated they would amount to $116,000, out of which the company had about $750,000 interest to pay, besides needing money for liquidation of floating debt and for the completion of unfinished plant. He was living in fools' paradise and very unfit for the position to which he had been elected. Our total loss for the year of 1910, including coupon interest, amounted to $661,000!

On March 29 Grenfell wired from New York asking what we were doing to provide for the next coupons in New York. As chairman of the company he ought to have known that it had not earned one dollar towards its interest coupons during the previous year, and that I was doing mighty well to meet the payrolls. I had been compelled the previous week to use billets as collateral with the Alabama Great Southern Railroad to prevent our traffic being stopped.

Grenfell wrote again insisting on a reduction in our general operating staff, and I wrote him that he could cut off myself and that the organization of the company was its strongest asset. I was taken very much aback by Grenfell's demand for immediate payment of $10,000 salary and prompt and regular payment of the succeeding installments, and said so. I [knew] that Mr. Grenfell's salary of $25,000 was . . . a liability, just as our coupons were liabilities. But [they were] not to be paid for in cash while the poor Negroes were sweating all day at the steelworks and needed their money with which to buy flour and meat and shoes.

Grenfell . . . caused the executive committee to vote him $40,000 in our bonds to be held by him as collateral security for the payment of his salary. This again was an act of bankruptcy, but no one on the outside knew about it. I learned that the assistant secretary, so-called, who was nothing but an office boy in Mr. Grenfell's office, had left suddenly without notice. This was explained afterwards when we found out that during Mr. Grenfell's absence in London, having left with him the key to his box, this young man had taken the greater part of the $40,000 of our bonds deposited with Mr. Grenfell as security for his salary, and had sold them on the "curb" market, using the money to speculate in oil and mining stocks and of course lost it all. I held Mr. Grenfell responsible for this $40,000 of bonds, but he would not admit the liability.

I received a reply from Grenfell ignoring his broken promises, minimizing my work, and saying that they had put $600,000 into the company for me, and that he would call a meeting of the executive committee to present my resignation. Heaven only knows where they put that money. It never reached Birmingham. I think the explanation was that they put the greater part of it on the table with one hand in exchange for new notes, and took it off the table with the other hand to pay the old ones which they held. [I am] quite certain we did not draw down over $300,000. I took this correspondence to President Harding at the First National Bank. Harding wrote Grenfell, resigning as a director in the company and [telling] him that any successor to me would have to carry $100,000 on hand for claims which I had been able to stand off.

June 15, 1911, [was] a pretty ... typical day as to my occupation: arrang[ed] with a railroad company to buy its steel scrap, taking nails and bars in payment; bluffed creditors on overdue account for leather belting out of bringing suit and made them take notes which they had once returned to us; got a $10,000 mortgage note then due on one of our mines extended four months; arranged to borrow from a bank on an account for steel billets and got the customer to take a monthly quota one month ahead of time so as to furnish the collateral; agreed to shut down operations for three weeks to reduce our wage outgo, as well as make some repairs. It was interesting work, but it was hard.

On July 8 Grenfell wrote me that New York parties had failed him and that he must get some of the underwriting [of new bonds] done in England, and asked me to keep the company out of the hands of a receiver until he cabled either his success or failure. So when he came down this way off his high perch, and recognized what I was doing, I immediately replied withdrawing my resignation and assuring him that I would see the company through its troubles. Grenfell's appeal ... filled me with new energy and determination.

In August 1911 our rod mill was down for want of billets, and still New York was wiring me to send storage warrants for billets that they might be lodged as security for some of the maturing interest coupons. I wired back that we could not spare them. I was determined that as the bondholders would get the property against their bonds, they might take it for their coupons also. I positively would not take the men's wages and money needed for supply bills and turn it over to the bondholders, and I did not, and in that way alone I succeeded in liquidating local accounts.

On July 10, 1912, at about 10:00 A.M., I was amazed at the newspaper telephoning me asking what I had to say "about the petition." I did not know what he was talking about, and he explained that a petition had been filed against the Southern Iron and Steel Company in bankruptcy. This turned out to be true. The petition was filed by two young attorneys on behalf of three petitioning creditors whose aggregate claims amounted to about $514,000 and who asked for the appointment of a Gadsden Coca-Cola salesman as receiver for the company!

On July 11 we filed an answer and demurrer demanding a jury at the hearing of the petition. The following day the railroads cut off all credit, refusing to deliver further goods except on cash payments of freights. Bankers in New York refused to handle our foreign exchange, and the moneylenders in St. Louis notified all our customers to remit to them direct. At the same time the business kept running along somehow or other. Orders were heavier and prices stiffening a little bit.

On July 15 the reorganization committee in New York announced that a separate reorganization of the Southern Iron and Steel Company would be undertaken on a basis of cutting off all the stockholders. I sent a reassuring circular to our customers telling them that we were going to be reorganized and that debentures were already deposited for that express purpose and that customers might continue dealing with us without any anxiety as all our obligations to them would be carefully attended to.

On July 17 they wired from New York that they had agreed to close the New York office of the company to reduce expenses. At the same time the committee asked us to take active steps to install all possible economies, and I had a meeting of four or five department heads on the subject of reduction of salaries. Four of our department heads accepted my proposed reduction of salaries. I proposed this reduction on a basis of 5 percent on salaries $3,000 up to $5,000, 10 percent on those above $5,000, and 20 percent for . . . myself.

On July 25 I had an outspoken conference with Otto Marx[2] and also with Walker Percy as attorney for the New York bondholders, and insisted that they could not afford to have the bondholders to throw the concern into receivership in their interest and freeze out the little fellows, the common creditors, who held no security. My attitude was that the unsecured creditors should be allowed to . . . [have] their accounts assumed by the new company. I was really amazed to find that the big bondholders were shylocks. They wanted the earth with a gilt fence around it, and in the long run they substantially got it.

On July 31 a local committee of creditors . . . sent for me, and I went over and spoke to them twenty minutes about the general situation. I was informed that afterwards Mr. Harding spoke and everyone present without dissent signed the petition to Judge W. I. Grubb[3] to appoint me as receiver. The same day I had a meeting of our eleven traveling [sales]men and told them to keep their feet warm and their heads cool, and we were going to see this thing through, and that they might just as well keep in touch with their customers.

On August 1 I was attending to my work when Henry Badham came into the office to congratulate me on having been appointed not one of the receivers but the sole receiver of the company on the petition of forty-five of the local creditors. I was not even present. Judge Grubb said he appointed me solely on account of my supposed ability to finance the business and keep it in operation. When it had failed in 1907, three different receivers and afterwards a fourth were nominated, at $8,000 each, and they shut the plants down and they stayed down for a year and a half. In this case, not a single plant was shut down for one hour, not a single payroll was postponed for one hour, and the business went straight on. It would only be true to admit that I laid awake about half the night planning and thinking. I had so many problems to solve that one might well pause to think and pray, and especially a man getting on nearly seventy years of age and without the energy of youth.

My first month as trustee showed $2,932 estimated profits. My operations as trustee for the month of October showed over $8,000 profit made for the creditors after paying one month's share of interest and taxes, and allowing for depreciation. I felt greatly encouraged! My November results showed a clean profit for the creditors of about $4,000, after bearing all idle expense, and the monthly quota for taxes and interest on the outstanding debts of the old company. I received an abusive letter from Mr. Grenfell for not paying his salary, although . . . he had held $40,000 of our bonds as security for it and allowed them by his carelessness to disappear. This was the last letter I . . . had from him until 1919.

January 31, 1913, was the date set by the court for the sale of the Southern Iron and Steel Company property in bankruptcy by me as trustee. Mr. James W. Platten arrived from New York . . . and made heavy deposit of bonds at the last minute aggregating . . . 97 percent of all the bonds outstanding. In November I held pro forma a meeting of the stockholders and ratified the sale of all its property to the [new company], Gulf States Steel Company. Notices were made on December 1 through the newspapers, bylaws accepted, customers notified, and all temporary arrangements thus brought to an end. So ended all interim business arrangements and so started another page, and one of the most interesting in the whole history of my long and interesting life.

The new board of directors . . . notified me not to borrow any money without express authority from the board. This was very amusing, as for half a century my principal occupation had been the borrowing of money for corporation purposes when the board of directors itself could not, or would not, find any. A meeting was held . . . of the reorganization committee at the Bankers' Trust Company, and I was not even invited in to sit with them, but sat outside amongst the hats and coats in an anteroom like a Negro porter.

Finally I got pretty tired of the situation and said to Judge Grubb, who was staying at the same hotel, that it looked to me as though the entire operations of the new company would be throttled, and it might be necessary for some of the stockholders to apply to him again for a receiver. He promptly said in that case he would appoint me again. With this knowledge, and feeling very keenly and rather bitterly the lack of personal confidence in a man who had already demonstrated his ability single-handedly to manage the property, I refused to return to Birmingham as president of the company unless I was at least given authority to conduct current affairs in the usual way by signing notes for purchases and endorsing receivables for rediscount. This authority was given me.

On February 4, 1914, Mr. Platten arrived on a visit. All of us went to meet him at the hotel and spend the evening, and visited the steelworks together the following day. He was generally pleased with his visit and what he saw and returned to Birmingham. He and I and President George Gordon Crawford of TCI dined together. Mr. Platten then asked me to excuse them and I said good night, and Crawford told me afterwards that they discussed me personally, as to my fitness for the position. He told Mr. Platten that he did not know anyone who could run concerns without money in the way that I could, as I had proved that for twenty years in the Tennessee Coal and Iron Company. If they had millions of dollars to spend, no doubt I would need assistance, but if they wanted the company developed without putting up any money, they had better let me do it my own way—all of which was very gratifying.

In March 1914 we entertained the vice-president of the National Suffrage Society, Mrs. Kimbrough, and then I had the pleasure of presiding over a most interesting meeting at the Jefferson Theatre, crowded with those who wished to hear the arguments in favor of woman suffrage. The theatre was packed to the doors, and an overflow meeting [was] held at the Cable Hall, which was also filled—the speakers alternating from one meeting to the other. The newspaper [reported]: "Jas. Bowron, who stands unique as the one Birmingham man with a 40 year vision of the suffrage question in England and America, will lend a very individual touch to the votes for women at the mass meeting at the Jefferson Theatre. He is to have the temporary chairmanship and will make the address of welcome." I had presided over a meeting in the interest of woman suffrage in England . . . which was addressed by the well-known English suffragist Mrs. Lydia Becker. I was most favorably impressed by the appearance, dignity, wit, good humor, and logic of the distinguished ladies whom it was my privilege to introduce [in Birmingham], including amongst others Miss Jane Addams.

A Birmingham newspaper, 1913:
WHO'S FOR WOMAN SUFRAGE [sic] CAUSE IN BIRMINGHAM AND WHY?
James Bowron said:

"I have been in favor of woman suffrage for fifty years and presided over a meeting in England in that interest more than forty years ago.

"I was accustomed there to see women voting in elections for poor law guardians, County Councillors [sic] and Boards of Education. I never saw the slightest trouble incident to such voting, and have never seen any reason why the same intelligence that could direct a vote on local politics should not be directed toward voting in national politics.

"Two-thirds of the members of all churches are women. They are naturally more inclined to policies of religion, morality and benevolence, than are men. If women had a vote there would be a higher standard of civic righteousness and observance of law. If their good will was necessary to sway elections there would be less official ignoring of law breakers. There would be a stricter enforcement of laws against vice, drunkenness and gambling. There would be a tendency toward greater cleanliness and better provisions for the protection of the weak and of the aged, or children. I can readily imagine many directions where the political influence of women would be helpful, and I know of none in which it would be hurtful. I am, therefore, a pronounced advocate of woman suffrage."

My brother Will wrote me [in 1911] that he was a member of the Unitarian church and had been for five years. As he is a votary of evolution, I suppose I might use his argument and say that [he] was coming up from the jellyfish to the lizard. I had much rather have heard from him that he had risen to the full stature of a man in Christ Jesus. I have more respect for the Jew than I have for the Unitarian. I [later] received a letter from one of my nieces asking that I would take Will into my family to remain with me for the rest of his life. One single reason prevented this: he had been through all his life more or less of an agnostic—sneering more or less openly at all

Henry Edmonds, minister of South Highland Presbyterian Church (courtesy of Birmingham Public Library Archives)

religious profession, and I could not afford to take anyone into my family whose bearing and conversation would offset and counteract the strong religious influence that I was trying to create.

In November 1913, in conference with Dr. Henry M. Edmonds, I consented to join the South Highland Presbyterian Church and to serve as an elder. My feelings on this matter were very mixed. One of my ancestors was a convert of George Fox, the founder of the Quaker religion. From that date down to myself the Bowron family had been strictly Quakers, and believing thoroughly in these principles, it became a question purely of expediency with me. I realized approaching seventy years of age that I should never pull up my roots in this country where my children were marrying and all becoming settled in life, and that I should never therefore be restored to my own people. Under these circumstances, the question was "Should I not be leading a more useful life if I joined the church of which my wife was an active member and where I myself had already been for eighteen years a teacher of the adult Bible class?" By doing so I would take my share of personal responsibility and activity, which otherwise I was allowing other people to carry for me. These considerations controlled, and I told Dr. Edmonds that I would be governed accordingly. On November 23 I was accepted at a meeting of the session of the South Highland Presbyterian Church as a member of that church, and at the following meeting of the congregation I was, after the service, elected an elder. How little Dr. Edmonds could realize that he was preparing the way for his own separation from the church as the result of that day's work.

On January 31, 1915, as I sat in my place in church, part of a crowded congregation, I heard . . . Edmonds preach that belief in the inspiration of the Bible, the story of Jonah, and the virgin birth of our Savior were nonessential. I was dreadfully shocked and said to my colleague, Mr. H. R. Todd, that I thought we ought to protest against it, and we went together to him after the sermon and Mr. Todd said to him, "Doctor, I am afraid your sermon will hurt the faith of many." Edmonds replied that he was sorry.

Dr. Edmonds returned from his vacation [in 1915] about the same time that I did, and instead of waiting to meet the session and telling us whether he had in any way changed the views which he had expressed at our last conference, he had broke out into print, publishing every Sunday morning in the *Age-Herald* a sermon in which he was expressing views inconsistent with the church whose standards he had vowed to preserve. One of his sermons began with these words: "We are not saved by anything that Christ did for us, but by what He does in us." His teaching [was] the well-known and hopeless error of assuming that the individual, by contemplating the image of beauty and virtue and holiness, will seek to imitate and be changed into the same image, which is a method of self-salvation by the sinner lifting himself into Heaven by his boot straps.

Dr. Edmonds dissented from the virgin birth of the Savior. [He] claimed that God was not angry with the sinners, although the Scripture says that he "is angry with the sinners every day." He claimed, therefore, that there was no need for anyone to die as a sacrifice, and took his stand on the text in Micah, "What doth the Lord require of thee but do justly, and to love mercy and walk humbly with thy God?" Of course, in taking such a position Dr. Edmonds was fatally contradicting the Lord's teaching in John 3:18 ["He that believeth on him is not condemned: but he that believeth not is condemned already, because he hath not believed in the name of the only begotten Son of God."] and Paul's teaching in Galatians 2:16 ["Knowing that a man is not justified by the works of the law, but by the faith of Jesus Christ, even we have believed in Jesus Christ, that we might be justified by the faith of Christ, and not by the works of the law: for by the works of the law shall no flesh be justified."].

On September 13, 1915, we met together, and Dr. Edmonds, as though nothing had taken place, went on with the current business and then suggested the engagement of a certain gentleman [for] a revival meeting . . . in the church. All voted "Aye" except myself, and I voted "No." Dr. Edmonds inquired why I so voted, and I said because I had seen a great deal of revival meetings in my life and I did not think that any would or could be successful unless Christ crucified for the sins of others was preached in that church, and that He was not being so preached at that time. This, of course, brought on a full, general, and frank expression of opinion.

Dr. Edmonds said . . . that he took the position now that he had as much right to push his views on the rest of the church as we had to push ours on him. Whilst he believed that he would be [condemned] by the Presbytery and again by the Synod and again by the General Assembly, still in twenty-five years he thought the church generally would think as he did, and he would therefore continue to advocate his own views. Upon this frank and open refusal to maintain the standards of the church, I at once moved a resolution that, in the discharge of our solemn duties as elders of the church, we were constrained to express our dissent from the sermons being published in the *Age-Herald* by the pastor of our church.

This resolution was supported by H. R. Todd, Samuel D. Weakley,

John W. Sibley, J. K. Brockman, C. Bradshaw, and myself, but to my surprise C. C. Heidt, S. W. Lee, A. W. Allen, V. S. Gage, and H. M. Archibald[4] voted against it. The attitude of elders Heidt and Lee was soon afterwards made clear. They were dreadfully afraid of the injury to come to the church as the result of a split. Mr. Gage said he did not understand what the trouble was, Allen and Archibald never opened their mouth except to vote, so I do not know what their reason was for taking that stand. This resolution going on record ... put the matter where it would necessarily come up on the examination of ... the next meeting of the Presbytery, which was something that Dr. Edmonds's supporters were extremely anxious to avoid.

On September 16 I had a visit from Henry L. Badham and Frank P. Glass ... to ask me to withdraw my opposition to the preaching of Dr. Edmonds. [They said] that he was a young man and that he might change his views and that I should give him time. I told them that Dr. Edmonds was a young man, but I was an old man, past three score and ten, and it could not be long before I was called upon to stand myself before the great white throne, and come what might, regardless of personal friendships or consequences, I could not take the position of denying my Savior. Either He was the Son of God and a part of the Godhead and made sin for us, although He knew none, and bore in His own person our sins upon the cross, or he was otherwise the illegitimate son of a carpenter, a wonderful preacher, but a monomaniac carried away with a sense of his own importance. Christians believed the first proposition and the Jews, Moslems, and Unitarians believed the second. Dr. Edmonds might take the second, but I must take the first, and the committee departed. Henry Badham remark[ed] that he told them before they came that they could not argue with me on such a question.

On October 8 John W. Sibley showed me a copy of the "Presbyterian Standard" published in Charlotte, North Carolina, quoting Dr. Edmonds's sermons and strongly condemning them. The situation had now become public and could no longer be hushed up as his friends desired. On October 10 Dr. Edmonds made a statement to the congregation of what he thought were his differences with the session and expressed the thought that he could stay and build up a "new Presbyterianism."

On October 20 ... the Presbytery was in session over at Fayette, Alabama. We of the South Highland Church who dissented from this teaching declined to send any representative to the Presbytery or to present any charges against Dr. Edmonds whatever. He went there attended by some thirty-five or forty of his friends who sent special communication to the *Age-Herald* and *News*, both of whose editors were his strong supporters, to the effect that they were interviewing the delegates to the Presbytery and pledging them to support Dr. Edmonds. This ... in common daily life would be called tampering with the jury. The Presbytery appointed its own committee to examine Dr. Edmonds as to his teaching, and after a session of several hours, voted that they found his teachings were not in accord with the standards of the Presbyterian Church.[5]

We held a special meeting of the session in my office, [at] which Dr. Edmonds ... notified us that he would not remain in the church under the decision of the Presbytery and handed over a briefly written resignation. This was entirely out of harmony with the law of the Presbyterian church, as only the Presbytery can install a minister or release him from his duties— the congregation may call him or might wish to dispense with him, but only the Presbytery can act. Notwithstanding Dr. Edmonds's written resignation, he was still, under church law, our pastor, and we could not call anyone else until the action of the Presbytery. We went to church on Sunday morning to find a huge banner floating upon the Jewish temple across the street, announcing the so-called Independent Presbyterian Church. How a church could be Presbyterian which did not belong to a Presbytery has never been explained.

About 60 percent of the congregation numerically, but representing nearly 70 percent of the financial supporters of the congregation, withdrew and followed Dr. Edmonds. I would not venture to assert in the slightest degree why they were doing it, except that they liked his interesting way of talking. I never met one who was willing to admit that he knew the grounds of difference between Dr. Edmonds and the Presbytery. So the word began to be published assiduously, by some of them that knew no better, that we the session had persecuted Dr. Edmonds and driven him out of the church. The reader of the preceding pages will realize that I had as much to do with it as any other man—perhaps a little more, and I have never felt otherwise than that I did right and would do it again. I could not do otherwise than stand for the honor and the dignity of the Savior, the Atonement, His mother, His word, and His day, and His name, and have striven and shall strive to maintain the same without fear of man.

On March 1, 1916, I went to Dr. John D. S. Davis for examination. I had been participating in indoor baseball at the YMCA gymnasium and during the previous week had actually run a foot race in a relay race on the gym-

Bowron with four younger sons who served in the army during World War I (courtesy of Birmingham Public Library Archives)

nasium floor one length and back, and am glad to say that I won it. I continued, however, to be so much out of breath that in running around the gymnasium I usually had to drop out about the second lap, and I wanted to find out the reason. Dr. Davis said my lungs were all right, but my blood pressure was too high—about 170, my pulse before exercise 96 and after slight exercise 144, and urine analysis showed albumen present. I was shocked at this of course, not having suspected such a thing, and was ordered to stop all exercise in the gym and to abstain from red meat.

I thereupon naturally conferred with my son-in-law Dr. McLester . . . who said that for a man of my age 150 blood pressure would be normal, and a pulse rate of 90 would be accepted by [an] insurance company. He made a very thorough examination of me, [saying] that my heart was all right in every respect, but that it was affected by kidney trouble. This, which is brought on very extensively by wrong diet, exposure, strain of any kind, frequently develops into Bright's disease and causes death of hundreds, perhaps thousands, of businessmen many years before their time. It is marvelous that I should have carried the strain of corporation finances practically since 1866 without any breakdown of my system, whilst nearly every colleague that I had ever had in any way approaching my own age, had fallen by the way.

I have had, however, great advantage over many of them in total abstention from Sunday work and having many other objects of thought other than business, so that my mind might be rested in all sorts of religious, sociological, athletic, musical, literary, or Masonic work, instead of everlastingly brooding over business cares. If I had attempted to carry my own cares for monthly notes and payrolls instead of living up to Matthew 11:28–30 ["Come unto me, all ye that labor and are heavy laden, and I will give you rest. Take my yoke upon you, and learn of me; for I am meek and lowly in heart: and ye shall find rest unto your souls. For my yoke is easy, and my burden is light."], I would have been buried many years ago. McLester then recommended that to ease the heart I should abstain from my usual habit of walking to the office, and also all of the forms of physical exercise including my morning sitting-up exercise, and that to rest the kidneys from their overwork I should restrict my eating of animal food to once per day. As I never do anything by halves, I went him one better and restricted my animal food to once every other day and have kept that up pretty well for the past four years.

It is fair to say that finding myself for the first time in my life face to face with a physical breakdown, I had to take stock of things pretty seriously. I knew of others who had kidney trouble who had passed away in a few weeks or few months at most. I was not at all concerned as to myself, having then and at all other times perfect confidence in the finished work of my blessed Redeemer, but I did not feel at that time that if I were taken away there would remain adequate provision for my large family to maintain its members in a reasonable condition of comfort and finish the education of the younger members. I had accomplished much since 1910, but felt that there was much left for me to do, so I desired to take every possible means of conserving my health and making such good use of the time that might be left to me as might be possible.

On December 9, 1917, [my daughter] Edith was not well. [Edith, twenty-eight years old, was in the late stages of pregnancy.] We felt anxious about her, and her mother took her down to the Davis Infirmary, feeling that it would be more satisfactory to have her in charge of someone. But at 12:45 A.M. Monday morning [we] received [a] message that she was in convulsions. I was quite unable to walk down . . . , suffering with my heart, and could only lie awake humbly waiting at the feet of God. At 3:00 A.M., as she was in repeated convulsions, Dr. Lupton took her little girl from her, who had been alive up to the time of her convulsions. The convulsions had been caused by uremic poison, and her kidneys were not acting. We got in touch with several of our dearest friends . . . that we might start a chain of prayer for her. As the afternoon progressed she was more restful—drank some water and recognized several of us. We went down on the Tuesday morning, finding her apparently improving, the kidneys apparently commencing to act, the heart and pulse and temperature seemingly improved. She was conscious and talking. I went to the office feeling more cheerful. [I] stayed there . . . until noon and . . . thence back to the infirmary, feeling much encouraged, but within a very few minutes after arrival she suddenly collapsed. Oxygen was administered, but she pushed the tube away saying they were choking her. That was her last expression. The respiration became slower and stopped at 2:00 P.M.

We went home, receiving friends that afternoon and evening. The following day, December 12, we received a wonderful number of kind and sympathetic business, social, and church friends. It was deeply interesting. I can count up from memory the birth of fifty-two of my own children, grandchildren, brothers, sisters, nephews, or nieces without such a tragedy befalling any of the families involved, so that the proportion of women who are taken away in childbirth must be very small, but when it does occur it is profoundly touching and pathetic. As the chairman of the sick visitation committee of our church, it had been my task to visit a great many other people in the hours of bereavement, and despite my large family the shadow of death had not crossed my own threshold since January 1883 until December 1917—nearly thirty-five years—a long time, but quite in accordance with the fullness and richness of the unmerited mercy and blessing which a bountiful, compassionate, and generous God has vouchsafed to my dear wife and myself. The Lord supported us both very much at this trying hour, and I think our testimony of faith and peace and rest in Him was helpful to some of our friends who came to comfort us and went away comforted.

On December 13 we had a service at the house by Dr. Albert Sidney Johnson and went to Elmwood [Cemetery] where we laid our dear one to rest in the cemetery lot that I had but recently purchased expecting, of course, to be the first one laid there. The eight brothers of our daughter had acted as the pallbearers; there might have been nine, but Paul [the youngest] was not needed.

Wartime

The second decade of the twentieth century brought political changes that James Bowron disliked intensely. Republicans had controlled national policy since 1897, and while Bowron had not always agreed with Theodore Roosevelt, he had enjoyed the relatively high tariffs and hard money of the Republican rule. Roosevelt accepted the idea of limited competition and large-business organization in basic industries like iron and steel. He had consented to U.S. Steel's emergency takeover of TCI in 1907. But after Roosevelt came political leaders less sympathetic to Bowron's view. William Howard Taft, though a conservative, allowed a full-scale investigation of U.S. Steel's policies. The election of Woodrow Wilson represented a triumph of anti-monopoly feeling, and his administration sponsored a wide range of economic policies that Bowron opposed. Some of the actions most objectionable to Bowron were the handiwork of Birmingham's own congressman, Oscar Underwood. The Underwood-Simmons tariff removed all protection on "monopoly" industries, including iron and steel, in the hope of creating keener competition. To replace the revenue lost in tariff reduction, an income tax on individuals and corporations was instituted for the first time.

Bowron objected strongly to the government's action against U.S. Steel. He had always believed that the iron and steel industry suffered from too much competition. He approved of the system of voluntary price supports cultivated by his friend, Judge Gary of U.S. Steel. Bowron saw no evidence of monopoly exploitation by U.S.

Steel, and in fact he continued to identify personally with Tennessee Coal and Iron, the enterprise that he believed he had helped bring to greatness. He knew that U.S. Steel had invested more capital than any previous owners of TCI and had brought the Birmingham district closer to realizing its potential than otherwise would have happened. He took issue with his longtime acquaintance Richard Edmonds of the *Manufacturers' Record*, who criticized U.S. Steel's failure to develop its properties while the antitrust suit was in the courts.

The case against U.S. Steel, the changes in tariffs, and the increase in taxes encouraged an increasing distrust of government among industrialists. Government-fixed freight rates, established when iron prices were very high in 1907, created a mounting burden as the price of iron fell after that year and thus contributed to a feeling of hostility against Washington. World War I then brought previously unimagined government involvement in the industrial economy. The national government intervened in labor relations, transportation, and the distribution of critical resources, all in an effort to maximize industrial output for the war effort. It even considered building its own armor plant to test whether the government could produce war material more cheaply than private industry.

James Bowron objected vociferously to government interference that he deemed both unprincipled and unproductive. He was convinced that the Democratic administration in Washington was unfairly harsh to the iron and steel industry, generally presided over by Republicans like himself. The government's intervention unnecessarily agitated labor relations and encouraged unionism. Perhaps because as a chief executive officer he now dealt more with labor problems, he manifested stronger antilabor views than he had in the past. He criticized his fellow industrialists for acceding too readily to the demands of labor when times were good, though he was himself guilty of making wage concessions to keep up production when profits were high. Bowron's antiunion attitude accurately reflected the commitments of the powerful "open-shop" movement among American manufacturers of the first three decades of this century, an effort that effectively stymied most unionization prior to the Great Depression.

I had a long interview with President Crawford of the Tennessee Coal and Iron Company, who told me that the U.S. Steel Corporation wanted my evidence on their behalf in the government suit for dissolution. At this time he opened up very confidentially and fully, showing me the future plans of the Tennessee Coal Company as to developments of Fairfield and Westfield . . . [and] the plans for [a company] hospital and the bringing of Dr. Lloyd Noland[1] from government service at Panama. On January 9, 1914, I was on the witness stand in the federal courtroom for four and one-half hours, giving evidence under direct and cross examination on behalf of . . . the U.S. Steel Corporation. Judge David Reid[2] of Pittsburgh, who conducted the direct examination, was good enough to say to President George Gordon Crawford that I was the best witness he had ever seen on the stand in his life.

Bowron's views in support of U.S. Steel were well known long before he gave evidence on the company's behalf. Doubtless his testimony in 1914 reflected the same opinions that had been reported earlier by the press.

Birmingham *Age-Herald*, October 27, 1911:

JAMES BOWRON THINKS IT PROFOUNDLY INJURIOUS

"I think the effect of the government's prosecution of the United States Steel Corporation will be profoundly injurious to this district and to the Iron and Steel trade at large," said James Bowron, vice-president, Southern Iron and Steel Co.

"For probably two years to come the right of that corporation and its subsidiaries to do business will be under a cloud, and their expenditures upon improvements in this district and elsewhere will probably be held in abeyance pending the decision of the suit in the court of last resort.

"Contrary to certain other corporations, who have earned the condemnation of the public by underhand and oppressive conduct towards their competitors, the United States Steel Corporation has maintained an attitude in the steel trade that may be likened to a balance wheel. It has been open and fair and above board in its conduct: confident of its own strength it has not sought to take advantage of its weaker competitors; its prices upon manufactured products have generally been known, freely given in the public through trade papers, and conservatively maintained.

"From my long association with the Tennessee Coal, Iron and Railroad Company I know very well how greatly this district has been

George Gordon Crawford, president of Tennessee Coal and Iron after U.S. Steel's takeover (courtesy of Birmingham Public Library Archives)

helped by the incoming of the Steel corporation. It has had the money and the courage to spend it on a large scale, introducing improvements in machinery and in methods and in the condition of work and the conditions of living on the part of its workmen, which the Tennessee Company could not do on the same scale for lack of funds, and in some cases for lack of experience.

"The removal of this conservative force from the trade—if the courts should sustain the government—will tend towards the old condition of numerous smaller concerns, with higher costs of production, with smaller profits on their product working to disadvantage, and reducing the wages of their employes [sic]. It is only by consolidation upon a large scale of capital and effort, that the best results can be obtained; and I think from an industrial standpoint the government is endeavoring to turn back the clock."

W. P. G. Harding . . . was and is a good banker. A young man of great energy and industry, not a many-sided man, but rather one devoted to business pure and simple. It is better for a man to be adaptable and have other interests in life besides finance. I had always befriended him with my influence when my friendship was of some value to him. From 1910 to . . . 1914 his friendship had been in turn of value to me, but from now onward his influence was turned against me so that he might make some large and handsome fee for himself by either selling our company to somebody else or unloading somebody else on us. I had to fight his efforts hard for the next year or two.

In June 1914 I frankly challenged Harding at the bank, telling him that he had gone back on his promise to support my administration [at Gulf States Steel]. He edged a little desk between us as if he thought perhaps I was going to hit him, and said that the welfare of the district was greater than the welfare or personal ambition of any one individual, and that in his opinion the district would be greatly helped by a combination of independents to compete with [U.S. Steel].

Bowron to Editor, *Manufacturers' Record*, December 2, 1915:
I am sorry that the ranks of the present workers in the Birmingham coal, iron and steel district do not contain, in the opinion of your editorial writer, men of equal standing with those whom you enumerate, and who have passed away from us within the past 20 years. For myself, however, looking back as I am able to do over the history of every iron and steel plant in this district . . . I am well content to believe that the developers of the present generation are carrying their task quite as well as the departed worthies. . . .

[Twenty years ago] the Mesaba [sic] ore fields had not been discovered, or at least developed, and the enormous lake commerce of today with the furnaces of Chicago, Toledo, Buffalo and Cleveland were unknown as a competitive factor. Today the South is holding its own and steadily growing, although deprived of the markets north of the Ohio and Potomac rivers for pig-iron. The iron and steel products of Birmingham, including Gadsden as part of the district, are going, to my knowledge, into Europe, Asia, Africa and South America. The development may be slow, but it is steady and continuous, and the people, I will venture to say, who have their money, their brain power and their hearts in the industry will continue to develop it, even with or without the stimulus of platitudinous resolutions or the spurring on of any newspapers. . . .

Because the South is blind to its own interest, because it is full of people who vote the Democratic ticket utterly regardless of the platform and swallow a free-trade platform . . . as a delicious morsel, and whose vote can be counted upon for the administration without the incentive of patronage or the expenditure of Government moneys, we have not had the Governmental development of our waterways that we should have. Birmingham is as much entitled to the slack watering of Valley Creek, bringing barge water to the suburban town of Bessemer, as Pittsburgh is entitled to the slack watering of the Ohio River. . . . The Birmingham district will take care of itself in the iron and steel trade, and it needs no such invidious comparison between the dead and the living to spur the present generation to do its duty, and to do it earnestly.

Edmonds's reply to Bowron:
In this day, when tens and tens of millions of dollars are being expended in the vast enlargement of the iron and steel interests of the East and the West, when new furnaces are going up and new steel plants being erected in other sections, the Birmingham district is not building a single new furnace or steel plant, nor enlarging any existing steel plant. Its magnificent advantages are being utilized by existing plants; but relatively Birmingham is not commanding the national attention it did in former years, and Mr. Bowron is in error when he suggests that in iron "the South is holding its own." As a matter of fact, the South has been steadily falling behind relatively in iron production for a decade or more. Its percentage of iron production compared with the total for the country is annually decreasing. The old plants . . . have been reshaped and most of them put on their feet, and are doing great things; but nothing new is being developed looking to a vast broadening of the metallurgical activities of the Birmingham district.

It is hard to realize how extremely depressed business was in November 1914 in the South. The stoppage of ocean commerce as to cotton movement was practically complete. German raiders attacked that which was going to English possessions, and the English blockaders stopped as contraband of war that which was going to Germany. This stoppage of shipments caused frozen credits throughout the South, and great depression and bewilderment. The Ensley steelworks shut down altogether for about two months— scores and hundreds of smaller business establishments closed. We continued to run three days per week at the Gulf States steelworks, so as to hold our organization together. We were selling, naturally, at anything we could get, but trying to get cost.

[In 1915] Gulf States Steel began to feel the increased demand from England for steel, due to the European war, selling 6,000 tons of billets to that country. We were sorely bothered, however, for want of ingot molds in which to make our steel. For some unknown reason the concern that had been furnishing them peremptorily cut off the supply, and but for the help of our accommodating neighbors, Tennessee Coal and Iron, we would have been in sore straits. Our operations were restricted anyhow by the detention of a carload cut off by high water around Cincinnati. So one's troubles, like the ripples in a pond, spread outward to affect others. Ought not our joys to do the same? We sold several thousand tons of painted barb wire to the French government. This was usually made to keep out four-legged hogs, but we had no objections to its use in France for keeping out two-legged hogs, and told them so. Our Gulf States Steel earnings . . . for the year 1915 [were] about $615,000.

At the end of 1915 [the Bessemer Coal, Iron and Land Company was] so hard up we could not sell land because there was no way of getting it clear from the mortgage. Whilst the steel trade was looking up vigorously, the coal trade was desperately in the dumps, and the Bessemer Company's outlook was most discouraging. [Then] in September 1916 Henry Badham told me that the Bessemer Company had earned $2,000 the previous month. After six years of heading off the sheriff and bankruptcy, we began to feel that perhaps the tide of adversity had turned. And indeed it had. In October [we were amazed] at a meeting of the Bessemer Company directors [to be] advised our profits for the previous month were $11,909. Such a thing seemed incredible.

Gulf States Steel's earnings for October . . . amounted to $351,000. At the November directors' meeting I found the directors were in high, good humor on account of our large earnings. They advanced my salary to $20,000. William Coverdale told me he had made $300,000 in two weeks on the rise of our stock, but he never collected any part of it, as he disregarded the suggestion I made to him that he should sell some on the top of market for the purpose of buying back again on when it might fall.

They commenced paying dividends on the common stock at the rate of 8 percent per annum, and I voted alone against it, as I thought it was not at all consistent to begin at such a high rate. Our new work was unfinished. We were spending a great deal of money, and I thought it would be quite adequate to have begun with it at 4 or 5 percent. My friend James Platten intimated before leaving the city that they were hurt at my opposing the dividend. I have always felt that every man ought to speak and vote exactly as he feels and not to vote against his own judgment because he thinks it would be pleasing to someone else, and I have so tried to govern my life.

I brought up the question as to our purchase direct of the property of the Pratt Consolidated Coal Company, which we could have bought . . . for about $1 million. It had at that time about $4 million of bonds and interest of $200,000 per annum. The average earning over ten years was $430,000, which if continued would have given us about $230,000 net in exchange for our $1 million of purchase money. It would have been a magnificent trade, but I could not put it through. Mr. Platten was so timid he objected to our having to take over a concern with a large bonded debt and to our having to go into the commercial trade. And yet during the next two years thereafter the company made more than $1 million per annum of net profits. We would have got all our money back within a year and within the next three or four or five years would have paid off all the bonded debt. It would have put us from being a third- or fourth-rate concern into the front rank as far as coal was concerned. It was not by any means the first time that I have been handicapped by the timidity of bankers. Well informed on their own matters, they are most timid as a class in dealing with technical affairs such as require knowledge of mining or manufacturing.

In December 1916, feeling very buoyant and optimistic, I did one of the most remarkable things in my life, showing, as a popular adage runs, there is no fool like an old fool. I had been running for years on a cash basis, making no notes, carrying nothing on margin, running no bills, owing nothing whatever except current household accounts from the first of each month. It was my rigid fixed idea never again to owe a dollar, so that I might never again have anything more to worry about financially. The stock market broke pretty violently, on rumors of peace, and our stock, which had been up to 193, fell as low as 130. Sitting at dinner . . . with Mr. Platten, we said what a good purchase it would be on our present earnings, and I remarked, really without thinking about it, that I would buy some but I hadn't any money available. He immediately said that they would lend me any money I wanted for that purpose, and so I just said, "Buy me 500 shares." I had no idea on earth of making any permanent investment or incurring a debt. I just thought it was a momentary fluctuation of the market and that the stock would go up again within the next three or four days, probably to 150, and that it was about as easy a way to make $10,000 as I knew of. I went to the train, leaving at midnight, and went to sleep just thinking in my mind that I could afford to give that profit partly to pay off the mortgage debt on the church and one or two other things of that sort, feeling in a most benevolent mood about the distribution of the chickens which had not hatched.

The next day I got a paper on the train and found that there had been a wild day on the exchange, which began by selling up to 136 first thing in the morning, at which price the 500 shares had been purchased for me, and closed at 129 that evening. I got home at midnight Saturday night, having missed connection in Atlanta [on] account [of a] train hung up for hours by a freight wreck—fifty hours on the way from New York to Birmingham, freezing weather—most uncomfortable outside and my mind a prey to re-morse and grief at having made such a fool of myself as to go back into debt again. I had to send my note to the Trust Company for $68,000, together with all my preferred stock as collateral, and I felt both distressed and humiliated beyond measure. This was immediately followed by a stock ex-change panic, the stock dropping to 100, showing me an apparent loss of $18,000 in three days!

I cannot account for, or excuse, giving way in a moment just to an impulse. Sometimes a man who has led an exemplary life is tempted for the moment and perhaps takes $100,000 of the bank's funds, and an hour afterwards realizes what he has done, but it is too late. Another man in a moment of impulse fires a pistol and his life is ruined—perhaps two lives—so we can-not afford to condemn severely other people who yield to a momentary im-pulse. Suppose stock had gone up twenty points; people would have said, "Why that man is a wise financial captain."

In March 1916 W. R. Fairley,[3] the well-known labor leader, who was at the same time in the employ of the Democratic administration Labor Bu-reau in Washington, proposed that the miners and coal operators should obtain legal permission to combine for putting up the price of coal sufficient to pay higher wages and still make decent profits. I fear if he had made his principles known in Washington he would have been packed off without ceremony. Mr. Fairley came here claiming his right as a U.S. government agent to intervene and insisted that we should make our recent wage advance retroactive. As I knew that in that matter he was acting solely for the United Mine Workers, I told him to put his demand in writing, and I would take up with the government the question as how he came to be drawing the government salary and simultaneously acting as a union representative. He naturally declined and never came back.

In August 1916 our by-product ovens [at Gadsden were] going up, the new machine and blacksmith shops in use, and the old ones being pulled down. At this time our machinists organized on us, and Charles A. Moffett[4] wanted to fight the question, but I suggested that we had better fight when we were not making $250,000 per month. And he agreed with me.

On August 3, 1917, I visited Virginia Mines to make an address to the miners, but found that union organizers had sent a committee around the previous night warning the men not to attend the meeting. I had an audience of fifty or sixty instead of threefold that number. It is ever thus—the laboring men are docile followers of their leaders and unwilling to hear both sides and judge for themselves.

Bowron to men at Virginia Mines, August 14, 1917:
When I visited Virginia Mines last week, after notice being posted of the same, I hoped to meet with you and all the other employes [sic] of this company, so that I might learn if there were any complaints against the management or any grievances to be redressed, or any reasons why you should discontinue work and interrupt or perhaps sever the friendly relations that have existed for an number of years between this company and its workmen. . . .

The [recent miners'] convention demanded an eight hours day. I do not know whether it was serious in making this request. If it were granted it would not affect the coal miners, as you know, for you are paid by a tonnage rate on the coal that you produce, whether you get it out in five hours or six or seven or eight. It would only affect the day men, and if the same rate per hour were paid to them that is paid now, which is the highest rate in the history of the state, they would, by the adoption on the eight hour rule, lose about 20% of their earnings; and you I think would be considerably handicapped if the outside men were to quit two hours sooner without weighing and dumping your coal and having the cars ready to put down to the working places the first thing in the morning, ready for you to start. . . .

There remains therefore only one single ground of so called offence [sic]; viz., that we do not recognize the union. Why should we recognize a union with headquarters in Indianapolis, having interests in 14 states or more in this Union, where the number of men employed is much greater than in Alabama, and the delegates are more numerous? The state of Alabama and its industries must compete, and does compete, against the states of Pennsylvania, Ohio, and Illinois. Why should our industries, and our production of fuel be regulated by the voice of a larger number of delegates from those states if they wanted to bring about conditions that would shut down the Alabama mines, and leave them to prosper in their own state?

Apart from this question, recognition of the union means a closed shop; viz., that we should not employ anyone who was not a member of the union; that we should condemn certain other men—as good Americans as you or I—to idleness, and refuse to allow them the privilege that every honest man is entitled to, both by the law of the state and the law of God, the privilege as an honest man of working for his living.

This company will never take the position that a man shall not be employed by it either because he does or does not belong to some particular union, or some particular lodge, or some particular church, or some particular political party. If a man can mine coal in accordance with the mining regulations of the state, and is a respectable citizen, living in peace, and order, in the community, we will employ him whatever may be his affiliations, and if our mines run at all they will run on this platform and no other.

Is it too much for us to hope that you, as . . . [men] of common sense, may consider carefully before you decide to go on strike and leave your present employment and your present home? It would seem to us to be a pity when we have worked together for years without any trouble or unfriendliness, when your earnings have increased to the highest point ever known, when the conditions surrounding your work are greatly improved, with other improvement now contemplated and in view, it would, I repeat, seem a pity for you to break off these relations and go to some other district to pick up such working places as you might find available, knowing . . . that the best places in other mines are already taken, and that you would only get what was left.

In February 1917 I [was] . . . a very active member of the local committee seeking to obtain the location of the U.S. government proposed armor plant. I met with the visiting board, Admiral Fletcher, and Commander Clark. I was made the chief witness for the district at the hearing at the Tutwiler Hotel, which lasted four hours, and was much applauded by the local people.

A Birmingham newspaper's report of Bowron's testimony:
"I may say that I feel very dubious as to the advantage in this district of a plant. If it should be run as other government plants are run today, under the demands of Mr. Gompers, which are so subserviently swallowed by Congress. . . . Every other manufacturing industry is considering today how in the modern race for results it can obtain the highest efficiency, both from labor and from machinery; but in the Government arsenals and navy yards apparently political expediency has decreed that no methods of efficiency are to be permitted. It is inevitable, therefore, that the results of industrial plants so operated would be unsatisfactory from an economical standpoint. . . .

"If the government wishes to waste money by operating a plant under such conditions anywhere, I am quite willing that it should spend the money, and buy the materials where the money will circulate in Jefferson County, but the examples of such methods of operating (as the Government employs) I am free to say, would not be to the highest interests of the success of other manufacturing plants. . . .

"The company which I serve does not make pig iron for sale, on the contrary we are buyers of additional pig iron beyond that which we produce, and the location in the district of an armor plate plant would not be of the slightest interest to our company. My sole object in appearing as a witness, therefore, was to testify to that which I know to be the truth, viz.: that steel of the very best possible quality can be produced from Birmingham pig iron. This fact had been wantonly challenged by people in the North, and it was fit and proper that we who know the facts, should rise to the occasion and defend the good name of the district."

On August 6 the U.S. government, under the powers of the Lever bill, undertook to define what were fair and reasonable prices for steel, which included allied and subsidiary products or materials—iron, ore, coke, coal. This bill, like most other war legislation, was absolutely unconstitutional and appeared so on its face even to an unlearned layman like myself. It [was later] declared unconstitutional by the Supreme Court of the U.S. But at that time, under the theory that everybody must submit to anything whatever imposed by the government as an act of patriotism to win the war, we, like all others, submitted as cheerfully as possible.

The whole thing was wrong in this way: only certain selected products were taken charge of by the government and prices fixed upon them. It may have been only a coincidence, but it is worthy of remark that the steel trade was the most severely restricted, the great majority of capitalists interested in it being northern Republicans, whilst on the other hand the cotton trade was left absolutely untouched by the government, the great bulk of the capitalists engaged in it being southern Democrats. Enormous fortunes were made by the southern mill owners, whilst we were left to sell some steel under government direction at a heavy loss, cash out of pocket. It has always seemed, and still seems to me grossly unjust, that manufacturers should be forbidden in this country alone, among all the civilized nations of the world, to agree with each other upon prices, whilst on the other hand producers of any product of agriculture and labor are permitted to sell their commodities at such prices as they may combine and agree upon. The wheat growers are permitted, as exempted from the Sherman antitrust law, to agree upon their own price for wheat, and labor is permitted to unite in trades' unions and fix its own rate of wages for operating the railroad to carry the wheat to market, and for operating the flour mill. But if the bakers unite to fix a profitable price upon their flour they might be indicted and put in jail. I have always contended that any sumptuary law should apply to every person, to every line of business, without distinction or discrimination.

On September 13 we were all compelled to advance wages to the coal miners by the action of the Woodward Iron Company. Mr. Woodward said that he was making more money than he had ever done before, and he wanted to run full and would pay whatever money was necessary to get miners. In 1921 . . . his concern was the first one in the district to shut down completely—perhaps as the result of such actions.

On December 27, 1917, [the] U.S. government took over all railroads—an action which might have been all right had it not been accompanied by the unwise and pusillanimous surrender to the dictation of organized labor which accompanied it. Our earnings were running very high at this time. The December earnings of the Gulf States were $370,000 and those of the Bessemer [Coal and Land] Company $50,000.

On January 14, 1918, we were shut down at the plant in about half of the departments, for want of gas coal, taken under government priority orders by the Southern Railway. The vagaries of the Fuel Administration under the government during the year 1918 were enough to turn any man's hair gray.

On January 17 the country was dazed by proclamation of [the] fuel administrator closing all manufacturing plants east of the Mississippi for five days. There was great public excitement. On January 31 the government dipped still further into our affairs: the steel administrator . . . forb[ade] our shipping any steel whatever to foreign countries without government permit. One part of the Fuel Administration said that no manufacturing plants might run on Mondays. Another section of it said that continuous processes such as blast furnaces, open-hearth steel furnaces, and coke ovens could. We decided to run and take the chance, as we were evidently to be blamed whether we ran or we did not.

On February 18 I went down to Virginia [Mines] with Moffett as I had promised a committee of miners who came up from there to interview me that we would [meet with them]. On arriving at the office [we] found no one to receive us, no meeting arranged, but a note on the table from the superintendent resigning his position. He objected so much to the miners' union that he would rather resign than to go into any negotiation with the miners. Therefore we got the men together and amicably discussed all points at issue with their committee, and then I addressed a mass meeting of the men and their families. They all seemed very much gratified.

February 26 was a day of trouble, as I was advised of the squeeze at Virginia Mines cutting off five entries and reducing the output from 1,000 tons per day to 500 per day. This was a terrible thing to happen at the moment when we were almost at our wit's end to obtain an adequate fuel supply, and between the fuel administrator in Washington and the railroad companies and public utilities and other holders of priorities, we could hardly count our own fuel as coming to us. The men [working were] somewhat disorganized. Our old experienced superintendent had just left us and taken the mine foreman with him.

To give an idea of the extraordinary tension and confusion caused by government control of both coal mines and railroads and car supply and miners, it was found in March on examination [that] there were thirty-six different coal mines furnishing our supply at the steelworks. No wonder that the mixture fed to our coke ovens and boilers and gas producers produced about as good result as a mixture of thirty-six medicines all poured into one bottle and shaken up together.

The government was undertaking to fix prices on both coal and coke, and John McQueen of the Sloss Company wanted us to continue to make coke and supply his company with it. We were asking the fuel administrator to fix a satisfactory price to us, and he named one which was quite inadequate and advised us that figure "was satisfactory to Mr. McQueen." This was about the government's way of doing things; of course it would be satisfactory to Mr. McQueen, because he wanted to buy it. I had to go to Washington . . . to get this and other matters satisfactorily straightened out with the fuel administrator, whose vagaries and muddles were profoundly distressing.

[We were] very much worried by the insistence of the U.S. government that we must make high carbon steel . . . especially eight-inch billets, which we did not believe our shear was strong enough to cut without breaking down and putting us out of business. We laid the situation before our executive committee in New York. We received instructions from the chairman of that committee that we were not to answer the government on any question of policy until the request had been first submitted to the executive committee and considered by it. On June 7, Saturday, [we] received demand that we must appear before the War Industrial Board for conference on Monday. I wired the chairman asking for instruction and waited all day but got no reply—about the usual outcome of people attempting a thousand miles away to manage a business.

On June 10 we arrived in Washington and were duly scarified, scoffed at, and bullied by various jacks in office, who said we might just as well be shut down one way as another. This was in answer to my plea that if our shear, which was old, should break on eight-inch high carbon blooms we could not get another, under war conditions, within a year, and the entire business would be stopped. [I was told] that if we did not make them they would commandeer our pig iron and take that away from us and that would shut us down.

At the steelworks I found we had 160 women employed on account of the wartime scarcity of men. These Negro women, as a rule, were not efficient. They were slow in their movements, and as might be supposed it required three of them to do the work of two men in lifting bars. They were largely employed in wheeling material to the warehouses. We were all glad when the end of the war and the return of men gradually to work permitted their discontinuance. It is perhaps needless to add that, in this country as in others, the higher wages paid for such work drew a large percentage of women from their usual tasks. Cooks [and] housemaids became very scarce and correspondingly independent.

On August 21, 1918, . . . [we] were greatly harassed, seeing that we were . . . making nothing at the steelworks. [This was due to] the action of the

U.S. Steel Corporation putting into effect a scale of wages which would advance our mechanics 20 to 30 percent and common labor 50 percent.

Bowron would later criticize Judge Gary, a man he genuinely admired, for giving in on wage increases. He wrote to the Manufacturers' Record *in 1923 that "it has sometimes appeared as though Judge Gary's company has advanced wages when there was really no necessity for it, and when the course of trade and the difficulty of sufficient orders would really rather have suggested the propriety of reducing both wages and prices."*

The end of the war brought a sudden end to the prosperity. Gulf States Steel, which had earned almost $32 per share on common stock in 1917, made just over $1 per share in 1919. Problems with labor and government intervention combined with declining profits to produce angry industrial executives in Birmingham. A strike of coal miners in late 1919 dramatized the hostility between management and labor. No one was angrier than James Bowron.

On November 12, 1919, at a meeting of the coal operators, it was the universal feeling that the district could not be run successfully on the open shop basis in view of the unfairness and aggressiveness of the union men and it must be run absolutely on a nonunion basis. Consequently we would not take any of the strikers back again. This was an eventful decision for many people, as many hundreds of strikers ... [were] still camped in tents or colonies throughout the district waiting to be taken back instead of going elsewhere for work.

On the first of April 1920, a suitable day for such folly, all our coal miners who were organized went out on strike at Virginia, Sayre, and Altoona [coal mines]. They had made no demand upon us of any description, they had no grievance, no complaint of any sort, but went out like so many sheep at the command of the United Mine Workers in Indianapolis. We had asked many of them at Sayre, which under the Sloss Company management had been a hotbed of unionism, whether they intended to go out, and the invariable answer was that they did not know, which, of course, was untrue. We did not attempt at this time to start Sayre, but concentrated our efforts on Virginia, gradually building up a force from day to day. In the meantime, we had known so well that there would be trouble on April 1 that we had accumulated a stock at the steelworks of about 60,000 tons to protect our operations.

Some of the strikers at Sayre began to vacate our houses, but only a few of them, the rest truculently refusing either to pay rent or to get out or to go away. They were being maintained by the union and stayed in the houses because they appealed from one court to another for the purpose of delay, so that we had to erect [a] boarding house and crowd up the workmen very badly in the few houses that we had available. By May 6 thirty more of our strikers had shipped their effects away from Sayre, and twenty more were getting ready. They had begun to realize what we meant. We would not again employ those men who were not in sympathy with us, who were not satisfied with our management, and who, without notice and without grievance and without any demand, would stop their work, endeavor to prevent other people coming in there and to injure our company because some union official up in the North said so. It was a matter of self-preservation to us to operate on a nonunion basis, and we determined to do so.

As an evidence of the disturbed conditions of workmen's minds, due to union teaching, we found that our men at the steelworks in the brass band, for which we had provided the instruments and the uniforms and paid the monthly salary of the military bandmaster, were not willing to practice any more unless we would pay for the time they spent in rehearsal. In other words, they wanted us to pay them for taking their own pleasure—which we naturally declined.

Bowron to *Manufacturers' Record*, April 1920:
Taking it as a whole, we find that labor is much less efficient than before the war. Men do not desire to work as many days or to work as long each day or to work as hard as they used to. This may be qualified in the case of tonnage men who are on piecework. We have some crews who show sufficient ambition to break records in one or two departments, but that is not the general characteristic of labor today. Take coal miners, for example, with all the force of the government, the newspapers and the public sentiment crying for large output of fuel. Our miners are not like those in domestic coal mines dependent on seasonable trade; our men can work every week-day throughout the year; but instead of working six days habitually, they average from four and a half to five days per week. At the present extremely high wages they could lay by money and on the instalment [*sic*] plan acquire homes.

We see no indication of this idea taking root among them, although one man came up the other day and bought $400 of good bonds. He was an exception. We find that coal miners do not mine the coal as a rule as clean and free from trash and bone and slate as they used to.

We have seen analyses of coal ranging up to twenty-five and even thirty percent ash; it should never exceed twelve in any merchantable fuel. The general average of coal or of ore or of limestone purchased by us have been below pre-war standards because the lack of care on the part of labor in preparing it.

At the steel works it is frequently the case that our fence weavers, nail cutters or barb wire operators are held back, sometimes losing half a day or a whole one, because of scarcity of wire. We have plenty of machines and plenty of wire rods. After last payday twelve of our wire drawers were idle, positively walking about utterly indifferent to the claims of their brother workmen, who were denied work by their indifference. One of our officials met and spoke with one of these men. His reply was: "What's the use of my making any more money? My wife would just blow it in. I may as well rest up in bed." Another of our officials met a negro woman and asked her if she wanted a job as cook. Her reply was: "Lawsy, white man, I doesn't have to cook for nobody; my nigger makes more money than me and him can spend."

A negro miner came into the office one day to ask us to make him a cash advance against his pay. Bear in mind that we pay in cash every fortnight, and men are not supposed to draw cash before paydays except in case of emergency. He explained his emergency as being that he had $40 worth of clothes at the express office which he had to take out. He was wearing a better suit than our general manager at the time. The word thrift seems to be forgotten. Laboring men are buying silk shirts for $7.50 to $12 each, silk hose, expensive clothing, automobiles, and are not content with Sundays and Saturday afternoons as time for riding around and showing off their finery. . . .

Manufacturing costs are out of sight; every one complains of the high cost of living. How can it be otherwise when, with a given amount of machinery and equipment, you get about eighty percent of the yield which the same equipment gave before the war? If men would turn around and be in earnest and had the desire to work as they did six years ago, and to put the money by in permanent assets, the condition of the country would be revolutionized; cost of production would be slashed in every direction, and the accumulating stocks of products entering into competition for the market would inevitably reduce prices, and this tendency would be accelerated by the thrift which would keep men back from making unnecessary purchases.

On January 30, 1920, I conferred with Vice-President Herbert Ryding as to the attitude of TCI, which was consenting to another advance in railroad freight rates on manufactured steel, whilst everyone else was strongly objecting to the same. Whilst I was in his office he received a telegram from New York of another 10 percent advance in wages ordered by his company. He was shocked. It was a mistake and injured the labor situation materially all over the country. On February 25 we were much annoyed by the steady grasping pressure of the railroads withdrawing our special rates for exports, as they had previously withdrawn special rates for handling raw materials. They seemed to wish to crush us out of existence. It seemed the more outrageous . . . that our export rates should be withdrawn, effective the very day that the government Railroad Administration ended.

On April 14 I had a long interview with Vice-President Evans [and] General Manager Starks of the Louisville and Nashville Railroad at Louisville regarding car supply and then a short interview with President Milton H. Smith. This [was] the last time I ever saw the grand old man. They plaintively pointed out that they were now so restricted by the rules of the Interstate Commerce Commission that they no longer had the control of their own railroad. Only 27 percent of their open-top cars were on their own railroad system, the others scattered all over America.

On July 2 we were having extreme difficulty conducting the business for want of railroad cars and were giving much time to negotiating either for the hire or for the purchase of 100 or 200 coal cars for our own use. To add to our other troubles, the smart aleck who represented the Interstate Commerce Commission in Birmingham on the distribution of cars stopped the Gadsden Car Works from turning over as it had been doing its empties to us so that they might be hauled to where they were wanted, carrying loads instead of being hauled empty. He said this was giving us an unfair advantage, and they must be hauled either to Chattanooga or Birmingham empty.

On October 8 I began a fortnight of a most distressing character. I was advised on that day that over 13,000 tons of coal had been shipped to us in seven days from Tennessee. [It was] intended to have been shipped over a period [but was] all shipped at once. I was perfectly paralyzed by the [subsequent] information that we had already received 26,000 tons of coal and 300 cars more were reported to be on the way to us. Our works were swamped, the sidetracks at Attalla and other places up to Chattanooga and beyond were reported full of cars addressed to us. Leslie Geohegan[5] at this time avoided us, staying away out of the office, [and] we had no opportunity of asking him the situation. He had shown himself a man of such splendid judgment, most fertile in resource, of indomitable courage, wonderful endurance and perseverance, that his extraordinary failure and mix-up on such a tremendous scale took my breath away. Counting the coal and the freight upon it, he had laid us open to the payment of literally half a million dollars within thirty days. It was a time when but for our excellent earnings, splendid credit, and strong friends we might have been seriously embarrassed ourselves.

I think the explanation was that Geohegan had been working so hard during the strike, night and day, that he had lost his sense of proportion for the time being and felt it necessary to secure coal in every direction. Just at that moment, however, an embargo was put on the shipment of coal for bunker purposes, and the shippers who had given Geohegan to understand they could ship a few cars each, took advantage with one accord of open orders and shipped whatever they could lay their hands on—50 or 100 cars when he expected 5 or 10. The trouble about it was that the previous day a heavy drop in prices went into effect, and all this coal was delivered to us at the top prices of the boom.

We fought the thing in a most vigorous way. Everyone cooperated splendidly. [We] worked with the railroad company and got it to confiscate and take over from us the coal that was blocking the sidetracks . . . which greatly relieved us, and we turned over to others quite a number of cars. Some we refused to accept at all on the grounds of lack of proper orders until the price was abated or adequate credit given for the payment. We had an officers' council and agreed definitely that all purchasing power should be lodged henceforth in the purchasing department alone and not mixed up with the executive duties of the assistant general manager.

Emeritus

In 1921, at the age of seventy-six, Bowron agreed to slow down his business career. He accepted the position of chairman of Gulf States, relinquishing responsibility for everyday operations. That left more time for travel, children, and his other business interests. He continued to be active in the management of the Bessemer Coal, Iron and Land Company, which prospered during the 1920s. He enjoyed extensive world travel, including trips to the Far East, Latin America, and sub-Saharan Africa. He attended to the early business and professional careers of his younger sons. Then, in November 1926, circumstances dictated that Bowron return to his old duties as chief executive officer of Gulf States Steel. Even as an octogenarian he managed with an active hand and a critical eye virtually to the day of his death in August 1928.

The recent war and the prolonged coal strike had left Bowron very unhappy about work relations in the iron and steel industry. His opinions on labor-related matters hardened further. Bowron opposed an end to the convict-lease system primarily because he believed that would constitute a victory for organized labor. He opposed a reduction of the twelve-hour day as an unnecessary increase in the cost of labor; he thought it was a false reform, another concession to a coddled labor force. Still, the iron and steel industry in Alabama relied traditionally on black labor, and the increasing migration of blacks to the North concerned him. Like most Birmingham industrialists, Bowron combined his concern for a ready supply of black labor with a paternalistic sympathy for the black community.

n March 20, 1921, I asked Charles Moffett what he thought we ought to recommend the board to do about salaries for the coming year. I thought they ought to be reduced in view of conditions of business, and he said that would depend on my answer to William Coverdale. I was rather surprised and asked him what he meant, and he [reminded me of] the proposition of my accepting the position as chairman of the board. Moffett and I dined that evening with Mr. and Mrs. Coverdale and were later joined by James Platten. I told them of the conversation I had with Moffett on the train, and they said he had correctly presented their view, so I agreed definitely that I would accept the position of chairman of the board at the next meeting, to be held in April, and Moffett then [would] be made president and general manager. Our duties would change gradually and conveniently. Messrs. Platten and Coverdale said that my salary should continue as it was, but I told them that it must be reduced.

On April 26, in session with Coverdale and Platten, they agreed they would fix the salaries $20,000 for me and $17,000 for Moffett. [This was] the first time they had ever agreed to accept any reduction on my part. At a directors' meeting the bylaws were amended creating the office of chairman of the board, and I was then elected to that position. And so ended my executive charge of the concern which I had stepped into at an hour's notice in its condition of impending bankruptcy in 1910, never dreaming at the time that the engagement could last possibly more than a year or two. The wildest fancy could not have then suggested that in a few years we would be making as much money in two or three months as the whole assets of the company at that time were worth. It was a case for the eleven years of going in at the little end of the horn and coming out at the big end. There was nothing about it to give me any feeling of exultation or pride, however, for I always felt that I knew very little practically about such matters and that the success of the company was due to the teamwork of many faithful and experienced men around me all pulling together. To them I was and still am grateful, but infinitely more so to God, Who directed my path as He has done through all these many long years.

On May 18, 1922, I arrived in Washington in pursuance of request from President Harding to meet him. There were about forty of us present who were individually introduced to the president and Secretaries Herbert Hoover, Andrew Mellon, and James J. Davis of the Departments of Commerce, Treasury, and Department of Labor, respectively. President Harding at dinner ... had Judge Gary and Mr. Charles Schwab on either side of him. The president stated that ... the twelve-hour day should be abolished if possible in the steel trade, because the public thought it oppressive and cruel. We pointed out to him that the twenty-four hours in any continuous process must be divided either by two, three, or four. We must have turns either of twelve, eight, or six hours. The latter was out of the question because it takes so long for men to come to their work and get back to their homes. It was pointed out that there was no such thing as twelve hours of continuous work, but that it was intermittent and that men did not work more than an average of eight hours on a twelve-hour turn. [Furthermore] the men themselves did not want any such change, because it would reduce their gross earnings.

The operators could not afford to pay twelve hours' wages if they only got eight hours' work. One woman told an operator she didn't want her man coming home to the house any sooner—he'd only be a nuisance, getting in the way and scolding the children. It was further pointed out that there was a scarcity of skilled labor in the country and that the immigration law prevented bringing in such people. When I spoke I only summarized these arguments, but also stated that the South was a place where we raised and taught labor [only] for northern competition to take [it] away from us by paying higher wages. They could take labor from us, but we couldn't take it back from them, as we were compelled to have cheaper production to be able to pay the freights to distant cities, not having dense populations around us as they had in the North.

James Bowron to *Manufacturers' Record*, June 1923:
"One of the Oldest Steel Makers in America, Who Is One of the Noblest Christian Men of America, Broadly Discusses the Whole 12-Hour Steel Labor Problem."

After examination of the subject, the highly representative committee appointed from the leaders of the Iron and Steel Institute have reported that 60,000 additional men would be required. These men are skilled or semiskilled. Men who are farm laborers, waiters, tram conductors, elevator runners, clerks, shopkeepers, teamsters, etc., cannot go to an open hearth furnace or a blast furnace and perform the duties required, which involve a co-ordination of strength, skill and experience. Such additional men simply are not to be had today in the United States. At this moment of writing there are mills reported partially shut down for lack of labor. If the 8-hour day were at this moment to be put in force throughout the trade, it would be necessary to close down one-third of the capacity of the plants which are running on the 12-hour basis so that the present available skilled and semiskilled labor would be adequate on an 8-hour basis for the remainder. This at a stroke would create such a scarcity of materials as to create a buyers' panic and disorganize all the consumers of steel to a degree that cannot be expressed. It would preclude the maintenance at present of even an ordinary scale of locomotive and car production and repair, of the supply of rails and other track materials, of steel for shipbuilding industries, for the automobile business, structural steel for building, and hundreds of thousands of men would be put on short time or deprived of occupation throughout the country because of the inability of their employers to obtain the necessary supplies of steel. . . .

The men who are thus engaged are satisfied; they are not complaining; they would complain very bitterly if they were required to work shorter time and earn less money. The public would complain if they were reduced at the expense of bringing in another crew, (that does not now exist in this country,) involving large increases in selling prices, and the clamor of the abolition of the turn arises from those who are not personally acquainted with the conditions and mistakenly suppose that it means, as it does not, continuous work.

In March 1921 the Bessemer Company directors [had discovered] that we had actually lost money the previous month on account of sales having practically stopped. Much of the coal we were mining [was] being put on the ground. The convicts [were] employed in the mine on dead work or narrow work. Of course it was necessary to continue working the convicts, as we had to pay for them just the same.

On December 8, 1922, at a meeting of Bessemer directors we declared an extra Christmas dividend in addition to the regular, putting the company on a 5 percent basis. It was reported that we had paid off in advance the last of [the company's] bonds . . . so that we had no liabilities of any description except current vouchers and had $1 million worth of quick assets on hand, besides all our lands. The book value was then reported as being $150 per share, although the stock was selling between $60 and $70. During 1923 we made . . . about $53,000 on coal and $153,000 in land sales, of which we had invested $101,000 in building houses to be sold on the installment plan. I always have felt that as we sold these lots and houses for payment over 100 months, 1 percent per month with 6 percent interest, we were helping people to the habit of saving and the habit of buying their own homes.

I [believe] the growth of socialism [shows] the necessity for increasing the ownership of homes. Every man who [owns] a home or a farm [has] given hostage to fortune and [is] interested in the preservation of order and the rights of property. This [is] affected in cities by the extension of suburban railroads, steam or trolley, and the construction of homes on the monthly installment plan, so that a workman might go cheaply from his work to his own home in reasonable time.

In May 1923 I had a conference with Badham and insisted that we should not renew the convict lease on the basis of paying so much per head per month, but that we should only have them if, at all, on the basis of so much per ton of coal upon cars. [I said] that we should tell the state we were willing to give them up any day, as we were losing money on their work. In fact, there were [many] days . . . when we had to pay for them [when] we had . . . no orders. [Sometimes] we had orders, [but] we had no [railroad] cars.

I appeared before a committee of the Junior Chamber of Commerce to discuss the convict question and addressed them for seventy minutes, advocating mining by the state for state use.

Birmingham *Age-Herald*, August 2, 1923:
In a speech during which the venerable industrial leader almost flashed fire, he said that the ministers, good women and others were being misled by various untruths, false facts and misinformation. . . .

"Many writers, good women, ministers and others," declared Mr. Bowron, "have apparently lost their senses on this subject. Their work is based on false facts, misrepresentations and they are being misled. Why was it that John L. Lewis of the United Mine Workers spent $3,000,000 in Alabama, necessitating the calling out of state troops costing the state $500,000, which the coal operators paid back to the state in a tonnage tax to make up this expense? It was to make this a closed district and I tell you that the same agency is directing this fight against convicts in the mines knowing that so long as coal is mined here by convicts the mine workers union will never close this district."

Bowron to Editor, *Manufacturers' Record*, August 9, 1923:
I have read with interest your editorial on pages 54 and 55 in your issue of July 26 and regret very much to see a man of your large judgement so carried away, undoubtedly by misinformation, as to speak of the Alabama legislature stamping an "infamy" upon this state, and you insist that Alabama should take its convicts out of every mine, lumber camp and turpentine farm in which convicts are leased. . . .

I well remember the time years ago in another state where the convicts slept in bunks two high and where questions of personal cleanliness were optional with themselves. Now they have entirely different sleeping accommodations, separate suits for working and wearing in prison quarters and a bath is compulsory after they come from their work. The food and other supplies are not provided by the state, but by the employers. The work is supervised absolutely by state officials. The odious and infamous statements, which are continually made to the contrary in the newspapers by persons in many cases of high social standing and good women, judges, preachers, etc., are obviously based on gross misinformation. Newspaper editors joined with the paid attorneys of the united miners in denouncing that corporate greed which tasks a man beyond his strength. The answer is to quote the facts. No prisoner is put to work underground unless in the opinion of the State physician the work is suitable for him. At the discretion of the physician he is either tasked for underground or overground or if neither one nor the other is suitable, he is sent to the state penitentiary. If he be found tubercular, he is segregated. . . .

The employment of convicts in coal mines producing the basic commodity of coal, which lies at the foundation of nearly all modern business, is guaranteed against such unspeakable conditions as would be produced by a universal strike. There are always men who are willing to work as non-union miners if they can be protected from intimidation and when trains of coal are seen moving even though it be convict produced coal this is an encouragement to other men who realize that the strike is not a complete one, and that they may participate in the mines without undue feeling of persecution. There is no other advantage in the employment of convicts instead of free labor.

Editor's reply:

Col. Bowron is noted far and wide for his good works, his devotion to the best interests of humanity and his love of his fellow man. We know of no man more thoroughly conscientious in all these respects. We appreciate his arguments and his explanations as to the way convicts are hired for work in coal mines. Nevertheless the leasing of convicts to mining or lumber companies or kindred activities is against the moral sentiment of the world and every state which does it creates a moral hostility in all other sections which in the long run does great material harm.

I have always had much sympathy for the Negro race. I feel that it is looked down upon by its white neighbors because of its inferiority in every respect, and so little opportunity is given it to improve itself. I think the white race has everything to gain and nothing to lose by improving the status of this great mass of people who, as a whole, are of a kindly disposition and when properly trained are reasonably industrious and loyal. I think we should make many great allowances for their faults, considering the absence of advantages which we possess but they do not.

I attended a meeting at the American Bank where about twenty interesting people were gathered together to discuss the status of the colored race amongst us and to consider what the difficulties were and to what extent they could be removed, so as to satisfy the Negroes and make their lives more happy and comfortable and their property more secure. We talked across the table in a heart-to-heart manner. I advocated their being taught thrift by their preachers and the avoidance of gambling, so that they might save some money to put into their houses instead of being kicked about from one old shack to another. This meeting was held in pursuance of the policy of the league for improving interracial relations [the Commission for Interracial Cooperation], headed by my friend John J. Eagan of Atlanta.

On July 25 we had another meeting with reference to [the] Negro situation, where three Negro preachers told us very frankly that 10,000 of their people were going up East in response to the letters that were coming from their friends saying how they might live on any street they thought fit if they had the money to pay the rent. They could go to the same schools with the white children and the same churches and theaters and sit amongst them on terms of perfect equality in street cars and everything else. Even if they could not make any more money they had the satisfaction up there of being treated as equals and not as inferiors.

Iron Trade Review, September 13, 1923:
Economic and social conditions have combined to bring into the northern industrial districts from the South more than 600,000 negroes within five years. . . . The movement northward for nearly two years has been of a sustained, mass character.

The major part of the migration has occurred since the 3 per cent limitation was placed on immigration from Europe and other countries. The department of labor estimates that 358,856 negro men and women have moved to the northern industrial centers since Dec. 1, 1922.

The negroes are remaining in the North; the influences that brought them here still are at work, and may continue, for the negroes are the North's immigrants, coming to a "promised land" of high wages and "equality," seeking to escape poverty and degradation. They are coming to the North essentially for the same reason [*sic*] that have led Europeans to seek entrance to this country. The destruction of cotton crops by the boll weevil may be likened in its effect on their lives to the blight of war. Living has become more difficult, hovels must serve for homes. In the North, there is prosperity, a call for labor, good pay, and what the average negro especially desires, greater tolerance from white people. . . .

Do the representatives of the South take note of the loss that their districts may sustain if the negroes continue to leave? . . .

The head of a large Alabama steelworks says:

"The migration of the negroes is demoralizing the southern farm labor market. The different southern industrial works, mines, etc., are experiencing difficulty in operating without the negroes who have gone North. Some of them are working shorter time in consequence—some have closed down so as to concentrate the available labor on fewer points and thus lessen the overhead."

The president of a large southern foundry states his views as follows:

"The South has already suffered on account of the exodus of its negro labor, and it seems that it must suffer considerably more. Our immigration laws, of course, as they now stand, prevent bringing in additional foreign laborers. Should further inroads be made on the southern labor market, the South must suffer greatly."

Georgia and Alabama have passed drastic laws making it a penal offense for labor agents to induce persons to leave those states, and similar laws are receiving strong endorsement elsewhere. . . .

Southern railroads are refusing to accept prepaid transportation or to deliver tickets. Southern banks have refused to cash checks written by northerners and sent South to finance "the darky's joyride." Southerners who have cashed such checks have been threatened by the Ku Klux Klan. The Southern Metal Trades association in a recent bulletin sounds this warning: "The negro belongs to the South, and he should stay here for his interest and for the interest of the country at large. Shut the barn door before the horses all get out. Help us to stop further depredations on the supply of labor remaining in the South. We have none to spare."

Another phase of the situation is the change of attitude, or the more emphatic assertion of opinion in the South in regard to the rights of negroes. A half dozen southern industrial leaders comment freely on the negro situation, and they are in agreement on the statement conditions affecting the negroes must be improved, that there is no other way of holding them, in view of the many advantages which may arise in the North. These leaders say the negroes have not received a square deal, they do not receive fair treatment at work, on the streets, in their homes, or in the courts. The negroes have been forced to live without proper sanitation, have been denied the use of the same schools as the whites, "always put off to take the leavings and the last of what there is." A prominent industrial manager says "the negro cannot be blamed for moving North at the first opportunity." "Who wouldn't under similar conditions?" he asks, and answers: "I would."

Bowron to Robert R. Moton, principal of Tuskegee Institute, 1928:
My dear Sir:
  I received your usual letter of reminder last week as to my annual subscription. I think you must excuse me this year as I have assisted within the past few weeks five different colored churches in this City with contributions towards their building or mortgage debts, and also $100 towards the building fund or purchase fund of the colored Y.W.C.A. of this City. . . . I shall hope to maintain my usual subscription next year to Tuskegee.

In May 1923 my wife went to a picnic at the Warrior River. The auto got stuck in the mud, and they were scared out of their wits by a procession of Ku Klux Klan in their uniform. In September we sat on the porch and watched more than 1,000 autos go past our house to attend a Ku Klux Klan meeting . . . until the entire road for miles was blocked.

In 1925 Bowron's son Edgar ran for a seat on the three-person Birmingham City Commission. An attractive thirty-two-year-old lawyer with a well-known name and the support of one local newspaper, Edgar gained a place in the run-off election. Just prior to the election, two influential Birmingham men, the banker W. Webb Crawford and the Birmingham News *editor Victor Hanson, offered Edgar a future appointment as city attorney in a Klan-dominated city administration if he would withdraw from the run-off election. James Bowron reported in his diary that he told Edgar that he could not "afford to desert*

6,000 friends who have a marked [preference] for him." Edgar stayed in the race and lost, though he subsequently would have a successful career in local politics.

Edgar polled nearly 10,000 votes in election for the City Commission, running about 1,000 votes behind the three successful candidates, who were reputed to have the vote of the Ku Klux Klan behind them. The newspapers had made a point, whether it was true or not, and had waxed so intense over it that . . . the Klan leaders felt they must oppose the newspaper nominees to save their own dignity and reputation. It was felt by everyone that Edgar's race was an extremely creditable one.

On January 31, 1927, I went to the Masonic lodge . . . at Wahouma [a predominantly white neighborhood in Birmingham]. I spoke for ninety-eight minutes to 100 people theoretically on Italy, Russia, Mexico, and Mussolini, . . . but I took the opportunity to talk about the Ku Klux Klan, knowing that it was a very hotbed and that probably many of those present were of the order. I told them frankly that in my judgment, whilst I approved quite extensively of their principles, I could not approve of their practices and methods, and I thought they were making a great mistake. I said that, if they would discard their masks and publish a list of their membership once a year, there was no officeholder in the county or in the state who could withstand the force of all their thousands of votes, and they could use that suasion instead of the threat measures of physical force.

Later that year Bowron gave a speech entitled "Masonry and Law and Order" at the Birmingham Masonic Temple:

I am next to enjoin you to be exemplary in the discharge of your civil duties, by never proposing, or at all countenancing any act, which may have a tendency to subvert the peace and good order of society; by paying due obedience to the laws of any state which may for a time become the place of your residence, or afford you its protection. . . .

Taking the law into your own hands . . . is mob spirit. Where the people undertake to be themselves the Grand Jury, judge, witnesses, and executioner they are barbarous. The base of Masonry in every case is to support the law as it exists and to lend every assistance to the suppression of law breakers. . . .

I learned in England . . . that the lash is an effective restraint from brutality and I would approve flogging inflicted in the punishment of any person convicted of violence, such as highway robbery, burglary and all crimes of violence against women and children, but such punishment should be inflicted after a trial by jury and officers of the law.

My judgment is that the Klan made a tremendous error in seeking secrecy. No force exists equal in power to public opinion. If the list of members were published once a year, it would be quite sufficient to notify any delinquent officer that he would be impeached or his reelection opposed by 10,000 members in Jefferson County, and in cases of drinking, wife beating, bootlegging, immorality, disorderly houses the proper course would be to bring such matters to the attention of the officers of the law and the Grand Jury, and impress upon men called for jury service to frankly accept and perform their full service and duty.

The public attention focused on the question of evolution by the Scopes "monkey trial" in Dayton, Tennessee, in 1925 inevitably brought an impassioned response from Bowron. In August of that year he spoke on the subject to "a large concourse of people" in the industrial suburb of Tarrant.

For those who find satisfaction in ascribing their ancestry to jelly fish, reptiles and monkeys, I have no word of criticism—I have no right to criticize them. But I would only say from the Great Book, "Ephriam is joined to his idols, let him alone." And to those who believe in the inspiration of the holy scriptures, from cover to cover as I do, I would say in encouragement "Hold fast that thou hast, let no man take thy crown." . . .

The allegations of the extraordinary antiquity of man are inexpressibly obscure to the student of geology—man could not have existed during the carboniferous age, he could not have breathed and lived in the atmosphere which nourished the development of enormous canebrakes, which are preserved and fossilized in our mines, neither could man have lived in the early Tertiary period during the extreme cold of the ice age, except in the very limited portion of the earth below, its reach indicated by Genesis as Mesopotamia. . . .

As I see it . . . the evolutionists are confronted with two impassable barriers—one at the beginning of his theory and the other at the end. If he ignores God and the teachings of Genesis 1:1, and John 1:1–3, and asserts that man has always been and was not created by divine fiat but that present conditions are the result of a movement of evolution upward, he is at once confronted with the profoundest enigma—why not this law of evolution work during the untold millions of years, which he asserts is the age of the world, and—why, was not the present condition of creation arrived at in by-gone ages, instead of being retained for the present?

Furthermore I assert fearlessly ... that the scientific knowledge available gives no assurance whatever that the law of so-called "upward evolution" has ever prevailed upon this earth! Observers of natural history, either biological or botanical, know very well that the process of development of high blooded stock, or of fruits or flowers by cross breeding or selection invariably leads to greater delicacy than characterized the parent stock, and that the Darwinian so-called "law of improvement," of natural selection is fully countered by the law of "reversion to type."

Is not this reversion to type eminently true of man? ...

If the history of mankind is "upward evolution" ... why should the Chinese know of gun powder and the mariner's compass before the Christian era, and lose them again? Why should we see today only the pitiful traces of the Mogul empire in the palaces and tombs of India?

Why should the Hindu race have gone backward for 400 years? Why should the stupendous ruins of the twelfth and fourteenth centuries of Angkor in Cambodia, and of Borobodaer in Java, be pointed to with amazement?

Why should modern Egyptians now be ignorant of the arts of astronomy and mathematics which enabled them to erect the great Pyramid of Cheops upon the principle of squaring the circle and at the point it should absorb its own shadow at noon time at the vernal equinox?

In August 1921 I strongly urged the Christian life on Harold, showing him Ridgeway's pamphlet of how practically 90 percent of the most successful businessmen of the country are earnest Christians. In May 1922 I had a session with Harold, whom we had been urging as strongly as possible to defer his proposed marriage until he got sufficiently settled in business to be able to run without assistance. However, he like several other of my sons,

Bowron with a part of his large family, c. 1927. Adah is seated immediately to his left. (courtesy of James French)

was so determined to discount the future there was no holding him back. I got him the money for his marriage expenses and wedding tour. In August I heard that Harold's business arrangements were in a condition of flux and that he must seek something else to do. This was what I had foreseen when I had vainly opposed his hasty marriage.

In October 1923 Harold stated that he had earned $520 so that he felt that he was breaking into the insurance business, and I felt that he was too, but it was an open proposition as to whether he would break into the business or the business would break him first. In May 1925 I helped Harold a good deal by getting him a policy of $50,000 on the life of President Dyer of the Nashville Bridge Company [a subsidiary of the Bessemer Company], this being paid by the Bessemer Company as the policy was its property. In July 1926 Harold complained that L. C. Brown got $400,000 of group insurance from Gulf States officials, which might have been given to him. Of course, my only answer was, why didn't he get it? It was not my fault. I knew nothing about it.

In November 1925 Tom was greatly annoyed and, of course, we were all sympathetically annoyed, to be told as he was by his president, Oscar Wells of the First National Bank of Birmingham, that he would not be recommended for the presidential succession. Mr. Wells thought it required a man of a different "temperament." Tom had certainly been up to that time one of the main factors in the success of the bank, being the most popular of its officials and having doubtless drawn more accounts to the bank than any other one person. They have shown their confidence in Tom, however, by continuing to advance his salary.

In October 1923 I had a conference with Bob on the subject of getting married to Margaret Jones. I told him to be sure of each other and to count the cost and that I hoped to give them $500 per annum as long as my salary last[ed]. He had saved $500. The following May I [conferred] with Bob as to his future plans. He insisted, against my judgment, on getting married before he had earned the money to support a home. I offered to advance him $1,500 to make [the] first payment on the purchase of one. In August 1924, to help Bob complete [the] purchase of his home, I gave him certificates of 2,000 shares of Bessemer Company stock and $1,500 cash.

In August 1925 Bob got $600 from me to start him off for Florida, but I cautioned him under no consideration to speculate. If he had heeded my earnest injunction he would have saved himself an enormous amount of perplexity and trouble. In December Bob and Margaret . . . motored up [from Florida] for Christmas, and [Bob] said he had earned in commission $4,000. The unfortunate thing was that he never got it. In April 1926 Bob said he was undecided whether to return here or to stay in West Palm Beach. Evidently the boom in Florida had broken, but they were all slow to appreciate it. In June Bob came in to see me in all kinds of trouble, as he owed $1,000 in Florida and about $600 or $700 here and since he came back had not sold a single house, although he had worked hard, for he is always an industrious worker. He had to part with his Bessemer stock for current expenses, and had to do something to earn an income. In addition to this he was tangled up as endorser on certain Florida plans which he considered void because the other people had not done what they promised.

In August Bob came in, telling me that he was negotiating for a position with the Nokol Company. I found this was a proposition where he would put some money up, or I would put it up for him, and he would get part of the profits and somebody else the other part, and I told him that I did not play that way. In July 1927 Bob told me he was physically unable on account of a former operation for appendicitis to stand up to the hard work at the sheet mill at [U.S. Steel], and he had an offer to go into the sales department of Odom, Bowers and White, clothiers. I did not think much of it but told him he must decide for himself, and that he ought to give up his car and cut his expense account to fit his earnings.

On September 23, 1926, Mr. Coverdale frankly charged Moffett with holding too many outside interests. Afterwards I discussed this with him and [Moffett] said he would . . . refuse the position as campaign manager to Bibb Graves [candidate for governor of Alabama]. I urged him to turn the details of the Coal Operators Association over to . . . the president of the association, instead of [Moffett's] doing the work . . . as vice-president. I suggested that he might ease up a little bit in some of his Masonic activities. It [was not] necessary to sit through a three-day reunion, for instance. But he said he would rather leave the company than to do so.

On October 13 Mr. Coverdale came to dinner with us, and he told me that he was perfectly shocked at Mr. Moffett's purchase of the new bar mill and his assumption of all power. All of his officers were against him and resented his management and autocracy, and . . . he, Coverdale, would not recommend any large further outlay under Moffett, regarding him as mentally unable to collaborate properly with his associates. On October 14 Coverdale told Moffett in my presence how he sized up the situation, and after he had gone, Moffett came into my room. We talked over things and agreed to try to make the best of things for the future. Moffett said he had done his best and was "ready to be shot at."

On October 21 James Platten was raging against Moffett like a lion, and I suggested, pending further action, that Geohegan be made vice-president and general manager in charge of operations. [Platten] approved, and . . . Coverdale also approved as soon as I told him. On October 26 [I] had a conference with Geohegan on New York proceedings, and he said that he had recommended Coverdale to restore me as president. That would have been far from my wish.

On November 10 we went down to Coverdale's office, and . . . to my astonishment, Coverdale said that Moffett told him I "had been against him because of [Moffett's] attitude on . . . [a] coal land purchase" [that Bowron had favored]. Melville's report [a management consultant's evaluation] amongst other things had a chart of two lines, one showing the market price of scrap, the other the tonnage bought by Moffett from month to month. [It] showed that the heaviest purchases were always made at the time of highest prices. His estimate submitted to the directors was that Moffett's assumption of the purchasing of scrap instead of leaving it to the general manager and purchasing agent had cost the company during the five years of his presidency about $400,000. This did not reflect in any way upon his integrity but upon his judgment and ability as a manager.

The works manager at [Gadsden] testified to Coverdale that he had appealed to Moffett to send the chief engineer [to the works because] they had problems in connection with the location and construction of the mill. Moffett replied, "This is one plant that I am going to build myself, and I do not want the chief engineer to set foot on the place." This produced a very unfortunate effect on the minds of the directors because of the absence of any other officer having had any share in the authority for locating and constructing the mill, or the responsibility for its original cost, amounting to $800,000 for installation apart from the purchase price instead of $300,000 as asked from the directors. All the responsibility from such unwise location and the excessive cost of conversion came back upon Mr. Moffett alone. There was no one with whom the responsibility could be divided and shared. His action in removing the building of the twenty-inch mill to act as a warehouse was taken in absolute contravention of the unanimous vote of myself, the general manager, the chief engineer, the works manager, the works engineer, the mill superintendent, the assistant works manager, and the roll designer. The removal handicapped the old mill, and the building, not being strong enough to carry an overhead crane, has always proved a source of difficulty, perplexity, and expense in its operation.

[Moffett's] resignation as president . . . was accepted to take effect at the end of his term. Mr. Geohegan was then elected vice-president in charge of operations. On November 15 I held a meeting of the three vice-presidents, who requested me to move back again into my old office, the president's room. I outlined a policy of cooperation, avoiding publicity and recrimination, [and] also suggested weekly meetings of the staff in Birmingham and at [Gadsden]. [We] agreed we should buy scrap by open competition. On November 16 I was eighty-two years old and celebrated my birthday by going to the plant, where we had a full meeting of officers.

In December, Mr. Coverdale and his associate sat in with our officials in the joint conference in the office, going over one after another the improvements proposed to be made, many of which were agreed to as we went on, such as a gas washer at the blast furnace and skewback tables at the bar mill. It was also agreed to start outside work on the Virginia escapeway; to make the proposed contract with the Weber Engineering Company to fight the water at Shannon [ore mine]; to provide new machine tools for [Gadsden] and transfer the old ones to Sayre, Virginia, and Shannon; to put twenty new houses at Sayre; and to electrify that mine, using power from the Alabama Power Company. It was understood that no money had been provided for these outlays but that some plan would be attempted.

Later the executive committee authorized the third slag pit, and I wrote Mr. Coverdale my idea of the right method of selling stock to our employees by joint units of one share each of preferred and common where the preferred dividend alone would pay more than the ordinary savings bank rate. At a meeting of directors . . . [in July 1927] we accepted my proposal [that we] should buy some preferred and common stock at low prices to resell on the installment plan to our own employees, something I had always wanted to do.

In February 1927 we were greatly encouraged to see pig iron cost down to $17.03 [per ton] on a record output of 11,606 tons, the largest by far in the history of the blast furnace since it was built. Our earnings for January were $86,492, being much better than we had anticipated, and our conversion cost at the bar mill reduced to $9.54 [per ton]. The blast furnace daily record was broken on February 5 with an output of 440 tons. On the strength of these good results in January we were able to reduce our prices and sold Connor's Steel 10,000 tons [of] four-inch billets at $29.00 delivered equal $28.32 at works against January cost of $25.84.

James Bowron continued to enjoy world travel into his old age, making several long voyages with his wife. In 1921 and 1922, they made a world tour that took them through the Far and Middle East, a highlight of which was an audience with Mahatma Gandhi. His last trip was to sub-Saharan Africa in early 1928. Ever the student, ever the teacher, Bowron liked to give his impressions in letters to newspapers.

Bowron to Birmingham *Age-Herald*, March 11, 1922, from Madras, India:

I had an interview three or four days ago with Mr. M. K. Gandhi, the man who has probably more influence in this country than any other living man. His influence is so great that 200,000 men at Ahmedabad, at his suggestion, passed a resolution to adopt his policy of "Mass civil

Bowron in Nepal during world tour in early 1922 (courtesy of Bowron Collection, Special Collections, University of Alabama)

disobedience." This policy, so I understand, is one of refusing to pay taxes or to pay any respect to laws made by the British ruler of this country and is associated with a policy of non-cooperation, that is refusing to work with or for English. He would have them withdraw from all services with European employers. I was one of a party of three gentlemen with their wives who were admitted to see Mr. Gandhi at home.

He is a very busy man and as natural, only gave us a short interview. My time was about five or six minutes. Mr. Gandhi received us sitting on the floor on a white cotton mat or rug, busily turning a small, crude spinning wheel drawing the cotton into yarn. He did not cease this occupation while talking with us. He was only wearing two articles of dress, a white loin cloth of khader and a loose white cotton cloth hung from his shoulders except when it fell down to his waist. He sat in the usual cross-legged attitude.

The following conversation took place:

Mr. Bowron: "Mr. Gandhi, will you permit me to ask you this question? How can the Indian nation become wealthy and prosperous, and therefore happy, whilst it continues to immobilize its savings in always building more and more temples and statues to Buddha, whilst other

nations invest their savings in buying plows and wagons, ships, loco-
motives and in making fine roads and irrigation ditches and other
things that earn money?"

Gandhi: "I do not think that all that expenditure is waste, because
many people live in the temples. Also it tends to maintain Indian art."

Mr. Bowron: "I cannot agree with you, Mr. Gandhi. Art is not promoted by duplicating one century after another the same images and
statues. But if your people were making something to sell they would
make all sorts of beautiful work which would bring money to the Indian
people and, I think, would much more promote Indian art."

Gandhi: "Oh, you people always reduce everything to pounds, shillings and pence, but there are higher things to live [for]."

Mr. Bowron: "I agree with you, Mr. Gandhi, but pounds, shillings
and pence are very useful even in promoting higher things. Look at all
the great public works, gifts to the people, parks, hospitals, libraries,
foundations for medical research, equipment for scientific expeditions
which could never have been done or gained without the assistance of
rich men."

Gandhi: "I knew too much of the way in which your large fortunes
have been made, by oppression of the people and driving competitors
out of business."

Mr. Bowron: "If one man commits murder today in Ahmedabad it
would be reported tomorrow in the newspaper. But if 100,000 men
behave themselves and keep the law it would not be reported. So you
hear of [bad] things done by corporations, but [they] do not write so
much of the good things. My corporation for which I work, the Gulf
States Steel Company, has no trouble in its steel works because we have
a representative council of 32 men, two from each department, who
meet monthly and discuss with the manager all pending questions and
settle them amicably."

This was the end of my five minutes. He gave my wife an auto-
graphed copy of his newspaper, "Young India." Reading it the next day
I saw his arguments that if the spinning wheels were introduced in the
60,000,000 Hindu homes it would save 60 crores of rupees from being
sent out of the country each year for foreign cotton goods. This means
that Mr. Gandhi is urging a boycott of all foreign cotton imports,
amounting to, he says, equivalent of $175,000,000 per annum. I think
his figure may be understated.

It seems very lamentable to me that a leader of his enormous influence should be taking such a step backward to recommend the people to withdraw from more remunerative work and give themselves to competing by hand with modern machinery in the production of cotton cloth, instead of recommending, as he might, that they should put their savings together and build in India cotton mills of their own, instead of spending all their money in thousands of duplicates of statues of their gods. I also noticed in his paper that he said he was opposed to the killing of flies.

I am sorry I had no more time so that I might have asked him whether it was better for coolies to kill flies or for flies to kill coolies. I have been so infinitely distressed at seeing these poor people in their great religious devotion bathing in the Ganges River right where the sewage of Benares was emptying into the river, and where dead bodies were floating down among the bathers, with crows sitting on and pecking at them.

Mr. Gandhi is obviously a man of much sincerity but not an economist and he is anxious to perpetuate that condition under which the great Indian nations have steadily sunk lower in wealth and health until today it makes one very sad to travel round and contrast the present conditions with those of the past.

Rand *Daily Mail*, March [?], 1928:
In extending the city's welcome to the party [of visiting Americans], Mr. W. H. Port [mayor of Johannesburg] communicated to them several interesting facts indicating Johannesburg's phenomenal growth and its present magnitude. In courtesy to his American audience he quoted financial figures in dollars, making the calculation for the conversion of pounds to dollars on the spot.

Mr. James Bowron, chairman of the Gulf States Steel Company, Birmingham, Alabama, presenting with white hair and white flowing beard a dignified and patriarchal figure, replied to the Mayor. "Many people, many minds, many men, many eyes," he began. "It would be hopeless for anyone to presume to express with one voice the thoughts, sentiments and impressions of a hundred fellow travellers, some of them interested in various manufactures, iron and steel, and textile industries; in the strange insects, the birds and their nests that we have seen; some of them interested in agriculture, in the vast open county here, and in the broad acres yet to be developed."

Mr. Bowron advocated the utilization of the by-products of South

Bowron and Adah at a costume party during 1924 voyage through Latin America
(courtesy of Bowron Collection, Special Collections, University of Alabama)

Africa's fuel resources. The surplus gases should be used for the production of electric power. As a casual traveller he had formed the opinion that electric power could be transmitted over large distances for the
installation of electric pumps, and thus help the development of large
arid districts.

"A country so young as this needs capital," he continued. "It is a
source of great interest to learn that a freight service is already in operation between New York and Cape Town. That is not enough. This
service should not only be for freight, but also for carrying passengers.
I am sure that if passage could be taken direct from New York to Cape-
town hundreds of thousands of people now going to other fields would
visit this country. If you offer facilities for people to come here an increased number of travellers will investigate the possibilities of the
country and attract large capital.

"All this will help to promote the feeling of friendship between the
two countries. For the Anglo-Saxons must ever stand for the unity of
the race on both sides of the water; for the creation of a hegemony of
the race above all other races of the world; for the uplift of humanity."

A Birmingham newspaper, late April 1928:
Mr. Bowron told of seeing many of the so-called native dances, varying
from the fierce and spectacular charge of the Zulu warriors in their war
dances to the plaintive cadences of the Madagascar maidens chanting
softly and alluringly in French.

"In Sierra Leone, Mrs. Bowron and I saw the most amazing exhibi-
tions of strength, endurance and agility among the men and women.
Wild gyrations, the creatures springing into the air with arms and legs
extended, up and down, like a rubber ball," said Mr. Bowron.

"I don't think that the Africans have any native music. We were
greatly surprised when the Royal Band, belonging to the sultan of Zan-
zibar, came aboard our train. Instead of native airs, they played the
latest American music."

Mr. Bowron found in Egypt gross injustice and much antipathy
shown to the English, who have given the Egyptians everything they
have, honest tax gathering and political liberty, which has saved them
from the Turks on one hand and the Sudanese on the other.

"Taking things into their own hands is shown particularly in the matter of the railroads," said Mr. Bowron. "The Egyptians are incompe-

tent, and some of our party suffered considerably in this way, the train in which they were travelling catching fire and burning up everything they had, bag and baggage.

"We escaped—Mrs. Bowron and I—because 25 years ago we had made the trip and it was those who were returning from Luxor who fared so badly. We did not go."

George Eastman, of Eastman camera fame, Mr. Bowron said, returned to Cairo, Shepherd's Hotel, clad in green pajamas with a red blanket wrapped around him and wasn't allowed to enter his suite at the hotel. Finally he persuaded the manager that he was really George Eastman and had a suite there.

"England, however, has control of the situation," said Mr. Bowron, "regarding the Sudan and the development of Port Sudan and the railroad to Khartoum and so could easily block the prosperity of Egypt materially, if so minded, by restricting the waters of the Nile."

On November 21, 1926, a cold, dark, rainy Sunday, in my Bible class it was too dark to read. We had a fine address that morning from Dr. J. M. Van der Meulen, the president of the Presbyterian Theological Seminary in Louisville, a very able man, whom I greatly admire. From 1894 to 1909 I had suffered on an average every eighteen or twenty days a violent attack of indigestion. This was caused by nervousness starting with the silver panic of 1893, the railroad men and coal miners strikes of 1894, Grover Cleveland's Venezuelan war panic of 1895, the William Jennings Bryan silver panic of 1896, and the Cuban war panic of 1897, and the anxiety and care devolving on me at that time permanently ruined my health, but saved the Tennessee Coal, Iron and Railroad Company, which has become one of the greatest institutions in the South. In 1909 Mrs. B. F. Tyler suggested to my wife a remedy which worked like a charm, Wampoles Glycolates, and until November 21, 1926, a period of seventeen years, I never had a single attack of indigestion, but I sometimes had very severe attacks of pain coming from overexertion affecting my heart.

The session having invited me to lay the foundation stone of the new Sunday School building, and to deliver an address in the open air at that time to the assembled crowd, I accepted the duty gladly. Imagine my horror and consternation, not having had an attack of indigestion for seventeen years, when as I stepped out of the car in front of the building I was struck with such a violent pain that I could neither move nor speak. After ten or fifteen minutes I managed to get into the church and sit there during the address of Dr. Van der Meulen, but when it came to be my turn to go through the ceremony and speak extemporaneously, as I always do, frankly and honestly, I do not know what I said. I was suffering such great pain that I was only half conscious of what I was saying. I think it was a clear case of the devil trying to get in his best work to hit me in such a way on such an occasion, and I have been trying to hit him a good many times since.

The attack in November 1926 was in all likelihood not indigestion but angina. Bowron's health began to decline at this point, though not rapidly, until the summer of 1928. Perhaps sensing that his death was near, he worked steadily to finish dictating his autobiography, all the while continuing in the management of Gulf States. He was able to take the autobiography up to August 1927. His diary reveals his concern for work and family during his last months.

BOWRON DIARY, May 1, 1928:
H. L. Badham called. Coal business very bad. Lost L and N contract. Geohegan urges that we seek market for 4,000 tons coal per month to keep down overhead.

May 8, 1928:
Margaret and Bob called [regarding their] finances. Says they cannot meet expenses on his $150 salary. I promise $100 [per month].

May 11, 1928:
Bess[emer Coal, Iron and Land Company] directors' meeting. Land sales almost stopped. Coal sales ditto. L and N contract lost.

May 14, 1928:
Home [3:30 P.M.]. Bad gas pain!

July 6, 1928:
Office—letters, reports, markets. Conf[erence with Geohegan] re Shannon [mine]. Most of water out but pressure is high. They are afraid. Men are leaving. Up [with] gas pain.

Bowron reviewing a volume of his diary (courtesy of Birmingham Public Library Archives)

July 11, 1928:
Miss Adair came. Dictated biography November 5 to December 31 [19]26.

August 1, 1928:
Edgar came. Told him to draw codicil [to] my will making Harold's share payable to Frances [Harold's wife].

August 7, 1928:

[Handwriting very unsteady]

Hoover campaign in Birmingham. Confer Brown on sale of pig iron. . . .
Awoke 10[:50] profuse sweat and back hurting.

August 16, 1928:

8:[30] to office. Letters, reports, markets. [Geohegan] re TCI's new
blast furnace and lessons for our own. Also he agrees to buy no more
scrap until we reduce down to 20,000 tons . . . 4 P.M. with [Adah] to
Public Library to see Africa exhibit. . . . Had difficulty in stopping the
heaving of my chest after gas pain.

August 17, 1928:

9:20 A.M. at office. Letters, reports, markets. . . . Wrote article for Gulf
Steel. Home 1:[15] . . . Gas pain . . . Blood coughed up . . . Dick here.
Anxious for me to go to TCI hospital. . . . Dick stayed all night.

August 21, 1928:

Visit of J. A. Bryan [Presbyterian minister and friend] and later of Charlie.
Harold called. . . . Rheumatism much worse with cooler weather.

August 25, 1928:

[In a different handwriting]

This diary—so faithfully kept for many years up to this, the day of the
Lord's summons to higher realms of activity—now ends!

[Signed Charles E. Bowron, the eldest child]

Bowron had died suddenly of a heart attack at home.

A Birmingham newspaper:

TRIBUTES GIVEN JAMES BOWRON AT FINAL RITES

City Industrialist Called Chief Fundamentalist

Christian of World

Simple, earnestly spoken tributes to the character and attainments of
James Bowron, late industrialist, patron of art and churchman, marked
the funeral services Sunday afternoon before a capacity congregation
at the South Highlands Presbyterian Church.

Those who paid the tributes were Dr. William R. Dobyns, pastor of
the South Highlands Presbyterian Church, where Mr. Bowron for

many years had been a ruling elder, and Dr. James A. Bryan, pastor of the Third Presbyterian Church.

Dr. Bryan declared that Mr. Bowron's Christian testimony and rugged defense of the divinity of the origin of the Bible, had been a great source of strength to the speaker.

"I say it solemnly and deliberately before the whole world that in my humble opinion this man, who entered into rest Saturday, was the greatest fundamentalist layman among Christian men throughout the entire world," declared Dr. Bryan.

Dr. Bryan declared in opening his address that "we do but celebrate the homegoing of our beloved friend."

"His chief joy was to see men and women give themselves unreservedly to the Master's service," Dr. Bryan continued.

Dr. Bryan concluded his address by singing two stanzas from "Sweeping Through the Gates."

Dr. Dobyns' tribute to Mr. Bowron took root in what that minister called "his absolute faith in God."

"Mr. Bowron was preeminently a man of the Word of God," said his pastor. "He never apologized for his beliefs. He just proclaimed them. He did not question the Bible. He believed it and treasured it in his heart. No man who knows the Bible doubts it. Mr. Bowron knew it as few others have been privileged to know it. He did not doubt it."

Pallbearers were the sons of the deceased, and burial was in Elmwood Cemetery, Johns in charge.

Hundreds of friends from all sections of the Birmingham district attended the services, and messages of condolence and sympathy have been received by the family from all parts of the country. Beautiful floral tributes came as expressions from many who knew Mr. Bowron through the years he has been so actively engaged in the development of the South, and particularly of the Birmingham district.

Notes

Introduction

1. A good discussion of the early literature on the New South is found in Paul M. Gaston, "The New South," in *Writing Southern History*, ed. Arthur S. Link and Rembert W. Patrick (Baton Rouge: Louisiana State University Press, 1965), 316–36.

2. Paul Bowron, interview with author, September 20, 1989.

3. Ethel Armes, *The Story of Coal and Iron in Alabama* (Birmingham: Birmingham Chamber of Commerce, 1910).

4. C. Vann Woodward, *Origins of the New South* (Baton Rouge: Louisiana State University Press, 1951), 107–41, 291–320.

5. For a lively discussion of Comer and railroad regulation, see Sheldon Hackney, *Populism to Progressivism in Alabama* (Princeton: Princeton University Press, 1969), 230–323.

6. Gavin Wright, *Old South, New South* (New York: Basic Books, 1986), 172–77; Woodward, *Origins*, 317.

7. For a thorough indictment of price-fixing in the steel industry, see George W. Stocking, *Basing Point Pricing and Regional Development: A Case Study of the Iron and Steel Industry* (Chapel Hill: University of North Carolina Press, 1954), 15–111.

8. Charles B. Dew, *Ironmaker to the Confederacy: Joseph R. Anderson and the Tredegar Iron Works* (New Haven: Yale University Press, 1966), 1–37; Lester J. Cappon, "Trend of the Southern Iron Industry Under the Plantation System," *Journal of Economic and Business History* 2 (February 1930): 352–81; James M. Swank, *History of the Manufacture of Iron in All Ages* (New York: Burt Franklin, 1892), 293–300.

9. Raimondo Luraghi, *The Rise and Fall of the Plantation* (New York: Franklin Watts, 1978), 123–32; Richard E. Beringer, Herman Hattaway, Archer Jones, and William N. Still, *Why the South Lost the Civil War* (Athens: University of Georgia Press, 1986), 214–18; Emory M. Thomas, *The Confederate Nation: 1861–1865* (New York: Harper & Row, 1979), 207, 208, 210–11.

10. Dew, *Ironmaker*, 303–10; Frank E. Vandiver, "Josiah Gorgas and the Brierfield Iron Works," *Alabama Review* 3 (January 1950): 16; Robert H. McKenzie, "Reconstruction of the Alabama Iron Industry, 1865–1880," *Alabama Review* 25 (July 1972): 178–91.

11. Morrow Chamberlain, *A Brief History of the Pig Iron Industry of East Tennessee* (Chattanooga: Tennessee Valley Authority, 1942); John B. Ryan, Jr., "Willard Warner and the Rise and Fall of the Iron Industry in Tecumseh, Alabama," *Alabama Review* 24 (October 1971): 261–79; Armes, *Story of Coal and Iron*, 301.

12. Armes, *Story of Coal and Iron*, 310–16, 255–58; Justin Fuller, "History of the Tennessee Coal, Iron, and Railroad Company, 1852–1907" (Ph.D. dissertation, University of North Carolina, 1966), 39–40.

13. *The Iron Age*, May 29, 1884.

14. Armes, *Story of Coal and Iron*, 301.

15. McKenzie, "Alabama Iron Industry," 188.

16. *The Iron Age*, May 22, 1884, May 28, 1885; *Report of the Committee of the Senate upon the Relations between Labor and Capital* (Washington: Government Printing Office, 1885), 6:260–61.

17. Ralph M. Tanner, "Notes and Documents: Some Characteristics of Eight Land Companies in North Alabama, 1863–1900," *Alabama Review* 29 (April 1976): 124–33; Victor S. Clark, *History of Manufactures in the United States* (New York: McGraw-Hill, 1929), 2:211–20.

18. Fuller, "Tennessee Coal and Iron," 64–67, 90–100.

19. Justin Fuller, "Notes and Documents: From Iron to Steel: Alabama's Industrial Evolution," *Alabama Review* 17 (April 1964): 137–48; Clark, *History of Manufacturers*, 3:22–24.

20. Fuller, "Tennessee Coal and Iron," 100–111.

21. Fuller, "From Iron to Steel," 138–42; W. David Lewis, *Iron and Steel in America* (Greenville, Del.: Hagley Museum, 1976), 39–41.

22. The steel-making effort at Chattanooga is best detailed in the Alfred M. Shook Papers at the Birmingham Public Library Archives, Birmingham, Alabama.

23. Fuller, "Tennessee Coal and Iron," 115–17, 250–67.

24. Ibid., 257–66.

25. Wright, *Old South, New South*, 171–72.

26. Fuller, "Tennessee Coal and Iron," 267–71.

27. Ibid., 140–67; Kenneth Warren, *The American Steel Industry, 1850–1970* (London: Oxford University Press, 1973), 188.

28. Melvin I. Urofsky, *Big Steel and the Wilson Administration* (Columbus: Ohio State University Press, 1969), 1–37.

29. Clark, *History of Manufactures*, 3:24–28; H. H. Chapman, *The Iron and Steel Industries of the South* (University: University of Alabama Press, 1953), 111–47.

30. Aaron Austin Godfrey, *Government Operation of the Railroads: Its Necessity, Success, and Consequences, 1918–1920* (Austin: San Felipe Press, 1974); David M. Potter, "The Historical Development of Eastern-Southern Freight Rate Relationships," *Law and Contemporary Problems* 12 (Summer 1947): 416–48; Stocking, *Basing Point Pricing*, 75–143.

31. Stocking, *Basing Point Pricing*, 60–111.

32. Warren, *American Steel Industry*, 192.

33. Ibid., 192, 209–10.

Chapter 1

1. The Pease family was perhaps northeastern England's wealthiest Quaker family. They had moved from the wool trade into banking in the mid-eighteenth century and by the 1830s had three branches of their operation.

Chapter 2

1. Leland Hamilton Jenks, *The Migration of British Capital to 1875* (New York: Knopf, 1938), 426.

2. Sir Charles Lyell, *A Second Visit to the United States of North America* (London: John Murray, 1849); *The Iron Age*, May 29, 1884.

3. David H. Pratt, *English Quakers and the First Industrial Revolution* (New York: Garland Publishing, 1985).

4. A New York banker.

5. A noted oceanographer, naval officer, Confederate statesman, and professor.

6. An industrial region in northeastern England encompassing the city of Middlesbrough.

7. A silvery metallic substance used primarily in the manufacture of paint.

8. Brother to banker Edward Quintard, the Episcopal bishop of Tennessee.

Chapter 3

1. Colyar was cited in Karin A. Shapiro, "'The Convicts Must Go!': Tennessee Miners and the State 1891–92" (Paper presented at the Southern Labor Studies Conference, Atlanta, Georgia, October 1986, cited with permission of the author).

2. Paul M. Gaston, *The New South Creed* (New York: Alfred A. Knopf, 1970); William D. Kelley, *The Old South and the New* (London: Knickerbocker Press, 1888).

3. John A. Garraty, *The New Commonwealth, 1877–1890* (New York: Harper & Row, 1968), 115–21.

4. Bowron's testimony before the Interstate Commerce Commission is taken from *Interstate Commerce Reports*, vol. 1, *Decisions and Proceedings . . . May, 1887, to June, 1888* (Rochester: Lawyers' Co-operative Publishing Company, 1887), 161–65.

5. A Michigan lawyer, Supreme Court justice, and professor prior to becoming chairman of the Interstate Commerce Commission.

6. Morrison had been a Democratic congressman from Illinois until he was defeated in 1886, after which President Grover Cleveland appointed him to the Interstate Commerce Commission.

Chapter 4

1. Fuller, "Tennessee Coal and Iron," 56–77.
2. Ibid., 75.
3. Ibid., 77–83.
4. Ibid., 83–89.
5. J. P. Williams, a banker.
6. George B. McCormack, a young furnace manager who later became a powerful TCI executive.
7. Nathaniel Baxter's brother.
8. A Pittsburgh metallurgist and inventor.
9. "Bearing" the stock was the effort to drive down the value of the stock by selling it and by spreading negative information about the company.
10. A Naylor and Company executive.
11. Testimony before the Joint Committee of the General Assembly, *Convict System of Alabama*, Alabama Legislative Session 1888–1889, 38.
12. Ibid., 39.
13. Thomas Seay was the conservative Democratic governor of Alabama from 1886 to 1890. He showed some concern about the scandals associated with the prison system.
14. A. C. Hutson, Jr., "The Coal Miners' Insurrections of 1891 in Anderson County, Tennessee," *The East Tennessee Historical Society Publication*, no. 7 (1935): 103–21, and "The Overthrow of the Convict Lease System in Tennessee," *The East Tennessee Historical Society Publication*, no. 8 (1936): 82–103; Shapiro, "The Convicts Must Go!"
15. Shapiro, "The Convicts Must Go!"

Chapter 5

1. Fuller, "Tennessee Coal and Iron," 101–13.
2. Armes, *Story of Coal and Iron*, 331.
3. Ibid., 343.
4. Robert D. Ward and William W. Rogers, *Labor Revolt in Alabama: The Great Strike of 1894* (University: University of Alabama Press, 1965).
5. An executive of Naylor and Company, New York iron brokers.
6. Thomas Seddon of Richmond, president of the Sloss Iron Company of Birmingham.
7. Nathaniel Baxter's brother, a Nashville railroad executive and land speculator.
8. James T. Woodward, head of the Hanover Bank and a TCI director.
9. A former president of the L&N Railroad, now a TCI director.
10. Joseph F. Johnston, an Alabama politician, later governor, and director of the Sloss Company.
11. A. S. Christian of Richmond, a Sloss director.

12. The DeBardeleben Company's other major stockholders, all Charleston businessmen except Roberts, who was a Welsh mining engineer.

13. Ward and Rogers, *Labor Revolt*, 75–138.

14. Letter in Alfred M. Shook Papers, Birmingham Public Library Archives, Birmingham, Alabama.

15. Quoted in Fuller, "Tennessee Coal and Iron," 283–84.

16. A mining engineer and company executive with DeBardeleben Coal and Iron.

17. A Charleston, South Carolina, lawyer and TCI director.

Chapter 6

1. Fuller, "Tennessee Coal and Iron," 124–34.

2. Bowron and Baxter had bought 900 shares of TCI stock in a partnership agreement in 1893. This stock had been a small part of the many shares that Henry DeBardeleben had dumped after his unsuccessful takeover bid.

3. An engineering firm that designed steel operations.

4. A design engineer for steel operations.

Chapter 7

1. A TCI plant superintendent.

2. A Birmingham industrial investor with roots in Nashville.

3. An Alabama industrialist who entered politics as a progressive Democrat in the first decade of the twentieth century, serving as a railroad commissioner and then, beginning in 1907, as governor. Comer challenged the Louisville and Nashville Railroad over what he thought were excessive rates, and he succeeded in getting some reductions.

4. *The Booker T. Washington Papers*, ed. Louis Harlan (Urbana: University of Illinois Press, 1975), 4:231–32.

5. Bowron's younger brother Harry.

6. A leading Ohio iron manufacturer.

7. A Columbus, Ohio, merchant.

8. A TCI subsidiary.

9. Son of the late James Warner, a former president of TCI.

10. A Memphis cotton merchant, banker, and business associate of Enoch Ensley.

11. An experienced pipe manufacturer.

Chapter 8

1. Virginia Foster Durr, interview with author, January 11, 1990.

2. A Birmingham investment banker.

3. A Republican-appointed federal district judge in Birmingham.

4. The members of the session of the South Highland Presbyterian Church included merchants, lawyers, and industrialists.

5. The Presbytery finally found Edmonds in error only on his view of the Atonement. Orthodox Calvinism taught that only through Christ's death could people make retribution for their sinfulness and thus receive salvation. Edmonds did not believe that God required such retribution, but that salvation came from a forgiving God without Christ's sacrifice. For a full explanation of the Edmonds controversy, see Marvin Yeomans Whiting, *The Bearing Day Is Not Gone: The Seventy-fifth Anniversary History of Independent Presbyterian Church of Birmingham, Alabama, 1915–1990* (Birmingham: Independent Presbyterian Church, 1990), 13–23.

Chapter 9

1. A noted epidemiologist who addressed the health problems Americans encountered in the building of the Panama Canal.

2. An attorney for U.S. Steel.

3. A longtime United Mine Workers' official in Birmingham.

4. A Gulf States executive second in charge to Bowron.

5. A Gulf States manager.

Index